Python Programming

The Most Complete Crash Course for Beginners to Learn Python with Hands-On Exercises and Practical Applications

- 4 Books in 1 -

D1519031

Andrew Park

© Copyright 2021 - All rights reserved.

The content contained within this book may not be reproduced, duplicated or transmitted without direct written permission from the author or the publisher.

Under no circumstances will any blame or legal responsibility be held against the publisher, or author, for any damages, reparation, or monetary loss due to the information contained within this book. Either directly or indirectly.

Legal Notice:

This book is copyright protected. This book is only for personal use. You cannot amend, distribute, sell, use, quote or paraphrase any part, or the content within this book, without the consent of the author or publisher.

Disclaimer Notice:

Please note the information contained within this document is for educational and entertainment purposes only. All effort has been executed to present accurate, up to date, and reliable, complete information. No warranties of any kind are declared or implied. Readers acknowledge that the author is not engaging in the rendering of legal, financial, medical or professional advice. The content within this book has been derived from various sources. Please consult a licensed professional before attempting any techniques outlined in this book.

By reading this document, the reader agrees that under no circumstances is the author responsible for any losses, direct or indirect, which are incurred as a result of the use of information contained within this document, including, but not limited to, — errors, omissions, or inaccuracies.

"Life is short (You need Python)"

— Bruce Eckel

Table of Contents

Python for Beginners

Introduction

Python is one of the top programming languages universities and industries are preferring to teach and use respectively. The charm of Python is hidden in the fact that it has extremely large applications in a wide range of fields. Most people abhor Python because of its use in building Artificial Intelligence models. They fear that these Python-powered AI models will drive people out of different industries and snatch their jobs. They quote the example of Tesla's driverless taxi program by which Tesla aims to replace Uber's taxis in the US market. But the reality is different. In fact, Python-powered AI models will create many more jobs instead of removing jobs. For example, building these models will become an independent industry. Also, the implementation of these AI models will become a new business sector.

Data Science is going to take the corporate world by storm. Data Science is based on the Python programming language, as more and more companies are now moving in neck-on-neck competition. All they crave is a way to gain an edge over their competitors. They do everything for power and to get ahead. In this regard, Python seems to be promising. Python-backed Data Science tends to equip industries with sophisticated data about past and present sales patterns, which can help corporate sector CEOs make wiser decisions about sales and development of marketing strategies.

The biggest advantage for learners of Python is that you don't have to compile the code. In C++, you have to compile the entire program first and then run it. Only then you will be able to see whether your program runs or returns an error. Python offers the same level of programming and even at a higher level, but still, it is an interpreted language that can be easily written, edited, and corrected.

Python is very easy to read and learn. You can easily read source codes for different programs that are created by other programmers. But no matter how easy it is on the outside to read and learn, it needs, like all the other programming languages, dedicated practice. You will have to get to the Python editor and practice all codes. In the beginning, you can take the code and just paste it in the editor to see the results. In the second phase, you can make minor edits to the code and see the results. In the third phase, you will be able to completely reshape a program and

8

see how it runs in the Python shell. Given the increasing applications of Python, learning it is extremely profitable from the angle of the global job market. Python can give you the much-needed edge over others when it comes to securing high paid jobs.

1. Python Installation

The up-to-date edition with the binaries, current source codes, documentation, latest news, etc. can be accessed at the official Python website: http://www.Python.org/

It is accessible in various formats like PDF, HTML, and PostScript. Python Documentation Website: www.Python.org/doc/

Python has two major versions: Python 2 and Python 3. Python 3 is a version with new features that Python 2 does not have. However, because Python 3 was not designed with backward compatibility in mind, Python 2 is still the main product in actual production (although Python 3 has been released for almost 10 years at the time of writing this book). The code in this book is compatible with both Python 2 and Python 3.

The following describes how to install Python and some important libraries.

Windows

The author does not recommend to develop under the Windows system. There are many reasons, the most important of which is that in the Big Data era data is stored under the Linux system. Therefore, in production, the programs developed by data scientists will eventually run in the Linux environment. Furthermore, the compatibility between Windows and Linux is not optimal. Thus, programs that run without any criticality under Windows (e.g. on a local machine) might then not run normally in the real production environment.

If you use a Windows system, he can choose to install a Linux virtual machine and then develop on the virtual machine. If you insist on using Windows, given the limitations of certain libraries (such as TensorFlow) under Windows, the only solution is to install the latest version of Python 3.

To see which one it is visit https://www.python.org/downloads.

Some applications available under Windows are IPython, Jupyter, Conda and Spyder. We will explain some of them in detail below.

Conda

Conda is a management system for the Python development environment and open source libraries. If you are familiar with Linux, Conda is equivalent to pip+virtualenv under Linux. You can see all the installed Python libraries by entering "Condolist" on the command line.

Spyder

Spyder is an Integrated Development Environment (IDE) specifically designed for scientific computing in Python. If you are familiar with the mathematical analysis software MATLAB, you can find that Spyder and MATLAB are very similar in syntax and interface.

Mac

Starting with Mac OS X version 10.2, Python is pre-installed on Macs. For educational purposes, you may choose to use the pre-installed version of Python directly. For development purposes, the pre-installed Python is likely to give problems when installing third-party libraries, and the latest version of Python must be reinstalled.

Unlike the Windows version, the Mac version does not contain the TensorFlow Deep Learning library, which must be installed using pip (preferred installer program). Although using pip requires a command line, it is very easy to use. Also, pip is more widely used, so it is suggested to install the required libraries with pip from the beginning.

Linux

There are many versions of Linux. Here we will describe only the installation on Ubuntu. Although most Ubuntu versions have Python pre-installed, the version is old, and it is recommended to install a newer one. To check the version of Python you have, open the terminal and type:

```
python -version
```

If the version you have is lower than 3.7.x you can install Python 3.8 with the command:

```
sudo apt install python3.8
```

Now everything is ready and we can start running our first Python commands!

Running Python

Python can be run in two different ways: through an interactive interpreter or an Integrated Development Environment (IDE).

Interactive Interpreter –Python Shell

Python is a dynamic language that is usually used in two ways: as a script interpreter to execute programs, or as an actual program that allows you to enter and execute any stream of instructions. To do this, Python provides a real-time interactive command window: the Python shell. This allows you to write code, debug, and test instructions.

To start the Python shell, type "python" in the terminal (Linux or Mac) or command prompt (Windows). Once started you will notice this symbol at the beginning of the line:

```
>>>_
```

You can then enter commands and begin to familiarize yourself. Some observations:

1. Any Python command can be executed in the shell, so some people use it as a calculator as well.

2. You can assign values to variables. For example by writing:

```
>>> a=5
>>> b=3
```

In this case you have assigned the value 5 to the variable "a" and 3 to the variable "b". You can use these variables until you close the shell, for example you can calculate the sum:

```
>>> a+b
5
```

Notice that Python is a **dynamic** type language, so there is no need to declare the type of a variable when assigning values to it.

3. You can also import and use a third-party library in the shell, such as "numpy" (numerical python), which contains a large collection of high-level mathematical functions and through which you can work with large matrices and multidimensional arrays:

```
>>> import numpy as np
```

```
>>> x=np.array([1, 2, 3])
>>> x
array([1, 2, 3])
```

We can see that, as shown in the code, the third-party library "numpy" can be given an alias, such as "np" while being imported. When "numpy" is needed later, it is replaced by "np" to reduce the amount of character input. In the example code, we used numpy to create an array of integers.

The following table shows a list of options that you can enter in the command line.

Option	Description
-d	Provide the output after debugging
-o	Optimized byte code generation i.e., the .pyo file is generated
-s	Don't run the import site for searching Python paths in a startup.
-v	Details of the import statement
-x	Disable the class-based built-in exceptions
-c cmd	This runs the Python script sent in cmd String
file	The python script is run from the given file

Integrated Development Environment (IDE)

An IDE, or Integrated Development Environment, is a software that facilitates the development of other applications. Designed to encapsulate all programming tasks in a single application, the IDE allows you to consolidate the different aspects of writing a program.

The main advantage of an IDE is that it offers a central interface with all the tools a developer needs, including:

- Code editor: designed to write and edit source code, these editors differ from text editors in that they simplify and improve the process of writing and editing code

- Compiler: compilers transform source code that is written in a human readable/writable language into a form that computers can execute.

- Debugger: debuggers are used during testing and help developers debug their application programs.

Requirements for a good Python IDE

There are several open source IDEs to use Python. Let's see what features an IDE must have:

- Save and reload source code

    An IDE should **save your work automatically** and reopen everything later, in the same state it was in when you left. This will save you development time.

- Running from inside the environment

    The IDE should have a **built-in compiler** to run your code. If you need to open another application to run it, then you are probably using a text editor.

- Debugger support

    The debugger must be able to partially run the code through the so-called **break points**.

- Syntax highlighting

    Being able to **quickly identify keywords**, variables, and symbols within the code, even with different text colors, makes reading and understanding the code much easier.

- Automatic code formatting

The code indents itself when the developer uses loops, functions, or any other block code.

In light of these features just mentioned, a good IDE is undoubtedly **Pycharm**. It is an integrated development environment developed by JetBrains. It stands out from the competition because of its productivity tools, such as quick fixes.

It is available in three versions, the Community version under Apache license, the Educational version and the proprietary Professional version. The first two versions are open source and therefore free, while the Professional version is paid.

Official website: https://www.jetbrains.com/pycharm/

Python Environment Variables

Variable	Description
PYTHONPATH	This is similar to PATH. This variable foretells the Python interpreter as to where it can locate the module files that you can import into a program. PYTHONPATH must have a Python source library directory and the directories in which your Python code is present. PYTHONPATH is sometimes set by the Python installer automatically.
PYTHONSTARTUP	This has the path for the initialization file, which contains Python source codes that are executed every time you work on the interpreter. This file is often named .Pythonrc.py in Unix, which usually has commands that can load the utilities or can modify the PYTHONPATH.
PYTHONCASEOK	This is used in Windows OS for instructing Python to find case-insensitive matches in an import statement. You can set this to any random value for activating it.
PYTHONHOME	This is an alternative search path that is embedded in PYTHONSTARTUP or PYTHONPATH directories for switching the module libraries very easily.

2. Python Variables

Understanding variables in Python, classes, and how they work is essential for both beginners and expert programmers looking to expand their programming skills.

What is a Variable in Python?

When you write complex code, your program will require some structure to make changes before running it.

Variables are sections of memory used to store certain values that will later be used during the development of the program. Unlike other programming languages, Python does not have the command to declare a variable.

Variables in Python are thus described as memory segments used to store data. As such, they act as memory units that feed the computer with data needed for processing.

Each value includes its own database, and all data is categorized as numbers, tuples, dictionaries, and lists, to name a few.

It's important to understand how variables work and how useful they are in creating an effective Python script. We will understand in the following how to declare, redeclare, and delete local and global variables.

Variables and Constants

Variables and constants are components used in Python, but they perform different functions. Variables, as well as constants, use values that are used to create code to be executed during the creation of the program. They act as essential storage places for data in memory, while constants are variables whose value remains unchanged. Variables therefore store reserves for data, while constants have a fixed value. A characteristic of constants is that they are written in capital letters and separated by underscores.

Variables and Literals

A literal is a raw data given in a variable or constant. In Python, there are several types of literals: numeric, string, and Boolean. There are also collections of Literals such as tuples, dictionaries, lists, and sets.

Both variables and literals deal with unprocessed data. The difference is that variables store them.

```
foo = 42
^        ^
|        |--- literal, 42 is *literally* 42
|
|--variabile "foo", the content may vary
```

Variabili e Array

Variables in Python have a unique feature: they store a value in memory so that it can be quickly retrieved and provided when needed.

On the other hand, Arrays (or collections) in Python contain a group of related values. These are data types used and categorized into lists, tuples, sets, or dictionaries which will be discussed shortly. Let's look at an example:

```
student = "Mark"
students[0] = "Alex"
students[1] = "Jack"
students[2] = "Albert"
# students is a string array of length 3
```

Naming Variables

Naming a variable is quite simple, both for beginners and advanced programmers. However, it is good to observe some rules in order to write the code in an optimal way, so that it can be easily read and modified by someone else. This is about consistency and common sense.

These are the rules that any variable name must follow:

- Names must have only one word, i.e., there must be no spaces within a single name

- Names should consist only of letters, numbers and underscores ("_")

- The first letter must never be a number

- Reserved words should never be used as variable names

Like most programming languages, Python is case sensitive. Therefore, you should avoid creating identical names within a single program so as not to create confusion.

Another important component when naming variables is the style. It is a good idea to always start a variable name with a lowercase letter. Also, if a name consists of several words, a good practice is to separate them with an underscore. For example:

```
my_number = 5
```

Creating variable names may seem very easy, but sometimes, when dealing with programs with a certain level of complexity, it may be a less straightforward process, especially for beginners.

Naming variables efficiently is a challenge that brings big benefits in the long run.

You can name variables as you like, with names of any length, using lower and upper case letters and numbers. Python also offers the full Unicode support, which is essential for Unicode features in variables.

As already mentioned, there are specific rules for naming variables. The purpose is to create code that is readable so to avoid confusion, especially when several people are working on the same project.

However, the technique of naming variables is subjective, as different programmers decide how to create their own type names.

Different Naming Methods

- Pascal case: the first letter of each word in uppercase to improve readability.

    Example: `ConcentrationOfWhiteSmoke`

- Camel case: the second and the following words have the first letter capitalized.

    Example: `concentrationOfWhiteSmoke`

- Snake case: The snake method for creating variable names involves a word separator using an underscore as mentioned earlier.

    Example: `concentration_of_white_smoke`

Variables Declaration

We have seen how variables are the naming and storing of data values (numeric, boolean, characters, strings, etc.) used when writing the program.

19

In Python, unlike other programming languages such as C/C++, you don't have to declare the variable before using it. It is sufficient to assign a value to it, and then the interpreter will automatically recognize the value and assign the correct data type to the variable.

Let's see two examples directly from the terminal.

Integer type example:

```
x = 5
print(type(x))
>> <class 'int'>
# the type of x is int
```

String type example:

```
x = 'Alex'
print(type(x))
>> <class 'str'>
# the type of x is str
```

Variables Assignment

As we have already mentioned, in Python variables do not need to be declared, so creating them is quite simple. Creating a variable simply means assigning a value to it and starting to use it. Just use the equal symbol ("=) for declarations and expressions.

For example, writing n=38 in Python means that 'n' is assigned the value '38' (a value that can be easily replaced).

As with literal values, the value (or content) of the variable can be displayed directly by the interpreter by typing the name of the variable and pressing enter, thus without using the print() function.

Finally, Python allows you to assign the same value to several variables at once. For example, just write a=b=c=d=38.

Re-declaring Variables

After declaring a variable in Python, you can make changes by declaring it again or assigning a replacement value to it. That is, you can replace or link a different value from the previous one through the re-declaration process.

Redeclaring variables is beneficial because, for example, you may want to change the code or make some changes during your project.

Assigning new values to variables is a delicate process when dealing with complex programs, especially if they were written by another programmer. The Python interpreter automatically discards the original value and adds the new value. The data type for the new value does not have to be the same as the previous one. For example, you can switch from a numeric value to a string value. Let's see an example:

```
x = 76
print(type(x))
>> <class 'int'>

x = 'white'
print(type(x))
>> <class 'str'>
```

In this example, the variable 'x' is assigned the value of an integer and then reassigned the value of a string.

Always keep in mind that it is good to write readable code in order to create clear programs. This will also make the re-declaration of variables more effective.

Global Variables

In Python, it is possible to make blocks of code that perform a specific task within the entire program. We'll delve into this important topic later when we will discuss functions and modules.

A variable declared outside of these blocks of code is called a **global variable**. This means that a global variable is always accessible. Vediamo un esempio:

```
z = "global variable"

def print_z():
    # print_z is a function that prints z
    print("z inside:", z)


print_z()
>> z inside: global variable

print("z outside:", z)
>> z outsed: global variable
```

21

Local Variables

A variable declared within a function, i.e. locally, is called a **local variable**.

Unlike global variables, local variables are therefore only used locally, declared within a specific block of code (function or module) and used exclusively within it.

If you try to use the variable outside of the code block in which it was declared, Python will not recognize it and will therefore throw an error message for undeclared values.

Let's see an example:

```
def LocalDeclare():
    y = "local"

LocalDeclare()
print(y)
>> NameError: name 'y' is not defined
```

The output shows an error since we are trying to access the local variable y, but it only works within `LocalDeclare()`.

Deleting Variables

Python provides a command to delete any variable: `del()`.

You may want to delete a variable, for example, to free up space for storing new values (especially in the case of complex programs). Or it could be that there are some unwanted or unnecessary variables that would be better to eliminate.

Before deleting a variable, make sure that it does not contain any essential values.

Finally, to confirm if the variable has been deleted, you can try printing it, and if an error message is displayed, it means that the variable has been deleted successfully.

Let's see an example:

```
z = 'awesome'
print(z)
>> awesome

del(z)
print(z)
>> NameError: name 'z' is not defined
```

3. Basic Operators of Python

Python is considered a high-level programming language with less complexity when it comes to using the basic operators in the code. It is built to read and implement computer language easily. Python provides various types of operators for performing tasks. Let's see the basic operators provided by Python.

Types of Operators

1. Python Arithmetic Operators
2. Python Assignment Operators
3. Python Comparison Operators
4. Python Logical Operators
5. Python Bitwise Operators
6. Python Membership Operators
7. Python Identity Operators

Python Arithmetic Operators

Arithmetic operators help us to solve several types of mathematical problems like addition, subtraction, multiplication, exponential values, floor divisions, etc. Let's suppose we have two variables whose values are x = 16, y = 4.

Operator	Description	Example
Addition (+)	This operator will be adding the values on both sides of operands.	x + y = 20
Subtraction (-)	This operator will be subtracting the right-hand side value from the left-hand side value of the operand.	x − y = 12
Multiplication (*)	This operator will be multiplying the two values on both sides of the operands.	x * y = 64
Division (/)	This operator will be dividing the left-hand side value by the right-hand side value of the operand.	x / y = 4
Modulus (%)	This operator will be dividing the left-hand side value by the right-hand side value of the operand and returns the remainder.	x % y = 0
Exponent (**)	This operator will be doing the 'exponential power' calculation on operands.	x ** y = 16 to the power 4
Floor division (//)	This operator will be dividing the operands, the quotient of a number which is divided by 2 is the result.	13 // 3 = 4, simultaneously 13.0 // 3.0 = 4.0;

Example

Let's see how the output comes. {values in [ ] are outputs}
Let x, y and z be three variables with the following values:
x = 25, y = 30, z = 0:

```
z = x + y
print(" result of z is ", z)
z = x - y
print("  result of z is ", z)
z = x * y
print(" result of z is ", z)
z = x / y
print(" result of z is ", z)
z = x % y
print(" result of z is ", z)
```

Output:
```
result of z is 55
result of z is -5
result of z is 750
result of z is 0.8333
result of z is 5
```

Now suppose
```
a = 4, b = 5, c = a**b;
print("value of c is", c)
a = 15, b = 45, c = b//a;
print("value of c is", c)
```

Outputs:
```
value of c is 1024
value of c is 3
```

As 4 to the power 5 is 1024 and the floor division between 45 and 15 is 3.

Python Comparison Operators

In Python, comparison operators are operators that compare two operands' values and returns true or false depending on whether the condition has matched or not. It is also called Python Relational Operator.

Let's take two variables having the values a = 20, b = 15:

Operator	Description	Example
(==)	This condition becomes true only if two given values (operands) are equal.	(a == b) ☐ not true
(!=)	This condition becomes true only if the two operands aren't equal.	(a != b) ☐ true
(>)	This condition becomes true only if the left operand is greater than the right operand.	(a > b) ☐ true
(<)	This condition becomes true only if the right operand is greater than the left operand.	(a < b) ☐ not true
(>=)	This condition becomes true only if the left operand is greater than or equal to the right operator.	(a >= b) ☐ true
(<=)	This condition becomes true only if the right operand is greater than or equal to the left operand.	(a <= b) ☐ not true

Example

Let's see what the output of the following code is:

```
i = 10
j = 15
if ( i ==j )
    print("i is equal to j")
else
    print("i is not equal to j")
if ( i != j)
    print("i is not equal to j")
else
    print("i is equal to j")
if ( i > j)
    print("i is greater than j")
else
    print("i is not greater than j")
if ( i < j)
    print("i is less than j")
else
    print("i is not less than j")
if ( i >= j)
    print("i is greater than or equal to j")
else
    print("i is neither greater than nor equal to j")
if ( i <= j)
    print ("i is less than or equal to j")
else
    print("i is neither less than nor equal to j")
```

Outputs of the recently used comparison operators:

```
i is not equal to j
i is not equal to j
i is not greater than j
i is less than j
i is neither greater than nor equal to j
i is less than or equal to j
```

27

Python Assignment Operators

These kinds of operators are used to assign several values to the variables. Let's check the different types of assignment operators.

Operator	Description	Example
Equal (=)	This operator will assign values from right side operand to left side operand.	c = a + b
Add AND (+=)	This operator will add the right operand with left operand and assigns the sum to the left operand.	c += a □ it is equivalent to c = c + a;
Subtract AND (-=)	This operator will subtract the right operand from the left operand and assigns the subtraction to the left operand.	c -= a □ it is equivalent to c = c - a
Multiply AND (*=)	This operator will multiply the right and left operand and assigns the multiplication to the left operand.	c *= a □ it is equivalent to c = c * a
Divide AND (/=)	This operator will divide the left operand with the right operand and assigns division to the left operand.	c /= a □ it's equivalent to c = c/a
Modulus AND (%=)	This operator takes modulus by using both sides' operand and assigns the outcome to left operand.	c %= a □ it's equivalent to c = c % a
Exponent AND (**=)	Does 'to the power' calculation and assigns the outcome to the left operand.	c **= a □ it's equivalent to c = c**a
Floor division AND (//=)	It does floor division and assigns the outcome to the left operand.	c //= a □ it's equivalent to c = c // a

Example

```
a = 15
b = 20
c = 0
c = a + b
print("value of c is", c)
c += a
print("value of c is", c)
c *= a
print("value of c is", c)
c %= a
print("value of c is", c)
```

Output: 35, 50, 525, 5 are the outputs of the operators respectively.

Python Bitwise Operators

Bitwise operators are used to perform bit operations. All the decimal values will be converted in the binary format here.

Let's suppose:

a = 0101 1010

b = 0001 1000

Then, it will be

(a & b) = 0001 1000

(a | b) = 0101 1010

(a ˆ b) = 0100 0010

(~a) = 1010 0101

Note: There is an in-built function [bin ()] in Python that can obtain the binary representation of an integer number.

Types of Bitwise Operators: [a = 0001 1000, b = 0101 1010]

Operators	Description	Example
Binary AND (&)	This operator executes a bit if it exists in both operands.	(a & b) is 0001 1000
Binary OR (|)	This operator executes a bit if it exists in one of the operands.	(a | b) is 0101 1010
Binary XOR (^)	This operator executes a bit if it is fixed in one operand but not in both	(a ^ b) is 0100 0010
Binary one's complement (~)	This operator executes just by flipping the bits.	~a = 1110 ~b = 0110
Binary left shift (<<)	This operator executes by moving left operand's value more left. It's specified by the right operand.	a << 100 (means 0110 0000)
Binary right shift (>>)	This operator executes by moving left operand's value right. It's specified by the right operand.	a >> 134 (means 0000 0110)

Let's see an example:

```
a = 50                    # 50 = 0011 0010
b = 17                    # 17 = 0001 0001
print('a=', a, ':', bin(a))
print('b=', b, ':', bin(b))
c = 0
c = a & b;                # 16 = 0001 0000
print("result of AND is", c, ':', bin(c))
c = a | b;                # 51 = 0011 0011
print("result of 0R is", c, ':', bin(c))
c = a ^ b;                # 66 = 0100 0010
print("result of XOR is", c, ':', bin(c))
c = a>> 2;                # 96 = 0110 0000
print("result of right shift is", c, ':', bin(c))
```

Output:
```
a=50: 00110010
b=17: 00010001
result of AND is 16: 0b010000
```

```
result of OR is 51: 0b110011
result of XOR is 66: 0b01000010
result of right shift is 96: 0b01100000
```

Python Logical Operator

The logical operator permits a program to make decisions according to multiple conditions. Every operand is assumed as a condition that can give us a true or false value. There are 3 types of logical operators.

(a = false operand, b = true operand)

Operators	Description	Example
Logical AND	If the given operands both are true, the condition becomes true	Condition is false
Logical OR	If one of the given operands is true, the condition becomes true.	Condition is true
Logical NOT	If the given operand is true, the condition becomes false.	Condition is true for a and false for b

Let's see an example:
```
>>> i = 25
# Logical AND Example
>>> if i < 30 AND i > 18:
print (" Condition is fulfilled ")
else:
print(" Condition is not fulfilled ")
# Logical OR Example
>>> if i < 18 OR i > 20:
print(" Condition is fulfilled ")
else:
print(" Condition is not fulfilled ")
```

Output:
```
Condition is fulfilled
Condition is fulfilled
```

Python Membership Operator

Membership operators are operators that validate the membership of a value. It examines for membership in a sequence like strings, lists, tuples, etc. Two types of membership operators are:

Operator	Description	Example
in	The condition becomes true if it can find a variable in a specified sequence.	Follow the example part given below.
not in	The condition becomes true if it can find no variable in a specified sequence.	Follow the example part given below.

Example

```
i = 40, j = 20;
listValues = {10, 20, 30, 40}
if( i is in the listValues )
print(" i is available in the list ")
else
print(" i is not available in the list ")
if(j is in the listValues)
print(" j is available in the list ")
else
print(" j is not available in the list ")
k = i / j
if( k is in the listValues)
print (" k is available in the list ")
else
print(" k is not available in the list ")
```

Output:
```
i is no available in the list
j is not available in the list
k is available in the list
```

Python Identity Operators

These are operators that are used to determine whether a value is of a particular class or type. To determine the type of data that contains several variables, this type of operator is used. There are two types of Identity operators as shown below:

Operator	Description	Example
is	The condition becomes true if the variables of each side of the operator are pointing to the same object.	If id(x) and id(y) are equal and x is y, the result is in 1.
is not	The condition becomes true if the variables of each side of the operator do not point to the same object.	If id(x) and id(y) are not equal and x is not y, the result is not in 1.

Example

```
x = 10, y = 10
print('x = ', 'x', ':', id(x), 'y = ', 'y', ':', id(y))
if (x is y)
print(" Both x and y are having same identity ")
else
print(" x and y are not having same identity ")
if( id(x) == id(y) )
print(" Both x and y are having same identity ")
else
print(" x and y are not having same identity ")
```

Output:
```
x = 10 : 2371593036   y = 10 : 2371593036
Both x and y are having same identity
Both x and y are having same identity
```

Python Operator Precedence

In the below table all the operators from higher to lower precedence are listed

Operator	Description
**	Exponentiation(raise to the power)
~ + -	First one is Complement, second is unary plus and last one is unary minus.
/ * % //	Division, multiplication, modulus, floor division
+ -	Addition and subtraction
>> <<	Right bitwise shift and left bitwise shift
&	Bitwise AND
^ |	Bitwise exclusive OR and bitwise regular OR
<= < > >=	Less than equals to, less than, greater than, greater than equals to (comparison operators)
== <> !=	Equality operators
= %= /= //= - = += *= **=	Assignment Operators
is is not	Identity Operators
In not in	Membership Operators
NOT OR AND	Logical Operators

Example

For example, x = 5 + 14 * 2; in this equation, the value of x is 33, not 38 because the operator * has higher precedence than +. For which it first multiplies 14 * 2 and then add it with 5.

4. Python Data Types

In programming, the concept of data type is an extremely important concept.

Python supports several data types. Variables can memorize data of different types, each one having unique characteristics that enable different operations.

We report below the different data types supported by Python by default:

- Numerical: `int, float, complex`

- Text: `str`

- Sequence: `list, tuple, range`

- Map: `dict`

- Set: `set, frozenset`

- Boolean: `bool`

We distinguish between simple data types and sequences, which in turn are divided into immutable and mutable.

We will discuss the most important data types below.

Numerical Type

These data types help in storing numeric values. The creation of numeric objects in Python happens after assigning them a value. Consider the example given below:

```
total = 55
age = 26
```

The following statement can be used for single or multiple variable deletions. This is shown below:

```
del total
del total, age
```

In the first instruction we are deleting a single variable, while in the second instruction we are deleting two variables. If the variables to be deleted are more than two, separate them with a comma and they will be deleted.

Python has three built-in numeric data types:

- integers: `int`
- floating-point numbers: `float`
- complex numbers: `complex`

In Python 3, all integers are represented as long integers.

Python's integer literals belong to the class int.

Execute the following instructions consecutively on the Python interactive interpreter.

```
>>> x=10
>>> x
10
```

Float is used to store numeric values with a decimal point.

```
>>> x=10.345
>>> x
10.345
```

If you run a multiplication operation between an integer and a float the result will be a float.

```
>>> 5 * 1.5
7.5
```

As shown above, the result of the operation is 7.5, which is a float.

Complex numbers consist of real and imaginary part, and the imaginary part is denoted by a j. They can be defined as follows:

```
>>> x = 4 + 5j
>>> x
(4+5j)
```

Strings

In Python, strings are a series of characters enclosed in quotation marks. You can use any type of quotes to enclose strings, i.e. single or double quotes.

They can only store characters and are a primitive data type. Note that strings are completely different from integers or numbers. Therefore, the string "111" has no relation to the number 111.

```
>>> print "hello"
hello
>>> print 'good'
good
```

We can access the elements of a string using square brackets ([ ]). The index of the string starts at 0 in Python.

```
>>> word = 'hello'
>>> word[0]
h
>>> word[2]
l
```

Indexes can also be negative numbers, to start counting from the right. Negative indexes start at -1 while positive indexes start at 0:

```
>>> word = 'good'
>>> word[-1]
d
>>> word[-2]
o
```

An important feature to note is that strings in Python are immutable (i.e., they cannot be changed).

```
thanks = 'Thank You'

print (thanks)
# it prints the whole string

print (thanks[0])
# it prints the first character of the string

print (thanks[2:7])
# it prints third to eighth character
```

```
print (thanks[4:])
# it prints from the fifth character onwards

print (thanks * 2)
# it prints the string twice

print (thanks + "Again!")
# it prints a concatenated string
```

The program prints the following when executed:

```
Thank You
T
ank Yo
k You
Thank YouThank You
Thank You Again!
```

Notice that we have text that begins with the # symbol. The symbol denotes the beginning of a comment. The program will ignore the part that goes from the hash mark to the end of the line. Comments are used to improve the readability of the code by giving explanations.

We have defined a string called 'thanks' with the value 'Thank you'. The instruction 'print (thanks[0])' helps us to access the first character of the string, so it prints 'T'. Also, note that the space between the two words is counted as a character.

String Operations

There are commands (or methods) created specifically for strings.

len: this method is used to compute the number of characters present in the string.

lower: this will convert all uppercase characters of the string to lowercase. Therefore, after using this function, all characters in the string will be lowercase only.

upper: contrary to 'lower', it will convert all lowercase characters in the string to uppercase letters. Therefore, after using this function, all characters in the string will be uppercase only.

split: this command splits the string into several parts using a delimiter. Examples of delimiter are spaces, lines, commas or tabs.

Let's see an example:

```
>>> s = 'wooden house'
>>> letter_1 = s[0]
>>> long = len (s)
>>> last_letter = s[long-1]  # alternative: s[-1]
>>> print (letter_1, last_ letter, long)
w e 12
```

The value 'wooden house' is an object of type string, which includes a sequence of 12 characters. This value is assigned to the variable s, which refers to the same object. We access the first element with index 0 (letter_1 = s[0]).

To calculate the number of elements, or length, of the string, we use the internal function 'len()'. The string has 12 elements and its last element is at position 11 or -1.

w	o	o	d	e	n		h	o	u	s	e
0	1	2	3	4	5	6	7	8	9	10	11
-12	-11	-10	-9	-8	-7	-6	-5	-4	-3	-2	-1

Table 1 String elements and indexes to access them, positive and negative

You can create an empty string: s = " (two single quotes without space). In this case the command 'len(s)' will give 0 as output.

Trimming or splitting sequences and other operations

To extract a subset of elements (or segment) of a string or any sequence, the trimming operator [n: m] is used, where n is the first element to be extracted and m-1 is the last.

Below we show some examples of accessing string elements and segments. We will write the result in the comments:

```
>>> s = 'wooden house'

>>> segm1 = s[0:3]
# segm1 <- 'woo'

>>> segm1 = s [:3]
# segm1 <- 'woo', equivalent to the previous slice

>>> segm2 = s[8:len(s)]
# segm2 <- 'hous'
```

39

```
>>> segm2 = s[8:]
# segm2 <- 'hous', equivalent to the previous slice

>>> segm3 = s[0:12:2]
# segm3 <- 'woe os', slice 0:12 in 2-by-2 steps

>>> letter_u = s[-1]
# letter_u <- 'e', last element

>>> letter_penu = s[-2]
# letter_penu <- 's', access penultimate element
```

In the slice operator, if the first index [: m] (before the colon) is omitted, the slice starts from the first element. If the second index [n :] is omitted, the slice starts from the first index to the end. Negative indexes are useful for accessing the last element [-1], without requiring the use of the len () function.

To concatenate strings in Python, we use the (+) operator, while the asterisk (*) is used for repetition.

Let's look at an example right away:

```
>>> s1 = 'house'
>>> s2 = s1 + 'big'
>>> print(s2)
'big house'

>>> s3 = 3 * s1 + '!'
>>> print(s3)
househousehouse!
```

The 'in' operator is considered a Boolean operator on two strings and returns 'True' if the string on the left is a segment (or substring) of the string on the right. If it is not, it returns 'False'. The 'not in' operator returns the opposite logical result:

```
>>> s = 'wooden house'
>>> 'house' in s
True
>>> 'housewood' in s
False
>>> 'housewood' not in s
True
```

Strings are immutable

Remember that this data type is considered immutable because we cannot change the values of its elements or change its size. If we want to do that, we have to create another variable (and another string value before it, of course). For example, if we want to capitalize the first letter of the string s from the previous example, we'll get an error:

```
>>> s = 'wooden house'
>>> s [0] = 'W'
Traceback (most recent call last):
  File "<stdin>", line 1, in <module>
TypeError: 'str' object does not support item assignment
```

Capitalizing the first letter of the string can be done automatically, as we will show later, by creating a new variable.

In object-oriented programming, objects have associated methods for manipulating their data. Methods receive arguments and return values. Strings have methods of their own. For example, the 'upper' method takes a string and returns another string with capital letters. To apply 'upper' to the string s just write s.upper(). The method is then applied to the values of the string.

Let's see some examples of applying string methods (there are methods with and without arguments):

```
s = 'wooden house'

s=s.upper()
# converts the letters to uppercase
WOODEN HOUSE

s.lower ()
# converts the letters to lowercase
wooden house

s.capitalize()
# first letter of the string in uppercase
Wooden house

s.title()
# first letter of each string word in uppercase
Wooden House
```

```
s.find('e')
# searches the index (position) of the first string 'e'
# if it doesn't find the string it returns -1
4

s.count('a')
# count how many times the element or string appears
0

s.replace('o','e')
# replace the first string with the second
weeden heuse

s.split (' ')
# split s using the string ' ' as divider
['wooden', 'house']

s1 = 'Hello'
s1.isupper()
# True if all characters in s1 are uppercase
False

s1[0].isupper()
True

s1.islower ()
# True if all characters in S are lowercase
False

s1[1].islower ()
True
```

The code above shows a group of common string methods. We solved the problem of capitalizing the first letter with the 'capitalize()' method. The split method divides the string into segments according to the delimiter used as an argument, which in this case is blank space. The ' ' (blank space) argument is the default argument, so 's.split()' can be used to separate words in a text. The resulting substring (words, in this case) is returned in a list with the substrings as elements.

String manipulation

We can use built-in functions to manipulate strings in Python. The "string" package provides other functions on strings.

For example:

```
name = "ABCD XYZ xyz"
print(len(name))
# It will return the length of the string name
12

name.startswith( 'A' )
# It will return True if name starts with A, False
otherwise
True

Print(name.endswith( 'Z' ))
# It will return True if name ends with Z, False
otherwise
False

print(name.index('C'))
# It will return the index of CD in name
2

Print('C'.isalpha())
# It will return True if C is a letter, False otherwise
True

print '1'.isdigit( )
# It will return True if 1 is a digit, False otherwise
True

print name.lower()
# It will return a string with lowercase characters in
name
abcd xyz xyz

print name.upper( )
# It will return a string with uppercase characters in
name
ABCD XYZ XYZ
```

The type() function

In Python there is a function called 'type()' that can be used to determine the type of a variable. All you need to do is pass the name of the variable within that function as an argument and its type will be printed:

```
>>> x=10
>>> type(x)
```

```
(class 'int')
```

The variable x is of class int as shown above. You can try this for other types of variables as shown below:

```
>>> name='nicholas'
>>> type(name)
(class 'str')
```

The variable 'name' is of class string ('str'), as show.

5. Data Structures

In the examples given so far, we have used simple data, which have only one associated value: an integer, a real, or a boolean in the case of numerical data types. They are scalar objects because they are indivisible, that is, they have no accessible internal structure.

We have also introduced compound data such as text or a sequence of characters, represented by strings. These types of data are not scalar because they can be divided into accessible elements, so they are structured data.

Structured data contains elements that can be simple data or other compound data. Recall that both simple and compound data in Python are treated as an object.

The elements can all be of the same type, such as strings containing characters, and in this case they are called homogeneous structured data. Other languages (C/C ++, Matlab, Pascal) have homogeneous structures such as matrix (or table), which are very useful for operations with vectors or matrices. The standard version of Python does not have a structure like a C or Pascal matrix, although Python's numerical library (NumPy) includes these options.

In Python, compound or structured data can be classified into two groups, according to the characteristic of being able to change, reduce, or expand their elements: mutable structured data and immutable structured data.

Immutable structured data (static)

Immutable structured data are characterized by the fact that the elements of their sequence cannot be changed or deleted, nor can new elements be added to the data structure. To modify this type of data we will have to use the appropriate built-in methods that are specific to that data type. In Python, immutable structured data are character strings, tuples and frozen sets.

Tuples

Tuples, like strings, are a sequence of elements arranged in a Python object. Unlike strings, which contain only characters, tuples can contain elements of any types. Elements are indexed like strings, through an integer. The syntax of tuples is a sequence of values separated by commas. Although not required, they are usually enclosed in parentheses:

```
# Example of tuples
>>> a = 1, 2, 3
>>> print(a)
(1, 2, 3)

>>> b = (3, 4, 5, 'a')
>>> print(b)
(3, 4, 5, 'a')

>>> type (a)
<class 'tuple'>

>>> type (b)
<class 'tuple'>
```

Items assigned to variables a and b are of type tuples. The important thing is to separate the elements by commas. For example:

```
>>> t = 'k',
>>> print(t)
('k',)

>>> type (t)
<class 'tuple'>

>>> t2 = 'k'
>>> print(t2)
'k'

>>> type (t2)
<class 'str'>
```

The object " 'k', " is a tuple, however 'k' is a string. An empty tuple can be created using parentheses without including anything: (). We can also use the internal tuple () function to convert a sequence, such as a string or list, into a tuple, or create an empty tuple:

```
>>> tuple ('Hello')
('H', 'e', 'l', 'l', 'o')

>>> tuple ([1, 2])
(1, 2)

>>> tuple ()
()
```

Indexing, trimming and other tuple operations

Accessing tuple elements, extracting elements, and other operations are performed in the same way as strings. Let's look at some examples:

```
>>> b = (3, 4, 5, 'a')
>>> b [0]
3

>>> b [-1]
'a'

>>> b [0: 3]
(3, 4, 5)

>>> t = ('the', 'tuples', 'are', 'immutable')
>>> t [0]
'the'

>>> t [1] = 'lists'
Traceback (most recent call last):
  File "<stdin>", line 1, in <module>
TypeError: 'tuple' object does not support item
assignment
```

Just like strings, tuples are static or immutable.

We can have tuples within tuples, concatenate them, and repeat them, like a string. In addition, concatenation (+), repetition (*) and the membership operators 'in' and 'not in' can also be used in tuples:

```
>>> b = (3, 4, 5, 'a')
>>> c = (b, 2)
>>> b + c
(3, 4, 5, 'a', (3, 4, 5, 'a'), 2)

>>> 3*b
(3, 4, 5, 'a', 3, 4, 5, 'a', 3, 4, 5, 'a')
```

47

Multiple assignments

Python allows multiple assignments through tuple assignments. These actions allow a tuple of variables on the left to be assigned a tuple of values on the right of it. The condition to be met is that the number of variables in the variable tuple is equal to the number of elements in the value tuple.

Also, the object to be assigned to the tuple of variables can be a string or a list (which we will discuss later), as long as the number of characters or elements is equal to the number of variables in the tuple to which the values are assigned. Let's look at some examples:

```
>>> a,b,c = (1,2,3)
>>> a
1

>>> type(a)
<class 'int'>

>>> d,e,f = 'xyz'
>>> d
'x'

>>> type(d)
<class 'str'>
```

In the first tuple of variables (a, b, c) the variables receive integer values. Although this object is a structured type, tuple, its elements are variables of type integer. Similarly, the tuple of variables (d, e, f) receives values of type string and its variables will be of type string.

This feature of tuple assignments makes it easy to solve the typical variable swapping problem, without requiring an auxiliary variable (as is the case in classical programming languages). For example, if we want to swap the values of the variables $x = 5$ and $y = 7$, in classical languages we would have:

```
>>> x = 5
>>> y = 7
>>> temp = x
# use of auxiliary (temporary) variable temp
>>> x = y
>>> y = temp
>>> print (x, y)
7    5
```

With multiple tuple assignments, the solution is straightforward:

```
>>> x = 5
>>> y = 7
>>> x, y = y, x
>>> print (x, y)
7       5
```

Tuples methodologies

As in strings, there are methods associated with objects of type tuple and lists. These are the 'count()' and 'index()' methods.

If the tuple (or list) is only of numerical values, you can use the internal functions 'max' and 'min'. If the elements are strings, these functions will calculate the largest or the smallest element depending on the position of the first character in the ASCII table.

Let's see a practical example:

```
>>> a = (2, 3, 4, 5, 79, -8, 5, -4)

>>> a.index (5)
# index of the first occurrence of 5 in a
3

>>> a.count (5)
# total occurrences of 5 in a
2

>>> max (a)
79

>>> min (a)
-8

>>> b = ('az', 'b', 'x')
>>> max (b)
'x'

>>> min (b)
'az'
```

49

Lists

Lists, like tuples and strings, are formed by a sequence of data. However, unlike tuples, the elements of a list can be modified, deleted, or increased. List elements can be simple data (numerical or Boolean), strings, tuples or other lists. Even in strings, the elements are indexed by an integer. The syntax of lists is a sequence of comma-separated values enclosed in square brackets:

```
>>> v1 = [2, 4, 6, 8, 10]
>>> type (v1)
<class 'list'>

>>> v2 = [7, 8.5, 'a', 'Hello', (2, 3), [11, 12]]
>>> v2
[7, 8, 'a', 'Hello', (2, 3), [11, 12]]

>>> games = ['tennis', 'baseball', 'football',
'volleyball', 'swimming']
>>> games
['tennis', 'baseball', 'football', 'volleyball',
'swimming']
```

The list 'v1' consists of integers, while 'v2' includes integers, real numbers, strings, tuples and a list as last element. The variable 'games' refers to a list object with 5 elements of type string. It is similar to the tuple defined above, but its elements can be modified. It is a dynamic structure.

```
>>> v = list (range (1,11))
>>> v
[1, 2, 3, 4, 5, 6, 7, 8, 9, 10]
```

In versions 2.x of Python, range () is a function that directly generates a list. However, in versions 3.x, range () is a type of data range. It can therefore be converted to a list with the 'list()' function. This function is also used to convert iterable data types, such as strings or tuples, to the list type. You can also create an empty list:

```
>>> t = (1, 2, 3)
>>> list (t)
[1, 2, 3]

>>> s = 'Hello'
>>> list (s)
```

```
['Hello']

>>> e = list ()   # empty list
>>> e = []        # empty list
```

Like strings, lists can also be indexed and trimmed.

```
>>> a = [5, 6, 7, 8, 9]
>>> a
[5, 6, 7, 8, 9]

>>> a[0]
5

>>> a[4]
9

>>> a[ 1:3 ]
[6, 7]

>>> a[ 2:4 ]
[7, 8]
```

As opposed to strings, lists are mutable, meaning that values can be changed.

```
>>> b = [11, 7, 22, 10, 8]
>>> b
[11, 7, 22, 10, 8]

>>> b[2] = 0
>>> b
[11, 7, 0, 10, 8]
# Here the index [2] is changed to 0 (the initial value
was 22)

>>> b[0] = 10
>>> b
[10, 7, 0, 10, 8]
# Here the index [0] is changed to 10 (the initial value
was 11)
```

Values in the list can be separated using a comma between square brackets. You can nest one list inside another, or add or remove items to the list:

```python
list1 = [11, 12, 13, 14, 15, 16]
print (len (list1))
# returns 6 - which is the length of the list

list1[2]
# returns 13 - which is third element in the list Starts

list1[-1]
# returns 16 - which is extreme last element in the list

list1[-2]
# returns 15 - which is second last element

list1[ 0:2 ] = [ 0, 5]
# replacing first two elements 11 and 12 with 0 and 5

list2 = [8, 4, 2, 1]
list2.append(10)
# inserting 10 from the last in the stack

print(list2)
# result is [8, 4, 2, 1, 10]

list2.pop()
#  removing 10 from the stack, Last In First Out

print(list2)
# result is [8, 4, 2, 1]

list3 = [8, 4, 2, 1]
list3.append(12)
# inserting 12 from the last in the queue

print(list3)
# result is: [8, 4, 2, 1, 12]

del(list3[0])
# removing 8 from the queue, First In First Out

print(list3)
# result is: [4, 2, 1, 12]
```

Dictionaries

Python dictionaries include indexed, editable but unordered elements, typically written in curly brackets with keys and values. You can access an element through the use of a keyword within the brackets, change values, add or remove elements, or perform iterations.

Key and values are separated by ":" and key pairs are separated by a comma and enclosed in curly brackets.

Lists cannot be used as keys.

```
capitals = { 'ES' : 'Madrid', 'MH' : 'Mumbai' }

capitals[ 'IT' ] = 'Rome'
# adding a new key to the dictionary

print (capitals[ 'ES' ])
# returns value of ES in the dictionary

del (capitals[ 'IT' ])
# deletes IT from the dictionary

capitals[ 'UP' ] = 'Luck now'
# adding UP to the dictionary

print ('ES' in capitals)
# checks whether ES key exist in dictionary
```

You can also copy the dictionary by writing 'dict2 = dict1'. In this case 'dict2' will become a representation of 'dict1', making any necessary changes automatically. Another way to create a copy is by using the dictionary's own method, namely 'copy'.

Python dictionaries can also have other dictionaries inside them. That is, you can have nested dictionaries.

Finally, you can generate a dictionary by using the 'dict()' function, which allows you to copy the previous dictionary or create a new one.

Frozen Sets

In Python, there is another group of data structures that tries to keep some relationship with set theory. These data structures are the sets: Set and Frozen Set. The former are presented in the following section of mutable or dynamic structured data.

A Frozen Set is a collection of unordered elements that are unique and unchanging. That is, it can contain numbers, strings, tuples, but not lists. The fact that they are unique elements means that they are not repeated. The Set and Frozen Set are not sequences of data:

```
>>> FS1 = frozenset ({25, 4, 'a', 2, 25, 'house', 'a'})
>>> FS1
frozenset ({2, 'a', 4, 'house', 25})

>>> type (FS1)
<class 'frozenset'>

>>> len (FS1)
5
```

The repeated elements (25 and 'a') that we included in the frozen set are only considered once.

Types of structured mutable (dynamic) data

Unlike strings, tuples, and frozen sets, mutable structured data, also called dynamic data, are characterized by the fact that their elements can change in value and elements can be added or deleted.

In Python, examples of mutable structured data are lists, sets and dictionaries. Lists and sets can be considered as the mutable equivalents of tuples and frozen sets, respectively.

Sets

A set has no duplicate elements in it and is a type of unsorted collection. It means that it will have all distinct elements in it without repetition:

```
fruits = ['apple', 'orange', 'apple', 'pear', 'orange', 'banana']
basket = set (fruits)
# removed the duplicate element apple

print ('orange' in basket)
# checking orange in basket, result is True
```

```
print ('pineapple' in basket)
# checking pineapple in basket, result is False

a = set('aioeueoiaeaeiou')
# create a set without duplicates

b = set('bcokcbzo')
# create a set without duplicates

print (a)
{'e', 'o', 'u', 'a', 'i'}

print b
{'o', 'c', 'k', 'z', 'b'}

print (a & b) # letters in both a and b   ( A AND B )
{'o'}

print (a | b) # letters in either a or b  ( A OR B )
{'u', 'e', 'k', 'z', 'o', 'a', 'c', 'b', 'i'}

print (a - b) # letters in a but not in b ( A\B )
{'a', 'u', 'i', 'e'}
```

6. Conditional or Decision Statements

In programming, we normally set certain conditions and decide which particular action to perform depending on the conditions. To do this, Python uses the "if statement" to check the program's current state before responding suitably to that state. However, in this chapter, you will be exposed to various ways to write conditional statements. Furthermore, you will learn basic "if statements," create complex "if statements" and write loops to handle items in a list. There is so much more loaded in this chapter for you to learn. Without further ado, let's begin with a simple example.

The program below shows how you can use an "if statement" to respond to a particular situation correctly. For instance, we have a list of colors and want to generate an output of different colors. Furthermore, the first letter should be in the title case of the lower case.

```
colors =["Green", "Blue", "Red", "Yellow"]
for color in colors:
print(color.title())
```

The output will be as follows:

```
Green
Blue
Red
Yellow
```

Consider another example where we want to print a list of cars. We have to print them in the title case since it is a proper name. Additionally, the value "Kia" must be in uppercase.

```
cars = ["Toyota," "Kia," "Audi," "Infinity"]
for car1 in cars:
if car1 == "kia":
print(car1.upper())
else:
print(car1.title())
```

The loop first verifies whether the current value of the car is "Kia." If that is true, it then prints the value in uppercase. However, if it is not kia, it prints it in title case. The output will look like this:

```
Toyota
KIA
Audi
Infinity
```

The example above combines different concepts which you will learn at the end of this chapter. However, let's begin with the various conditional tests.

Conditional Tests in Python

In the center of any if statement lies an expression, which must be evaluated to be either true or false. This is what is normally known as a conditional test because Python uses both values to determine if a particular code should be executed. If the particular statement is true, Python executes the code that follows it. However, if it is false, it ignores the code after it.

Checking Equality

At times, we may test for the equality of a particular condition. In this situation, we test if the value of the variable is equal to the other variable we decide. For instance:

```
>>>color = "green"
>>> color == "green"
True
```

In this example, we first assign the variable color with the value "green by using the single equal sign. This is not something new, as we have been using it throughout this book. However, the second line checks if the value of color is green, which has a double equal sign. It will return true if the value on the left side and that on the right side are both true. If it doesn't match, then the result will be false. When the value of the color is anything besides green, then this condition equates to false. The example below will clarify that.

```
>>>color = "green"
>>> color == "blue"
False
```

Note: When you test for equality, you should know that it is case sensitive. For instance, two values that have different capitalizations won't be regarded as equal. For instance,

```
>>>color = "Green"
>>> color == "green"
False
```

If the case is important, then this is advantageous. However, if the case of the variable isn't important, and you want to check the values, then you can convert the value of the variable to lowercase before checking for equality.

```
>>>color = "Green"
>>> color.lower() == "green"
True
```

This code will return True irrespective of how the value "Green" is formatted because the conditional tests aren't case sensitive. Please note that the lower() function we used in the program does not change the value originally stored in color.

In the same way, we can check for equality, we can also check for inequality in a program code. In checking for inequality, we verify if two values are not equal and then return it as true. To check for inequality, Python has its unique symbol, which is a combination of the exclamation sign with an equal sign (!=). Most programming languages use these signs to represent inequality.

The example below shows the use of an if statement to test for inequality:

```
color = "green"
if color != "blue"
print("The color doesn't match")
```

In the second line, the interpreter matches the value of color to that of "blue." If the values match, then Python returns false; however, if it is true, Python returns true before executing the statement following it "The color doesn't match"

```
The color doesn't match
```

Numerical Comparison in Python

We can also test numerical values in Python, but it is very straightforward. For instance, the code below determines if a person's age is 25 years old:

58

```
>>>myage = 25
>>>myage == 25
True
```

Additionally, we can also test if two numbers are unequal. Consider the code below.

```
number = 34
if number != 54:
print("The number does not match. Please retry!")
```

The first line declares the number as a variable and stores the number "34" in it. The conditional statement begins in line two and passes through the line because the number 34 is not equal to 54. Since the code is indented, the code is then executed to produce

```
The number does not match. Please retry!
```

In addition this, you can perform various mathematical comparisons inside your conditional expressions including greater than, greater than or equal to, less than, and less than or equal to.

```
>>> number = 22
>>> number <25
True
>>> number <= 25
True
>>> number > 25
False
>>> number >= 25
 False
```

Every mathematical comparison you want can be included as part of an "if statement" that allows you to detect the particular condition in question.

Creating Multiple Conditions

When writing code, some situations may warrant you verifying multiple conditions simultaneously. For instance, you require conditions to be false to take action. At times, you may want only one condition to be satisfied. In this situation, you can use the keyword "or" and "and". Let's first use the "and" keyword to check multiple conditions in Python programming.

Using "AND"

If you want to verify that two expressions are both true at the same time, the keyword "and" serves that purpose. The expression is evaluated to be true when both conditions test to return true. However, if one of the conditions fails, then the expression returns false.

For instance, you want to ascertain if two students in a class have over 45 score marks.

```
>>> score_1 = 46
>>> score_2 = 30
>>> score_1 >=45 and score_2 >= 45
False
>>> score_2 = 47
>>> score_1 >= 45 and score_2 >= 45
True
```

The program looks complicated but lets me explain it step-by-step. In the first two lines, we define two scores, score_1, and score_2. However, in line 3, we perform a check to ascertain if both scores are equal to or above 45. The condition on the right-hand side is false, but that of the left-hand side is true. Then in the line after the false statement, I changed the value of score_2 from 30 to 47. In this instant, the value of score_2 is now greater than 46; therefore, both conditions will evaluate to true.

To make the code more readable, we can use parentheses in each test. However, it is not compulsory to do such but makes it simpler. Let's use parentheses to demonstrate the difference between the previous code and the one below.

```
(score_1 >= 45) and (score_2 >=45)
```

Using "OR"

The "OR" keyword allows you to check multiple conditions like the "AND" keyword. However, the difference here is that the "OR" keyword is used when you want to ascertain that one expression is true for multiple conditions. In this situation, if one of the expressions is false, the condition returns true. It returns false when both conditions are false.

Let's consider our previous example using the "OR" keyword. For instance, you want to ascertain if two students in a class have over 45 score mark.

```
>>> score_1 = 46
>>> score_2 = 30
```

```
>>> score_1 >=45 or score_2 >= 45
True
>>> score_1 = 30
>>> score_1 >= 45 or score_2 >= 45
False
```

We began by declaring two variables score_1 and score_2 and assign values to them. In the third line, we test the OR condition using the two variables. The test in that line satisfies the condition because one of the expressions is true. Then it changed the value of the variable score to 30; however, it fails both conditions and therefore evaluates false.

In additionIn addition to using the "And" and "OR" conditional statements to check multiple conditions, we can also test the availability of a value in a particular list. For instance, you want to verify if a requested username is already in existence from a list of usernames before the completion of online registration on a website.

To do this, we can use the "in" keyword in such a situation. For instance, let's use a list of animals in the zoo and check if it is already on the list.

```
>>>animals = ["zebra", "lion", "crocodile", "monkey"]
>>> "monkey" in animals
True
>>> "rat" in animals
False
```

In the second and fourth lines, we use the "in" keyword to test if the requested word in a double quote exists in our list of animals. The first test ascertains that "monkey" exists in our list, whereas the second test returns false because the rat is not in the list of animals. This method is significant because we can generate lists of important values and check the existence of the values in the list.

There are situations where you want to check if a value isn't in a list. In such a case, instead of using the "in" keyword to return false, we can use the "not" keyword. For instance, let's consider a list of Manchester United players before allowing them to be part of their next match. In other words, we want to scan the real players and ensure that the club does not field an illegible player.

```
united_player = ["Rashford," "Young," "Pogba," "Mata,"
"De Gea"]
player = "Messi"
if player not in united_player:
```

```
print(f "{player.title()}, you are not qualified to play
for Manchester United.")
```

The line "if player, not in united_player:" reads quite clearly. If the value of the player isn't in the list united_player, Python returns the expression to be True and then executed the line indented under it. The player "Messi" isn't part of the list united_player; therefore, he will receive a message about his qualification status. The output will be as follow:

```
Messi, you are not qualified to play for Manchester
United.
```

Boolean Expressions in Python

If you have learned any programming language, you might have come across the term "Boolean Expression" because it is very important. A Boolean expression is another term to describe the conditional test. When evaluated, the outcome can only be either True or False. However, they are essential if your goal is to keep track of specific conditions like if a user can change content or a light is switched on or not. For instance,

```
change_content = False
light_on = False
light_off = True
```

Boolean values provide the best means of tracking the particular condition of a program.

Exercises

Conditional Testing – Write various conditional expressions. Furthermore, print a statement to describe each condition and what the likely output of each test will be. for instance, your code can be like this:

```
car = "Toyota"
print("Is car == 'Toyota'? My prediction is True."(
print (car == "Toyota")
print("\nIs car == 'KIA'? My prediction is False.")
print(car== "KIA")
```

1. Test the following condition to evaluate either True or False using any subject of your choice to form a list.
2. Test for both inequality and equality using strings and numbers
3. Test for the condition using the "or" and "and" keywords
4. Test if an item exists in the list

5. Test if an item doesn't exist in the list

If Statements

Since you now know about conditional tests, it will be easier for you to understand if statements. There are various types of if statements to use in Python, depending on your choice. In this section, you will learn the different if statements possible and the best situation to apply them, respectively.

Simple If Statements

In any programming language, the "if statement" is the simplest to come across. It only requires a test or condition with a single action following it, respectively. The syntax for this statement is as follows:

if condition:
        perform action

The first line can contain any conditional statement with the second being the action to take. Ensure to indent the second line for clarity purposes. If the conditional statement is true, then the code under the condition is executed. However, if it is false, the code is ignored.

For instance, we have set a standard that the minimum score for a person to qualify for a football match is 20. We want to test if such a person is qualified to participate.

```
person = 21
if person >= 20
print("You are qualified for the football match against
Valencia.")
```

In the first line, we define the person's age at 21 to qualify. Then the second line evaluates if the person is greater than or equal to 20. Python then executes the statement below because it fulfills the condition that the person is above 20.

```
You are qualified for the football match against
Valencia.
```

Indentation is very significant when using the "if statement" like we did in the "for loop" situations. All indented lines are executed once the condition is satisfied after the if statement. However, if the statement returns false, then the whole code under it is ignored, and the program halted.

We can also include more code inside the if statements to display what we want. Let's add another line to display that the match is between Arsenal and Valencia at Stamford Bridge.

```
person  =21
if person >= 20
print("You are qualified for the football match against
Valencia.")
print("The match is between Arsenal and Valencia.")
Print("The Venue is at the Emirate Stadium in England.")
```

The conditional statement passes through the condition and prints the indented actions once the condition is satisfied.

The output will be as follow:

```
You are qualified for the football match against
Valencia.
The match is between Arsenal and Valencia.
The Venue is at the Emirate Stadium in England.
```

Assuming the age is less than 20, and then there won't be any output for this program. Let's try another example before going into another conditional statement.

```
name = "Abraham Lincoln"
if name = "Abraham Lincoln"
print("Abraham Lincoln was a great United State
President.")
print("He is an icon that many presidents try to emulate
in the world.")
```

The output will be:

```
Abraham Lincoln was a great United State President.
He is an icon that many presidents try to emulate in the
world.
```

If-else Statements

At times, you may want to take certain actions if a particular condition isn't met. For example, you may decide what will happen if a person isn't qualified to play a match. Python provides the if-else statements to make this possible. The syntax is as follows:

if conditional test
    perform statement_1
else
    perform statement_2

Let's use our football match qualification to illustrate how to use the if-else statement.

```
person  =18
if person >= 20:
print("You are qualified for the football match against
Valencia.")
print("The match is between Arsenal and Valencia.")
print("The Venue is at the Emirate Stadium in England.")
else:
print("Unfortunately, you are not qualified to
participate in the match.")
print("Sorry, you have to wait until you are qualified.")
```

The conditional test (if person>=20) is first evaluated to ascertain that the person is above 20 before it passes to the first indented line of code. If it is true, then it prints the statements beneath the condition. However, in our example, the conditional test will evaluate to false then pass control to the else section. Finally, it prints the statement below it since it fulfills that part of the condition.

```
Unfortunately, you are not qualified to participate in
the match.
Sorry, you have to wait until you are qualified.
```

This program works because of the two possible scenarios to evaluate – a person must be qualified to play or not play. In this situation, the if-else statement works perfectly when you want Python to execute one action in two possible situations.

Let's try another.

```
station_numbers = 10
if station_numbers >=12:
print("We need additional 3 stations in this company.")
```

```
else:
print("We need additional 5 stations to meet the demands
of our audience.")
```

The output will be:
```
We need an additional 5 stations to meet the demands of
our audience.
```

The if-elif-else Chain

At times, you may want to test three different conditions based on certain criteria. In such a situation, Python allows us to use the if-elif-else conditional statement to execute such a task. We have many real-life situations, require more than two possibilities. For instance, think of a cinema hall with different charge rates for different sets of people.

- Children under 5 years are free
- Children between 5 years and 17 years are $30
- People older than 18 years is $50

As you can see, there are three possible situations because the following set of people can attend the cinema to watch the movie of their choice. In this situation, how can you ascertain a person's rate? Well, the following code will illustrate that point and print out specific price rates for each category of people.

```
person_age = 13
if person_age < 5:
print("Your ticket cost is $0.")
elif person_age < 17:
print("Your ticket cost is $30.")
else:
print("Your ticket cost is $50)
```

The first line declares a variable "person_age" with value 13. Then we perform the first conditional statement to test if the person is below the age of 5. If it fulfills the condition, it prints the appropriate message, and the program halts. However, if it returns false, it passes to the elif line, which tests if the person_age is less than 17. At this post, the person's minimum age must be 5 years and not above 17. If the person is above 17, then Python skips the instruction and goes to the next condition.

In the example, we fix the person_age to 13. Therefore, the first test will evaluate false and won't execute the block of line. It then tests the elif condition, which in this case is true, and will print the message. The output will be:

```
Your ticket cost is $30.")
```

Nevertheless, if the age is above 17, then it will pass through the first two tests because it will evaluate to false. Then the next command will be the else condition, which will print the statement below.

We can rewrite this program in such a way that we won't have to include the message "Your ticket cost is…" all we need is to put the prince inside the if-elif-else chain with a simple print() method to execute after the evaluation of the chain. Look at the line of code below:

```
person_age = 13
if person_age < 5:
cost = 0
elif person_age < 17:
cost =30
else:
cost = 50
print(f "Your ticket cost is ${cost}.")
```

In the third, fifth, and seventh lines, we defined the cost based on the person's age. The cost price is already set within the if-elif-else statement. However, the last line uses the cost of each age to form the final cost of the ticket.

This new code will produce the same result as the previous example. However, the latter is more concise and straightforward. Instead of using three different print statements, our reverse code only uses a single print statement to print the cost of the ticket.

Multiple elif Blocks

You can also have more than one elif block in your program. For instance, if the manager of the cinema decides to implement special discounts for workers, this will require additional, conditional tests to the program to ascertain whether the person in question is qualified for such a discount. Assuming those above 55 years will pay 70% of the initial cost of each ticket. Then the program code will be as follows:

```
person_age = 13
if person_age < 5:
cost = 0
elif person_age < 17:
cost =30
elif person_age < 55
```

```
cost = 50
else:
cost = 35
print(f "Your ticket cost is ${cost}.")
```

The cost is identical to our previous example; however, the only inclusion is the "elif person_age < 55" and is a respective else condition. This second elif block checks if the person's age is less than 55 before assigning them the cost of the ticket for $50. However, the statement after the else needs to be changed. In this situation, it is applicable if the person's age is above 55 years, which is this situation fulfills the condition we want.

The "else" statement isn't compulsory because you can omit it and use the elif statement instead. At times, it is better to use additional elif statements to capture specific interests. Let's see how to implement it without using the else statement.

```
person_age = 13
if person_age < 5:
cost = 0
elif person_age < 17:
cost =30
elif person_age < 55:
cost = 50
elif person_age >= 55:
cost = 35
print(f "Your ticket cost is ${cost}.")
```

The additional elif statement helps to assign the ticket cost of "$30" to those above 30 years. This format is a bit clearer when compared with the else block.

Performing Multiple Conditions

Using the if-elif-else statement comes in handy especially when you want to pass only one test. Once the interpreter discovers that this test is passed, it skips other tests and halts the program. With this feature, you test a specific condition in a line of code.

Nevertheless, some situations may warrant you to check all the conditions available. In such a scenario, you can use multiple if statements without adding the elif or else blocks. This method becomes relevant when more than one of the conditions returns true. For instance, let's consider the previous example of players in Manchester

United to illustrate this. In this, we want to include the players in an upcoming match against their rivals Manchester City.

```
united_players = ["Rashford," "Young," "Pogba," "Mata,"
"De Gea"]
if "Young" in united_players:
print("Adding Young to the team list.")
if "De Gea" in united_players:
print("Adding Dea Gea to the team list.")
if "Messi" in united_players:
print("Adding Messi to the team list.")
print( "Team list completed for the match against
Manchester City!")
```

In the first line, we defined united_players as a variable with values Rashford, Young, Pogba, Mata, and De Gea. The second line uses the "if statement" to check if the person requested Young. The same applies to the lines with the "if statement" and the condition is run regardless of the outcome of the previous tests. For this program above, the output will be:

```
Adding Young to the team list.
Adding De Gea to the team list.
Team list completed for the match against Manchester
City!
```

If we decide to use the if-elif-else block, the code won't function properly because once a particular test returns true, the program will stop.

Let's try it and see.

```
united_players = ["Rashford," "Young," "Pogba," "Mata,"
"De Gea"]
if "Young" in united_players:
print("Adding Young to the team list.")
elif  "De Gea" in united_players:
print("Adding Dea Gea to the team list.")
elif  "Messi" in united_players:
print("Adding Messi to the team list.")
print( "\ Team list completed for the match against
Manchester City!")
```

In this code, Python will evaluate the first condition, and once it is true, the program stops. The output for this program will be:

```
Adding Young to the team list.
```

```
Team list completed for the match against Manchester
City!
```

Exercise

Consider the list of colors we have in the world. Create a variable name-color and assign the following colors to it – blue, red, black, orange, white, yellow, indigo, green.

Use an "if statement" to check if the color is blue. If the color is blue, then print a message indicating a score of 5 points.

Write a problem using the if-else chain to print if a particular selected is green.

Write another program using the if-elif-else chain to determine the scores of students in a class. Set a variable "score" to store the student's score.

If the student's score is below 40, indicate an output a message that such student has failed.

If the student's score is above 41 but less than 55, print a message that the student has passed.

7. Lists in Python

We create a list in Python by placing items called elements inside square brackets separated by commas. The items in a list can be of mixed data types.

Start IDLE. Navigate to the File menu and click New Window.

Type the following:

```
list_mine=[] #empty list
list_mine=[2,5,8] #list of integers
list_mine=[5,"Happy", 5.2] #list having mixed data types
```

Exercise

Write a program that captures the following in a list: "Best", 26, 89, 3.9

Nested Lists

A nested list is a list as an item in another list.

Example

```
list_mine=["carrot", [9, 3, 6], ['g']]
```

Exercise

Write a nested list for the following elements: [36, 2, 1], "Writer", 't', [3.0, 2.5]

Accessing Elements from a List

In Python, the first element in a vector is always indexed as zero. A list of five items can be accessed by index0 to index4. An index error will occur if you fail to access the items in a list. The index is always an integer, so using other numbers will also create a type error.

Example

```
list_mine=['b','e','s','t']
print(list_mine[0])#the output will be b
print(list_mine[2])#the output will be s
print(list_mine[3])#the output will be t
```

Exercise

Given the following list:
```
your_collection=['t','k','v','w','z','n','f']
```

a. Write a Python program to display the second item in the list
b. Write a Python program to display the sixth item in the last
c. Write a Python program to display the last item in the list

Nested List Indexing
```
nested_list=["Best',[4,7,2,9]]
print(nested_list[0][1])
```

Python Negative Indexing

For its sequences, Python allows negative indexing. The last item on the list is index-1, index -2 is the second last item and so on.
```
list_mine=['c','h','a','n','g','e','s']
print(list_mine[-1])#Output is s
print(list_mine [-4])##Output is n
```

Slicing Lists in Python

Slicing operator (full colon) is used to access a range of elements in a list.

Example
```
list_mine=['c','h','a','n','g','e','s']
print(list_mine[3:5]) #Picking elements from the fourth
to the sixth
```

Example

Picking elements from start to the fifth.
```
print(list_mine[:-6])
```

Example

Picking the third element to the last.
```
print(list_mine[2:])
```

Exercise

Given class_names=['John', 'Kelly', 'Yvonne', 'Una','Lovy','Pius', 'Tracy']

a. Write a Python program using the slice operator to display from the second students and the rest.

b. Write a Python program using the slice operator to display the first student to the third using the negative indexing feature.

c. Write a Python program using the slice operator to display the fourth and fifth students only.

Manipulating Elements in a List using the Assignment Operator

```
list_yours=[4,8,5,2,1]
list_yours[1]=6
print(list_yours) #The output will be [4,6,5,2,1]
```

Changing a Range of Items in a List

```
list_yours[0:3]=[12,11,10] #Will change first item to
fourth item in the list
print(list_yours) #Output will be: [12,11,10,1]
```

Appending/Extending Items in the List

The append() method allows extending the items on the list. The extend() can also be used.

Example

```
list_yours=[4, 6, 5]
list_yours.append(3)
print(list_yours)#The output will be [4,6,5, 3]
```

Example

```
list_yours=[4,6,5]
list_yours.extend([13,7,9])
print(list_yours)#The output will be [4,6,5,13,7,9]
```

The plus operator (+) can also be used to combine two lists. The * operator can be used to iterate a list a given number of times.

Example

```
list_yours=[4,6,5]
print(list_yours+[13,7,9])# Output:[4, 6, 5,13,7,9]
print(['happy']*4)#Output:["happy","happy",
"happy","happy"]
```

Removing or Deleting Items from a List

The keyword del is used to delete elements or the entire list in Python.

```
list_mine=['t','r','o','g','r','a','m']
```

```
del list_mine[1]
print(list_mine) #t, o, g, r, a, m
```

Deleting Multiple Elements
```
del list_mine[0:3]
print(list_mine) #a, m
```

Delete Entire List
```
delete list_mine
print(list_mine) #will generate an error of lost not
found
```

The remove() method or pop() method can be used to remove the specified item. The pop() method will remove and return the last item if the index is not given and helps implement lists as stacks. The clear() method is used to empty a list.

Example
```
list_mine=['t','k','b','d','w','q','v']
list_mine.remove('t')
print(list_mine)#output will be
['t','k','b','d','w','q','v']
print(list_mine.pop(1))#output will be 'k'
print(list_mine.pop())#output will be 'v'
```

Exercise
Given list_yours=['K','N','O','C','K','E','D']

a. Pop the third item in the list, save the program as list1.
b. Remove the fourth item using remove() method and save the program as list2
c. Delete the second item in the list and save the program as list3.
d. Pop the list without specifying an index and save the program as list4.

Using an Empty List to Delete an Entire or Specific Elements
```
list_mine=['t','k','b','d','w','q','v']
list_mine[1:2]=[]
print(list_mine)#Output will be ['b','d','w','q','v']
```

Summary of List Methods in Python

Method	Description
insert()	Inserts an item at the defined index
append()	Adds an element to the end of the list
pop()	Removes and returns an element at the given index
index()	Returns the index of the first matched items
remove()	Removes an item from the list
copy()	Returns a shallow copy of the list
count()	Returns the count of number of items passed as an argument
clear()	Removes all items from the list
sort()	Sorts items in a list in ascending order
extend()	Adds all elements of a list to another list
reverse()	Reverses the order of items in the list

Inbuilt Python Functions to manipulate Python Lists

Method	Description
enumerate()	Returns an enumerated object and contains the index and value of all the items of the list as tuple
sorted()	Returns a new sorted list but does not sort the list itself
sum()	Returns the sum of all the elements in the list
max()	Returns the largest item in the list
len()	Returns the length of the list
any()	Returns True if any element of the list is true – if the list is empty, returns False
min()	Returns the smallest item in the list
all()	Returns True if all elements of the list are True

Exercise

Use list access methods to display the following items in reverse order list_yours=[4,9,2,1,6,7]

Use the list access method to count the elements in list_yours.

Use the list access method to sort the items in list_yours in an ascending order/default.

8. Modules in Python

Modules, also known as packages, are a set of names. This is usually a library of functions and/or object classes that are made available to be used within different programs. We used the notion of modules earlier in this chapter to use some function from the math library. In this chapter, we are going to cover in-depth on how to develop and define modules. To use modules in a Python program, the following statements are used: import, from, reload. The first one imports the whole module. The second allows importing only a specific name or element from the module. The third one, reload, allows reloading a code of a module while Python is running and without stopping it. Before digging into their definition and development, let's start first by the utility of modules or packages within Python.

Modules Concept and Utility Within Python

Modules are a very simple way to make a system component organized. Modules allow reusing the same code over and over. So far, we were working in a Python interactive session. Every code we have written and tested is lost once we exit the interactive session. Modules are saved in files that make them persistent, reusable, and sharable. You can consider modules as a set of files where you can define functions, names, data objects, attributes, and so on. Modules are a tool to group several components of a system in a single place. In Python programming, modules are among the highest-level unit. They point to the name of packages and tools. In additionIn addition, they allow the sharing of the implemented data. You only need one copy of the module to be able to use across a large program. If an object is to be used in different functions and programs, coding it as a module allows sharing it with other programmers.

To have a sense of the architecture of Python coding, we go through some general structure explanation. We have been using so far in this book very simple code examples that do not have a high-level structure. In large applications, a program is a set of several Python files. By Python files, we mean files that contain Python code and have a .py extension. There is one main high-level program and the other files are the modules. The high-level file consists of the main code that dictates the control flow and executes the application. Module files define the tools that are needed to process elements and components of the main program and maybe elsewhere. The main program makes use of the tools that are specified in the modules.

In their turn, modules make use of tools that are specified in other modules. When you import a module in Python, you have access to every tool that is declared or defined in that specific module. Attributes are the variables or the functions associated with the tools within a module. Hence, when a module is imported, we have access to the attributes of the tools as well to process them. For instance, let's consider we have two Python files named file1.py and file2.py where the file1.py is the main program and file2.py is the module. In the file2.py, we have a code that defines the following function:

```
def Xfactorial (X):
P = 1
for i in range (1, X + 1):
P *= i
return P
```

To use this function in the main program, we should define code statements in the file1.py as follows:

```
import file2
A = file2.Xfactorial (3)
```

The first line imports the module file2.py. This statement means to load the file file2.py. This gives access to the file1.py to all tools and functions defined in file2.py by the name file2. The function Xfactorial is called by the second line. The module file2.py is where this function is defined using the attributes' syntax. The line file2.Xfactorial() means fetch any name value of Xfactorial and lies within the code body of file2. In this example, it is a function that is callable. So, we have provided an input argument and assigned the output result to the variable A. If we add a third statement to print the variable A and run the file file1.py, it would display 6 which is the factorial of 3. Along with Python, you will see the attribute syntax as object.attribute. This allows calling the attributes that might be a function or data object that provides properties of the object.

Note that some modules you might import when programming with Python are available in Python itself. As we mentioned at the beginning of this book, Python comes with a standard large library that has built-in modules. These modules support all common tasks that might be needed in programming from operating system interfaces to graphical user interface. They are not part of the language. However, they can be imported and come with a software installation package. You can check the complete list of available modules in a manual that comes with the installation or goes to the official Python website: www.Python.org. This manual is kept updated every time a new version of Python is released.

How to Import a Module

We have talked about importing a module without really explaining what happens in the background in Python. Imports are a very fundamental concept in Python programming structure. In this section, we are going to cover in depth how Python really imports modules within a program.

Python follows three steps to import a file or a module within the work environment of a program. The first step consists of finding the file that contains the module. The second step consists of compiling the module to a byte-code if required. Finally, the third step runs the code within the module file to build the objects that are defined. These three steps are run only when the module is imported for the first time during the execution of a program. This module and all its objects are loaded in the memory. When the module is imported further in the program, it skips all three steps and just fetch the objects defined by the module and are saved in memory.

At the very first step of importing a module, Python has to find the module file location. Note that, so far in the examples we presented, we used import without providing the complete path of the module or extension .py. We just used import math, or import file2.py (an example from the previous section). The Python import statement omits the extension and the path. We just simply import a module by its name. The reason for this is that Python has a module that looks for paths called 'search path module'. This module is used specifically to find the path of the module files imported by using import statements.

In some cases, you might need to configure the path search of modules to be able to use new modules that are not part of the standard library. You need to customize it to include these new modules. The search path is simply the concatenation of the home directory, directories of PYTHONPATH, directories of the standard library, and optionally if the content of files with extension .pth when they exist. The home directory is set automatically by the system to a directory of Python executable when launched from the interactive session, or it can be modified to the working directory where your program is saved. This directory is the first to be searched when import a module is run without a path. Hence, if your home directory points to a directory that includes your program along with the modules, importing these modules does not require any path specification.

The directory of the standard library is also searched automatically. This directory contains all default libraries that come with Python. The directories of PYTHONPATH can be set to point toward the directory of new modules that are developed. In fact, PTYHONPATH is an environment variable that contains a list of directories that contains Python files. When PTYHONPATH is set, all these paths are included in the Python environment and the search path directory would search these directories too when importing modules. Python also allows defining a file with .pth extension that contains directories, one in each line. This file serves the same as PTYHONPATH when included appropriately in a directory. You can check the directories' paths included when you run Python using sys.path. You simply print sys.path to get the list of the directories that Python will be searching for.

Remember, when importing a module, we just use the name of the module without its extension. When Python is searching for a module in its environment paths, it selects the first name that matches the module name regardless of the extension. Because Python allows using packages that are coded in other languages, it does not simply select a module with .py extension but a file name or even a zip file name that matches the module name being imported. Therefore, you should name your modules distinctly and configure the search path in a manner that makes it obvious to choose a module.

When Python finds the source code of the module file with a name that corresponds to the name in the import statement, it will compile it into byte code in case it is required. This step is skipped if Python finds an already byte code file with no source code. If the source code has been modified, another byte code file is automatically regenerated by Python while the program runs in other further executions. Byte code files have typically .pyc extension. When Python is searching and finds the module file name, it will load the byte code file that corresponds to the latest version of the source code with .py extension. If the source code is newer than the byte code file, it will generate a new one by compiling the source code file. Note that only imported files have corresponding files with .pyc extension. These files, the byte code files, are stored on your machine to make the imports faster in future use.

The third step of the import statement is running the module's byte code. Each statement and each assignment in the file are executed. This allows generating any function, data objects, and so on defined in the module. The functions and all attributes are accessed within the program via importers. During this step, you will see print statements if they exist. The 'def ' statement will create a function object to be used in the main program.

To summarize the import statement, it involves searching for the file, compiling it, and running the byte code file. All other import statements use the module stored in memory and ignore all the three steps. When first imported, Python will look in the search path module to select the module. Hence, it is important to configure correctly the path environment variable to point to the directory that contains newly defined modules. Now that you have the big picture and the concept of modules, let's explore how we can define and develop new modules.

How to write and use a module in Python

Modules in Python can be created very easily and do not require any specific syntax. Modules are simply files with a .py extension that contains Python code. You can use a text editor like Notepad++ to develop and write modules, then save them in files with the .py extension. Then, you just import these files like we have seen in the previous section to make use of the contained code.

When you create a module, all the data object including functions that are defined becomes the module attributes. These attributes are accessed and used via the attribute syntax like follows: module.attribute. For instance, if we define a module named ' MyModule.py ' that has the following function:

```
def Myfct (A):
print (' A by 2 is: ', A * 2)
return A * 2
```

The function 'Myfct' becomes the attribute of the module 'MyModule.py'. You can call a module any Python code that you develop and save in a file with a .py extension if you are importing them in later use. Module names are referenced variables. Hence, when naming a module, you should follow the same rules as for variable naming. You might be able to name your module anything you want.

But if the rules are not respected, Python throws up an error. For instance, if you name your module $2P.py, you will not be able to import it and Python would trigger a syntax error. Directory names that contain the module and Python packages should follow the same rules. Also, their names cannot contain any space. In the rest of this section, we are going to provide some code examples of defining and using modules.

Two statements can be employed to make use of a module. The first one is the import statement we have covered in the previous section. Let's consider again the previous example to illustrate a module 'MyModule.py' that contains ' Myfct' function:

```
def Myfct(A):
print (A, 'by 2 is: ', A * 2)
```

Now, to use this module, we import it using the following statements:

```
>>> import MyModule
>>> MyModule.Myfct(2)
2 by 2 is: 4
```

Now, the MyModule name is being used by Python to load the file and as a variable in the program. The module name should be used to access all its attributes. Another way to import and use a module attribute is by using the 'from import' statement. This statement works in the same manner as the import statement we have been using. Instead of using the module name to fetch its attributes, we can access the attributes by their names directly. For example:

```
>>> from MyModule import Myfct
>>> Myfct (2)
2 by 2 is: 4
```

This statement makes a copy of the function name without using the module name. There is another form of 'from import' statement that uses an *. This statement allows copying all names that are assigned to objects in the module. For example:

```
>>> from MyModule import *
>>> Myfct (2)
2 by 2 is: 4
```

Because modules names become variables (i.e. references to objects), Python supports importing a module with an alias. Then we can access its attributes using the alias instead of its name. For instance, we can attribute an alias to our module as follows:

```
>>> import Mymodule as md
>>> md.Myfct(2)
2 by 2 is: 4
```

Data objects other than functions are accessed the same way with attribute syntax. For instance, we can define and initialize data objects in modules than used them later in the program. Let's consider the following code to create a module named ExModule.py.

```
A = 9
Name = 'John'
```

In this example, we initialize both variables A and Name.

Now, after importing the module, we can get both variables as follows:

```
>>> import ExModule
>>> print ('A is: ', ExModule.A)
A is: 9
>>> print ('Name is: ', Exmodule.Name)
Name is: John
```

Or we can assign attributes to other variables. For instance:

```
>>> import ExModule
>>> B = ExModule.A
>>> print ('B is: ', B)
B is: 9
```

If we use the 'from import' statement to import the attributes, the names of the attributes become variables in the script. For example:

```
>>> from Exmodule import A, Name
>>> print ('A is: ', A, 'and Name is: ', Name)
A is 9 and Name is John
```

Note that the 'from import' statement supports importing multiple attributes in one single line. Python allows changing objects that are sharable. For instance, let's consider the following code to define the module named ExModul1.py:

```
A = 9
MyList = [90, 40, 80]
```

Now, let's import this module and try to change the values of the attributes to see how Python behaves.

```
>>> from ExModule1 import A, MyList
>>> A = 20
```

```
>>> myList [0] = 100
```

Now, let's re-import the module and print those two attributes and see what changes Python has made.
```
>>> import ExModule1
>>> print ('A is: ', ExModule1.A)
A is: 9
>>> print ('My list is: ', ExModule.myList)
My list is: [100, 40, 80]
```

You notice that Python has changed the value of the first element of the list but did not change the value of the variable 'A' to the value we assigned before. The reason is that when a mutable object like lists is changed locally, the changes apply also in the module from which they were imported. Reassigning a fetched variable name does not reassign the reference in the module from which it was imported. In fact, there is no link between the reference variable name copied and the file it was copied from. To make a valid modification in the script and the module it is imported from, we should use the import statement like follows:
```
>>> import ExModule1
>>> ExModule1.A = 200
```

The difference between changing the attributes 'A' and 'myList' is the fact that 'A' is a variable name and 'myList' is an object data. That is why modification to the variable 'A' should use import to be applied in the module file, too.

We have mentioned that importing a module for the first time in a script implies going through three steps that are searching for the module, compiling the module, and running the module. All other imports of the module later in the script skip all these three steps and access to module loaded in the memory. Now, let's try an example to see how this works. Consider we have a module with the following code and named ExModule2.py:
```
print (' Hello World\n')
print (' This is my first module in Python')
A = 9
```

Now, let's import this module and see how Python behaves when importing this module:
```
>>> import ExModule2
Hello World
```

This is my first module in Python

You can notice that when importing this module, it displays both messages. Now, let's try to reassign a value to the attribute ' A', then re-import the module with the import statement.

```
>>> ExModule.A = 100
>>> import Exmodule2
```

As you can note from the example, Python did not display the messages, 'Hello World' and 'This is my first module in Python' because it did not re-run the module. It just used the module that is already loaded in the memory.

To make Python goes through all steps of importing a module for the second time in a script, we should use the reload statement. When using this statement, we force Python to import the module as it would for the first time. In addition, it helps make modifications in the program while it is running without interrupting it. It also helps to see instantly the modifications that are made. The reload is a function and not a statement in Python that takes as argument a module that is already loaded in memory.

Because reload is a function and expects an argument, this argument should be already assigned an object which is a module object. If for some reason the import statement failed to import a module, you will not be able to reload it. You have to repeat the import statement until it imports the module successfully. Like any other function, the reload takes the module name reference between parentheses. The general form of using reload with import is as follows:

```
import module_name
list of statements that use module attributes
reload(module_name)
list of statements that use module attributes
```

The module object is changed by the reload function. Hence, any reference to that module in your scripts is impacted by the reload function. Those statements that use the module attributes will be using the values of the new attributes if they are modified. The reload function overwrites the module source code and re-runs it instead of deleting the file and creating a new one. In the following code example, we will see a concrete illustration of the reload functioning. We consider the following code to create a module named ExModule3.py:

```
my_message = 'This is my module first version'
def display ():
```

```
print (my_message)
```

This module simply assigns a string to the variable 'my_message' and print it. Now, let's import this module in Python and call the attribute function:

```
>>> import ExModule3
>>> Exmodule3.display()
This is my module first version
```

Now, go to your text editor and edit the module source code without stopping the Python prompt shell. You can make a change as follows:

```
my_message = 'This is my module second version edited in
the text editor'
def display ():
print (my_message)
```

Now, back to the interactive session of Python in the prompt shell, you can try to import the module and call the function:

```
>>> import ExModule3
>>> Exmodule3.display()
This is my module first version
```

As you can see, the message did not change although the source code file was modified. As said before, all imports after the first import use the already loaded module in memory.

To get the new message and access the modification made in the module, we use the reload function:

```
>>> reload (ExModule3)
<module 'ExModule3)>
>>> Exmodule3.display()
This is my module second version edited in the text
editor
```

Note that the reload function re-runs the module and returns the module object. Because it was executed in the interactive session, it displays < module name> by default.

9. Learning about Functions

So far, we have learned quite a lot of things. If you have already started to lose track of all the knowledge, you shouldn't be alarmed. It is natural for everyone to find themselves in such a situation when they are in the learning process. No one is perfect and that is what makes us all human beings, right?

We have seen dictionaries and learned they are nothing like the ones we use to learn new words and meanings. We have learned about a rather funny thing called tuples and understood that they are essentially a list with parentheses and do not allow anyone to add, remove, or modify values. We have gone initially through some functions too, but now it is time for us to start looking into functions a little more closely.

Rules to define a function in Python

In Python, a function is defined using the keyword def. The arguments will be placed within the parenthesis ().

Now let's see an example:

```
>>> def printdetails(name, age):
...     print "Name:", name;
...     print "Age:", age;
...     return;
...
>>> printdetails(name = "Mary", age = 30);
Name: Mary
Age: 30
```

In the above example 'printdetails' is the function name and 'name' and 'age' are the parameters.

Syntax of user defined method

def < function name> :

[< declaration of local variables >]

[< statements >]

Now let's see an example:

```
Language = "Python"
def printString( input ) :
print input
```

```
def multiply ( x, y ) :
return x * y

def power( x, y):
return x ** y

printString( Language )        # returns Python
z = multiply( 10, 20 )
print z      # returns 200 - which is equal to 10 * 20
print power(10, 2) # returns 100 - which is equal to 10^2
```

Accepting inputs during the runtime

raw_input() is a built-in Python function that provides the facility to accept input during the execution of the script

Now let's see an example:

```
name = raw_input( "\n Please enter your name : " )
```

This statement provides a message to the user to provide input for a name.

Understanding the Concept of Function

A function is a block of organized and reusable code that is used to perform certain tasks. We can break our huge lines of programming code into smaller modules with the help of functions. It also helps in avoiding repetitions of code, as we don't need to write the same lines of code again and again. Instead, we can write it once inside a function and then use the function anywhere in the program.

Furthermore, the name of the function must be unique.

Functions are either user-defined or pre-defined. In either case, their job is to organize codes within a recallable function name. There are tons of pre-defined functions available within Python. We have already been using some of these again and again.

We already have a decent idea about functions that are built-in and pre-defined. These include and are not limited to input(), print(), and so many more. However, let's now look at how to create our function.

Let's begin with a traditional approach and write a block of code that welcomes the user with a friendly greeting. We will store this as a function named "welcome_message" so that we can call on this function later on.

```
def welcome_message():
```

```
    print("Hello and welcome")
    print("Hope you have a great time")
print("Begin")
welcome_message()
print("End")
```

Let's begin learning and see what is happening in the block of code above. Firstly, for us to create our function, we need to define it. The 'def' is a keyword that Python will look at and immediately understand that you are about to 'define' a new function. Next, we will need to name the function. While you can always name the function as you please, it is highly recommended and encouraged that you use names that are easy to understand and have a descriptive name. If we were to name this function anything other than welcome_message, we may know what it is as we wrote it, but for any other programmer out there, they may not understand.

Whenever you create a function, you need to use parentheses. You do not have to pass any information through it so leave them as they are. Now, we need to add the colon mark.

What happens when you use a colon at the end of a statement? Your cursor gets indented in the following line. That means your cursor will be slightly far from the actual starting point. This is to denote to the programmer that he/she is about to type something that would hold value for a command or a statement above it. In this case, we are trying to define the function.

Let's then use two print commands and place our greeting messages. That is it! You have now created your very first function. You can now recall it as many times as you like. However, should you try to call on this function a line or two before the 'def' command, Python will have no idea what you're talking about. Why? That has everything to do with the fact that Python reads a program line by line. By the time it arrives at the line where you called a function, it would check with the previous lines and not find anything relatable as the actual 'def' step was carried out in a step following this.

After this, let's now use our function and see how it works. Remember, the function holds two printable messages for our users. For our reference, we will now create a 'begin' and an 'end' message. This would allow us and the programmer to know where the regular messages are and where the function lies. Use your function with empty parentheses between the two print commands as shown above. If you like, you can remove these print commands and just type in your function number to see the results.

A quick tip for all! If you come across the annoying wiggly lines, simply hover your mouse over them and you will find out what the expected or suggested solution is. In this case, if you remove the two-line spaces, you should see a suggestion saying this:

Whenever you define a function, you will always be required to leave at least two blank lines before proceeding on with the codes.

Now, let's run the program and you should see all the messages and our function in action. Python initiated the sequence and first read the definition. This is where Python only understood for itself what the function was. The actual program was executed when Python reached line six, where our print("Begin") message started. In the next line, we placed our function and this is where Python recalled what it had just learned. It quickly carried out the set of codes we defined within the function and executed the same. Lastly, it executed the last line before finishing the program.

This is how functions are created and used. Now, we can use this function as many times as we like within the same file. Note that you cannot use this newly created function if you were to open a new file or work on an older file where you did not define this function.

When things start to get tougher for you in your programming future, remember to create your functions and use them where applicable. They will save you quite a lot of time and help you in places as well. These are used when certain actions or operations need to be carried out every now and then.

Using Various Functions

Python was created with simplicity in mind. It was also created to minimize the work and maximize the output. If you use the codes and the functions wisely, you will make the most out of this programming language. It is also noticeable that most of the things you learn about Python and its functions, parameters, methods, and such will help you learn other languages quicker, so do pay attention.

Parameters

Our eagle-eyed readers may have noticed something about the function we just created a few minutes ago. Unlike most of the functions, we did not pass any information through the parentheses at all. Why that happens is something we will come to learn about once we understand exactly what parameters are in Python.

Parameters are used as place-holders for receiving information. These are what we, as well as users, provide to the program in order for it to work more accurately. There are some cases and functions where arguments are not required for them to do their basic operation. However, if you provide an argument to these functions, they will provide you with a more specific output. Of course, it does depend on the availability of the said parameter. You cannot force a function to do something it is not designed to do.

Now, let's look at our function. It is certainly missing something. If you currently print the welcome_user function, it would say everything but will not contain the name of the user at all. Surely, it would look a lot nicer for us if we could somehow use this function to use the name of the user and add it to the greeting.

Luckily, we can do just that! For that, we first need to add the 'name' parameter in the first line, where we began defining our function. Simple type name between the parentheses and you will see the text turn grey. This confirms that the word has been added as a parameter. Now, we wish to print the name of this user along with the greetings we have defined within the function. For this example, let's assume that the user is named Fred.

```
def welcome_message(name):
    print("Begin")
    print("Hello and welcome {name}!")
    print("Hope you have a great time")
    print("End")
welcome_message('Fred')
Begin
Hello and welcome Fred!
Hope you have a great time
End
```

Finally! We have a name to add to our greetings. You can add another line of code by using our function and use a different name now. See what happens then.

When we set a parameter for a function and then call upon the function without providing it with an argument or the bit of information that goes between the parentheses, it will provide us with an error, except for a few.

Now, let's make our function a little more dynamic and add another parameter. Let's add a parameter that allows the program to print out the last name of the user. Now, our code should look something like this:

```
def welcome_message(name, last_name):
    print("Hello and welcome {name} {last_name}!")
    print("Hope you have a great time")
print("Begin")
welcome_message('Fred', 'William')
print("End")
```

The point to learn here, apart from being able to add parameters, is the fact that 'Fred' and 'William' are being used in a specific order. Should you type it the other way around, Python will print these as they are. This is because of their position concerning the defined parameters. The first value Python reads here, it will automatically link it with the first parameter. This can cause a little confusion, especially if the last name becomes the first name.

These arguments are called as positional arguments. To further show their importance, let's remove the last name from the argument above.

```
print("Begin")
welcome_message('Fred')
print("End")
Traceback (most recent call last):
Begin
  File
"C:/Users/Smith/PycharmProjects/MyFirstGo/PosArg.py",
line 7, in <module>
    welcome_message('Fred')
TypeError: welcome_message() missing 1 required
positional argument: 'last_name'
```

So, the system does not allow us to continue as we have removed an element. This time, type in the last name first followed by the first name and see if it makes any difference. When you run the program now, you should be able to see this:

```
print("Begin")
welcome_message('Fred', 'William')
print("End")
Begin
Hello and welcome William Fred!
Hope you have a great time
End
```

Now, the sequence kind of worked. The only issue is that it has gotten the name wrong. Now, the last name is being portrayed and printed as the first name. That is rather embarrassing, isn't it?

The above errors either state that we are missing one required positional argument or show that we placed the wrong name in the wrong place. Positional arguments are such arguments whose position matters a lot. If you miss out on the position altogether, you will end up with an error. If you type in something else, as we did in our last example, you will produce incorrect results. To correct it, simply provide the last name after the first name.

There is one more way you can have these dealt with by using what is termed as 'keyword arguments'. These are the kind of arguments whose position does not matter at all and Python will still continue to function properly regardless of their position in the parentheses. To pass a keyword argument, you will need to do the following:

```
print("Begin")
welcome_message(last_name='William', name='Fred')
print("End")
Begin
Hello and welcome Fred William!
Hope you have a great time
End
```

Now that's more like it. Things are looking right how we want them. Notice how, even though we wrote in the wrong order, Python picked up and sorted the order for us. That is because we made our entries or arguments into keyword arguments using the name= or last_name= parameter and combining it with arguments. This allows Python to draw information and understand which of these two comes first in order as defined originally in our function.

Factually speaking, you will not be using these quite a lot, but it is always an advantage to know the ways to overcome certain issues. Normally, you or any other programmer would be able to see the data and read it easily if you simply follow the rules and type the first name followed by the last name. Make the code as easy as you can for everyone to read and understand.

"Well, what if I was using numbers instead of names?"

That is one fine question. This is where you will need to use keyword arguments to represent what those values are for. You might be running a function that involves multiple values that only you might be able to understand, but others will have no idea where they came from. You must label each one of them with the relevant keyword argument so that the readability increases.

We are currently just beginning and for the sake of demonstration, we used a simple example to showcase how to create functions and use them. Your functions, when the time comes, might be quite vast or equally short, depending on the kind of function you create in any specific situation.

Creating functions certainly helps us organize our codes and be more efficient and effective. If we were unable to do this, we would have had to resort to writing the same bunch of lines every now and then.

Return Statement

We could have covered what a return statement is when we were discussing 'if' statements and others. However, it makes more sense to learn this after you have understood the concept of parameters and functions.

So far, we have created a function that has allowed us to send information via the use of parameters. However, when we talk about return statements, these are designed to do certain calculations and provide us with the results instead of us feeding it with values.

Let's look a little deeper into how this works by creating our second function. The purpose of this function is based on a simple math trick which most of us might have heard of or played with when we were young. Ask the user to think of any number and you would ask them to add and subtract a few simple numbers. Eventually, you would provide them with an accurate result and everyone would be shocked. Now, let's reveal what happens with the use of this function we are about to create.

```
def magic_number(number):
    return number + 6 - 4 + 5 - number
```

This simple calculation would always return you the value of seven. Go ahead, try it out yourself by doing this. However, for us to be able to get these values back, we have used the return statement here. This tells Python that it is supposed to do the calculation for us and then only return the resulting value instead of printing each of these individually.

Let's give our second function a test run:

```
result = magic_number(8329)
print(result)
```

See how the result now shows as seven? You can try and change the values to whatever you please, the result will continue to remain as seven. That is only made possible owing to the return statement we have provided here. If you take away the keyword return, you end up with a value that says 'None'. The program will still function, but the result would no longer be calculated or of any use to us. This is because Python would not execute a return phase and thus will not carry out the calculations as we would like it to.

Using these can greatly enhance your experience as a programmer or a user. However, before you dive in and start creating your functions, here are some which are pre-defined and may come in handy. There is no point in creating a function and finding out Python already had one for you.

1. min() and max() - In case you run into various values and you quickly wish to find out the minimum value in existence within a list or collection of data, use the min() command and run the numbers through. The minimum number will be printed for you. The max() function is the opposite, of course!

2. sum() - This is quite a nifty function and allows you to quickly add up all the numbers in the list and produce the result for you right away. The accuracy with floats might not be what we like, but hey, it gets you going.

3. type() - There may come lines and lines of codes with variables that are scattered all over the place. You now wish to find out where the variable started from and what kind of a variable it is. Using the type() function, you can quickly find out what kind of variable you are dealing with. It will return values such as 'bool' to indicate that the variable in question is a bool in type.

There are hundreds of functions that you will start to learn as you proceed into advanced Python learning and machine learning. However, to understand most of them, you will need to practice these and develop a thorough understanding of how these work. You should then have no problems venturing into a more advanced version of Python learning and developing complex programs.

Test your knowledge

This time, let's raise the stakes a bit and test your knowledge. This will involve a combination of everything you have learned so far. However, this time you will not be provided with solutions to keep you on a quest to search for answers and use the trial-and-error method to perfect the program.

Exercise

Here is the updated version of a program we designed to check insurance prices a person would have to pay if he/she was above or below a certain age. Your objective is to convert this into a function. Your function should have three fields set to receive input from the user.

- Name
- Age
- Actual insurance cost

Updated code:

```
Insurance = 1000
age = int(input('Your age: '))
is_old = age > 40
is_young = age <= 28
has_license = input('Do you have a license? ')
if has_license.lower() == 'Yes':
    has_license = True
elif has_license.lower() != 'Yes':
    has_license = False
if is_old and has_license:
    Insurance = Insurance / 2
    print("Your insurance cost is ${Insurance}")
elif is_young and has_license:
    Insurance = Insurance // 1.50
    print("You will need to pay ${Insurance}")
else:
    print('You are not eligible for insurance at this
time')
```

10. Functions and Modules – Recap

In Python programming, functions refer to any group of related statements that perform a given activity. Functions are used in breaking down programs into smaller and modular bits. In that sense, functions are the key factors that make programs easier to manage and organize as they grow bigger over time. Functions are also helpful in avoiding repetition during coding and make codes reusable.

The Syntax of Functions

The syntax of functions refers to the rules which govern the combination of characters that make up a function. These syntaxes include the following:

- The keyword "def" highlights the beginning of every function header.
- A function is named to identify it distinctly. The rules of making functions are the same as the rules which apply for writing identifiers in Python.
- Parameters or arguments via which values are passed onto a function are optional in Python.
- A colon sign (:) is used to highlight the end of every function header.
- The optional documentation string known as "docstring" is used to define the purpose of the function.
- The body of a function is comprised of one or more valid statements in Python. The statements must all have a similar indentation level, (typically four spaces).
- An optional return statement is included for returning a value from a function.

Below is a representation of the essential components of a function as described in the syntax.

```
def function_name(parameters):
'''docstring'''
statement(s)
```

How Functions are Called in Python

Once a function has been defined in Python, it is capable of being called from another function, a program, or the Python prompt even. Calling a function is done by entering a function name with a proper parameter.

Docstring

The docstring is the first string that comes after the function header. The docstring is short for documentation string and is used in explaining what a function does briefly. Although it is an optional part of a function, the documentation process is a good practice in programming. So, unless you have got an excellent memory that can recall what you had for breakfast on your first birthday, you should document your code at all times. In the example shown below, the docstring is used directly beneath the function header.

```
>>> greet("Amos")
Hello, Amos. Good morning!
```

Triple quotation marks are typically used when writing docstrings so they can extend to several lines. Such a string is inputted as the __doc__ attribute of the function. Take the example below.

You can run the following lines of code in a Python shell and see what it outputs:

```
>>> print(greet.__doc__)
This function greets to the person passed into the name
parameter
```

The return statement

The purpose of the return statement is to go back to the location from which it was called after exiting a function.

This statement can hold expressions that have been evaluated and have their values returned. A function will return the Noneobject if the statement is without an expression, or its return statement is itself absent in the function.

For instance:

```
>>> print(greet('Amos'))
Hello, Amos. Good morning!
None
```

In this case, the returned value is None.

11.   Working with Files

The next thing that we need to focus on when it comes to working with Python is making sure we know how to work and handle files. It may happen that you are working with some data and you want to store them while ensuring that they are accessible for you to pull up and use when they are needed later. You do have some choices in the way that you save the data, how they are going to be found later on, and how they are going to react in your code.

When you work with the files, you will find that the data is going to be saved on a disk, or you can re-use in the code over and over again as much as you would like. This chapter is going to help us learn a bit more about how to handle some of the work that we need to do to ensure the files behave the way that they should, and so much more.

Now we are going to enter into file mode on the Python language, and this allows you to do a few different options along the way. A good way to think about this is that you can think about it like working on a file in Word. At some point, you may try to save one of the documents that you are working with so that it doesn't get lost and you can find them later on. These kinds of files in Python are going to be similar. But you won't be saving pages as you did on Word, you are going to save parts of your code.

You will find with this one that there are a few operations or methods that you are able to choose when it comes to working with files. And some of these options will include:

- Closing up a file you are working on.
- Creating a brand new file to work on.
- Seeking out or moving a file that you have over to a new location to make it easier to find.
- Writing out a new part of the code on a file that was created earlier.

Creating new files

The first task that we are going to look at doing here is working on creating a file. It is hard to do much of the other tasks if we don't first have a file in place to help us out. If you would like to be able to make a new file and then add in some code into it, you first need to make sure the file is opened up inside of your IDLE. Then you can choose the mode that you would like to use when you write out your code.

When it comes to creating files on Python, you will find there are three modes that you are able to work with. The three main modes that we are going to focus on here include append (a), mode(x), and write(w).

Any time that you would like to open up a file and make some changes to it, then you would want to use the write mode. This is the easiest out of the three to work with. The write method is going to make it easier for you to get the right parts of the code set up and working for you in the end.

The write function is going to be easy to use and will ensure that you can make any additions and changes that you would like to the file. You can add in the new information that you would like to the file, change what is there, and so much more. If you would like to see what you can do with this part of the code with the write method, then you will want to open up your compiler and do the following code:

```
#file handling operations
#writing to a new file hello.txt
f = open('hello.txt', 'w', encoding = 'utf-8')
f.write("Hello Python Developers!")
f.write("Welcome to Python World")
f.flush()
f.close()
```

From here, we need to discuss what you can do with the directories that we are working with. The default directory is always going to be the current directory. You are able to go through and switch up the directory where the code information is stored, but you have to take the time, in the beginning, to change that information up, or it isn't going to end up in the directory that you would like.

Whatever directory you spent your time in when working on the code is the one you need to make your way back to when you want to find the file later on. If you would like it to show up in a different directory, make sure that you move over to that one before you save it and the code. With the option that we wrote above, when you go to the current directory (or the directory that you chose for this endeavor, then you will be able to open up the file and see the message that you wrote out there.

For this one, we wrote a simple part of the code. You, of course, will be writing out codes that are much more complicated as we go along. And with those codes, there are going to be times when you would like to edit or overwrite some of what is in that file. This is possible to do with Python, and it just needs a small change to the syntax that you are writing out. A good example of what you can do with this one includes:

```
#file handling operations
#writing to a new file hello.txt
f = open('hello.txt', 'w', encoding = 'utf-8')
f.write("Hello Python Developers!")
f.write("Welcome to Python World")
mylist = ["Apple", "Orange", "Banana"]
#writelines() is used to write multiple lines into the
file
f.write(mylist)
f.flush()
f.close()
```

The example above is a good one to use when you want to make a few changes to a file that you worked on before because you just need to add in one new line. This example wouldn't need to use that third line because it just has some simple words, but you can add in anything that you want to the program, just use the syntax above and change it up for what you need.

What are binary files?

One other thing that we need to focus on for a moment before moving on is the idea of writing out some of your files and your data in the code as a binary file. This may sound a bit confusing, but it is a simple thing that Python will allow you to do. All that you need to do to make this happen is to take the data that you have and change it over to a sound or image file, rather than having it as a text file.

With Python, you are able to change any of the code that you want into a binary file. It doesn't matter what kind of file it was in the past. But you do need to make sure that you work on the data in the right way to ensure that it is easier to expose in the way that you want later on. The syntax that is going to be needed to ensure that this will work well for you will be below:

```
# write binary data to a file
# writing the file hello.dat write binary mode
F = open('hello.dat', 'wb')
# writing as byte strings
f.write("I am writing data in binary file!/n")
f.write("Let's write another list/n")
f.close()
```

If you take the time to use this code in your files, it is going to help you to make the binary file that you would like. Some programmers find that they like using this method because it helps them to get things in order and will make it easier to pull the information up when you need it.

Opening your file up

So far, we have worked with writing a new file and getting it saved, and working with a binary file as well. In these examples, we got some of the basics of working with files down so that you can make them work for you and you can pull them up any time that you would like.

Now that this part is done, it is time to learn how to open up the file and use it, and later even make changes to it, any time that you would like. Once you open that file up, it is going to be so much easier to use it again and again as much as you would like. When you are ready to see the steps that are needed to open up a file and use it, you will need the following syntax.

```
# read binary data to a file
#writing the file hello.dat write append binary mode
with open("hello.dat", 'rb') as f:
data = f.read()
text = data.decode('utf-8')
print(text)
```

The output that you would get from putting this into the system would be like the following:

```
Hello, world!
This is a demo using with
This file contains three lines
Hello world
This is a demo using with
This file contains three lines.
Seeking out a file you need
```

104

And finally, we need to take a look at how you can seek out some of the files that you need in this kind of coding language. We already looked at how to make the files, how to store them in different manners, how to open them and rewrite them, and then how to seek the file. But there are times where you are able to move one of the files that you have over to a new location.

For example, if you are working on a file and as you do that, you find that things are not showing up the way that you would like it to, then it is time to fix this up. Maybe you didn't spell the time of the identifier the right way, or the directory is not where you want it to be, then the seek option may be the best way to actually find this lost file and then make the changes, so it is easier to find later on.

With this method, you are going to be able to change up where you place the file, to ensure that it is going to be in the right spot all of the time or even to make it a bit easier for you to find it when you need. You just need to use a syntax like what is above to help you make these changes.

Working with all the different methods we've talked about in this chapter will help you do a lot of different things within your code. If you want to create a new file, you want to change the code, move the file, and more; you can do it all using the codes we have discussed in this chapter.

12. Conditional and Loops in Python

This chapter describes moderate level topics like conditionals and loops in detail. We will use different examples to explain these topics in detail. Let's dive into learning more about these concepts.

What is a sequence in Python?

The sequence of program execution is not a highway linking the north and the south. It can run from the north to the south to the end. The sequence of program execution may be as complicated as a highway in a busy area, with nine turns and 18 turns, which is easy to make people dizzy.

To write a good program, it is very important to control the process of program execution. Therefore, it is necessary to use the process control structure of the program. Without them, it is impossible to use the program to complete any complicated work.

The programming language has been continuously developed for decades. Structured Programming has gradually become the mainstream of program development. Its main idea is to execute the entire program in sequence from top to bottom. Python language is mainly executed from top to bottom according to the sequence of program source code, but sometimes the execution sequence will be changed according to needs.

At this time, the computer can be told which sequence to execute the program preferentially through flow control instructions. The process control of the program is like designing a traffic direction extending in all directions for the highway system.

It is recognized that most program codes for process control are executed in sequence from top to bottom line after line, but for operations with high repeatability, it is not suitable to execute in sequence. Any Python program, no matter how complex its structure is, can be expressed or described using three basic control processes: sequence structure, selection structure, and loop structure.

The first line statement of the sequence structure program is the entry point and is executed from top to bottom to the last line statement of the program. The selection structure allows the program to select the program block to be executed according to whether the test condition is established or not. If the condition is True, some program statements are executed. If the condition is False, other program statements are executed.

Colloquially, if you encounter a situation A, perform operation A; if this is case b, operation b is executed. Just like when we drive to the intersection and see the signal lamp, the red light will stop, and the green light will pass. Also, different destinations also have different directions, and you can choose the route according to different situations. In other words, the selection structure represents that the program will determine the "direction" of the program according to the specified conditions.

The function of loop flow control with loop structure is to repeatedly execute the program statements in a program block until the specific ending conditions are met. Python has a for loop and a while loop.

Selection Process Control

Selection Process Control is a conditional control statement that contains a conditional judgment expression (also referred to as conditional expression or conditional judgment expression for short). If the result of the conditional judgment expression is True (true), a program block is executed. If the result of the conditional judgment expression is false (True), another program block is executed.

The following describes the statements and their functions related to the selection process control in Python language.

If...Else Conditional Statement

If...else conditional statement is a fairly common and practical statement. If the conditional judgment expression is True (true, or represented by 1), the program statement in the if program block is executed. If the conditional judgment expression is not true (False, or represented by 0), the program statement in the else program block is executed. If there are multiple judgments, elif instruction can be added.

The syntax of the if conditional statement is as follows:

If the conditional judgment expression holds, execute the program statement in this program block

Else :

If the condition does not hold, execute the program statement in this program block. If we want to judge whether the value of variable a

is greater than or equal to the value of variable b, the condition judgment expression can be written as follows:

If a >= b:

If A is greater than or equal to B, execute the program statement in this program block

Else :

If a is NOT greater than or equal to b, the program statement if ... if...else conditional statement in this program block is executed.

In the use of the if...else conditional statement, if the condition is not satisfied, there is no need to execute any program statement, and the else part can be omitted

If conditional judgment expression

If the condition is satisfied, execute the program statements in this program block. In addition, if the if...else conditional statement uses logical operators such as "and", it is suggested to add parentheses to distinguish the execution order to improve the readability of the program,

For example: if (a==c) and (a>b):

If A equals C and A is greater than B, execute the program statement in this program block

Else :

If the above condition does not hold, the program statement in this program block is executed.

Also, Python language provides a more concise conditional expression of if...else in the following format: X if C else Y returns one of the two expressions according to the conditional judgment expression. In the above expression, X is returned when C is truc; otherwise, Y is returned.

For example, to determine whether the integer x is odd or even, the original program would be written as follows:

```
If (first % 2)==0:
second= "even number"
Else:
second= "odd number"
```

If print('{0}'.format(second)) is changed to a concise form, only a single line of program statements is required to achieve the same purpose.

The statements are as follows:

```
print('{0}'.format ("even" if (first% 2)==0 else "odd"))
```

If the if condition determines that the expression is true, it returns "even"; otherwise, it returns "odd." In the following sample program, we will practice the use of the if...else statement. The purpose of the sample program is to make a simple leap year judgment program.

Let the user enter the year (4-digit integer year), and the program will determine whether it is a leap year. One of the following two conditions is a leap year:

1. leap every 4 years (divisible by 4) but not every 100 years (divisible by 100).
2. leap every 400 years (divisible by 400).

[example procedure: leapYear.py]

Determine whether an input year is a leap year or not

```
01 # -*- coding: utf-8 -*-
02 """""
03 program name: leap year judging program
04 Topic Requirements:
05 Enter the year (4-digit integer year) to determine
whether it is a leap year
06 condition 1. Every 4 leap (divisible by 4) and every
100 leap (divisible by 100)
07 condition 2. Every 400 leap (divisible by 400)
08 One of the two conditions met is a leap year.
09 """""
10 year = int(input ("Give year:"))
12 if (year % 4 == 0 and year % 100 ! = 0) or (year % 400
== 0):
13 print("{0} is a leap year ."format(year))
14 Else:
```

The execution results of the
```
15 print("{0} is the year of peace ."format(year))
```

Program Code Resolution:

Line 10: Enter a year, but remember to call the int () function to convert it to an integer type.

Line 12-15: Judge whether it is a leap year.

Condition 1: every 4 leaps (divisible by 4) and every 100 leaps (not divisible by 100).

Condition 2: every 400 leaps (divisible by 400). One of the two conditions is a leap year. Readers are asked to inquire whether the following years are leap years: 1900 (flat year), 1996 (leap year), 2004 (leap year), 2017 (flat year), 2400 (leap year).

Multiple Choices

If there is more than one conditional judgment expression, elif conditional statement can be added. Elif is like the abbreviation of "else if." Although using multiple if conditional statements can solve the problem of executing different program blocks under various conditions, it is still not simple enough. Then, elif conditional statements can be used, and the readability of the program can be improved.

Note that if the statement is a logical "necessity" in our program. Elif and else do not necessarily follow, so there are three situations: if, if/else, if/elif/else.

The format is as follows:

If condition judgment

Expression 1:

If the conditional judgment expression 1 holds, the program statement in this program block is executed

Elif condition judgment

Expression 2:

If the conditional judgment expression 2 holds, execute the program statement in this program block

Else :

If none of the above conditions hold, execute the program statement in this program block,

For example:

If first==second:

If first equals second, execute the program statement in this program block

Elif first>second :

If first is greater than second, execute the program statement in this program block

Else :

If first is not equal to second and first is less than second, execute the program statement in this program block.

110

The following example program is used to practice the use of IF multiple selection. The purpose of the sample program is to detect the current time to decide which greeting to use.

[sample procedure: currentTime.py]

Detects the current time to decide which greeting

```
01 # -*- coding: utf-8 -*-
02 """"
03 Program Name: Detect the current time to decide which
greeting to use
04 Topic Requirements:
05 Judging from the current time (24-hour system)
06 5~10:59, output "good morning"
07 11~17:59, output "good afternoon"
08 18~4:59, output "good night"
09 """"
11 import time
13 print ("current time: {}." format (time.strftime
("%h:% m:% s"))
14 h = int( time.strftime("%H") )
16 if h>5 and h < 11:
17 print ("good morning!" )
18 elif h >= 11 and h<18:
19 print ("good afternoon!" )
20 else:
21 print ("good night!")
```

The execution results of the program will be shown on the screen.

The output shows the current time in the sample program to judge whether it is morning, afternoon, or evening, and then displays the appropriate greeting. Python's time module provides various functions related to time. The Time module is a module in Python's standard module library.

Before using it, you need to use the import instruction to import and then call the strftime function to format the time into the format we want. For example, the following program statement is used to obtain the current time.

```
import time
Time.strftime ("%h:% m:% s")
 # 18: 36: 16 (6:36:16 p.m. 24-hour)
Time. strftime ("%i:% m:% s")
# 06:36:16 (6: 36: 16 p.m. 12-hour system) format
parameters to be set are enclosed in parentheses.
```

Pay attention to the case of format symbols. The following program statement is used to display the week, month, day, hour, minute, and second.

Print (time.strftime ("%a,% b% d% h:% m:% s")) execution results are as follows: Monday, sep17 15: 49: 29 4.2.3 nested if sometimes there is another layer of if conditional statement in the if conditional statement. This multi-layer selection structure is called nested if conditional statement.

Usually, when demonstrating the use of nested if conditional statements, it is more common to demonstrate multiple choices with numerical ranges or scores. In other words, different grades of certificates will be issued for different grades of achievements.

If it is more than 60 points, the first certificate of competency will be given, if it is more than 70 points, the second certificate of competency will be given, if it is more than 80 points, the third certificate of competency will be given, if it is more than 90 points, the fourth certificate of competency will be given, if it is more than 100 points, the all-round professional certificate of competency will be given.

Based on nested if statements, we can write the following program:

```
available= int(input ("Give a score:")
if available >= 60:
print ('First Certificate of Conformity')
if available >= 70:
print ('Second Certificate of Conformity')
if available >= 80:
print ('Third Certificate of Conformity')
if available >= 90:
print ('Fourth Certificate of Conformity')
if getScore == 100:
```

Print ('All-round Professional Qualification Certificate') is actually an if statement that is explored layer by layer. We can use the if/elif statement to filter the multiple choices one by one according to conditional expression operation and select the matching condition (True) to execute the program statement in a program block.

The syntax is as follows:

If Conditional Expression 1:

The program block to be executed under conditional expression 1

Elif conditional expression 2:

The program block to be executed under conditional expression 2

Elif conditional expression n:

The program block to be executed according to the conditional expression n

Else:

If all the conditional expressions do not conform, this program block is executed. When the conditional expression 1 does not conform, the program block searches down to the finally conforming conditional expression.

The elif instruction is an abbreviation of else if. Elif statements can generate multiple statements according to the operation of a conditional expression, and its conditional expression must be followed by a colon, which indicates that the following program blocks meet this conditional expression and need to be indented.

The following example program is a typical example of the combined use of nested if and if/elif statements. This program uses if to determine which grade the query results belong to. Also, another judgment has been added to the sample program. If the score integer value entered is not between 0 and 100, a prompt message of "input error, the number entered must be between 0 and 100" will be output.

Comprehensive use of nested if statements example:

```
01 # -*- coding: utf-8 -*-
02 """"""
03 Examples of Comprehensive Use of Nested if Statements
04 """"""
05 result = int(input ('Give final grade:')
06
07 # First Level if/else Statement: Judge whether the
result entered is between 0 and 100
08 if result >= 0 and result <= 100:
09 # 2nd level if/elif/else statement
10 if result <60:
11 print('{0} below cannot obtain certificate of
competency'. format(result))
12 elif result >= 60 and result <70:
13 print('{0} result is d'. format(result))
14 elif result >= 70 and result <80:
15 print('{0} result is c'. format(result))
16 elif result >= 80 and result <90:
17 print('{0} result is level b'. format(result))
18 else:
19 print('{0} result is grade a'. format(result))
20 else:
21 print ('input error, input number must be between 0-
100')
```

Program code analysis:

Lines 7-21: first-level if/else statement, used to judge whether the input result is between 0 and 100.

Lines 10-19: the second-level if/elif/else statement, which is used to judge which grade the inquired result belongs to.

In the next section, we will discuss loops one of the most important concepts.

The Loop Repeat Structure

This mainly refers to the loop control structure. A certain program statement is repeatedly executed according to the set conditions, and the loop will not jump out until the condition judgment is not established. In short, repetitive structures are used to design program blocks that need to be executed repeatedly, that is, to make program code conform to the spirit of structured design.

For example, if you want the computer to calculate the value of $1+2+3+4+...+10$, you don't need us to accumulate from 1 to 10 in the program code, which is tedious and repetitive, and you can easily achieve the goal by using the loop control structure. Python contains a while loop and a for loop, and the related usage is described below.

While loop

If the number of loops to be executed is determined, then using the for loop statement is the best choice. However, the while loop is more suitable for certain cycles that cannot be determined. The while loop statement is similar to the for loop statement and belongs to the pre-test loop. The working model of the pre-test loop is that the loop condition judgment expression must be checked at the beginning of the loop program block.

When the judgment expression result is true, the program statements in the loop block will be executed. We usually call the program statements in the loop block the "loop body." While loop also uses a conditional expression to judge whether it is true or false to control the loop flow. When the conditional expression is true, the program statement in the loop will be executed. When the conditional expression is false, the program flow will jump out of the loop.

The format of the While loop statement is as follows:

While conditional expression:

If the conditional expression holds, the flow chart of executing the while loop statement in this program block.

The while loop must include the initial value of the control variable and the expression for increasing or decreasing. When writing the loop program, it must check whether the condition for leaving the loop exists. If the condition does not exist, the loop body will be continuously executed without stopping, resulting in an "infinite loop," also called "dead loop."

The loop structure usually requires three conditions:

(1)   The initial value of the loop variable.
(2)   Cyclic conditional expression.
(3)   Adjust the increase or decrease the value of cyclic variables.

For example, the following procedure:

```
first=1
While first < 10: # Loop Condition Expression
print( first)
first += 1 # adjusts the increase or decrease value of
the loop variable.
```

When first is less than 10, the program statement in the while loop will be executed, and then first will be added with 1 until first is equal to 10. If the result of the conditional expression is False, it will jump out of the loop.

For loop

For loop, also known as count loop, is a loop form commonly used in programming. It can repeatedly execute a fixed number of loops. If the number of loop executions required is known to be fixed when designing the program, then the for-loop statement is the best choice. The for loop in Python language can be used to traverse elements or table items of any sequence. The sequence can be tuples, lists or strings, which are executed in sequence.

The syntax is as follows:

For element variable in sequence:

Executed instructions

The program block of #else can be added or not added, that is, when using the for loop, the else statement can be added or not added. The meaning represented by the above Python syntax is that the for loop traverses all elements in a sequence, such as a string or a list, in the order of the elements in the current sequence (item, or table item).

For example, the following variable values can all be used as traversal sequence elements of a for loop.

```
first= "abcdefghijklmnopqrstuvwxyz "
second= ['january', 'march', 'may', 'july', 'august',
'october', 'december']
result= [a, e, 3, 4, 5, j, 7, 8, 9, 10]
```

In addition, if you want to calculate the number of times a loop is executed, you must set the initial value of the loop, the ending condition, and the increase or decrease value of the loop variable for each loop executed in the for-loop control statement. For loop every round, if the increase or decrease value is not specifically specified, it will automatically accumulate 1 until the condition is met.

For example, the following statement is a tuple (11 ~ 15) and uses the for loop to print out the numeric elements in the tuple: x = [11, 12, 13, 14, 15]

```
for first in x:
    print(first)
```

A more efficient way to write tuples is to call the range () function directly. The format of the range () function is as follows:

range ([initial value], final value [,increase or decrease value])

Tuples start from "initial value" to the previous number of "final value." If no initial value is specified, the default value is 0; if no increase or decrease value is specified, the default increment is 1.

An example of calling the range () function is as follows: range (3) means that starting from the subscript value of 0, 3 elements are output, i.e., 0, 1 and 2 are three elements in total.

Range(1,6) means starting from subscript value 1 and ending before subscript value 6-1, that is, subscript number 6 is not included, i.e., 1, 2, 3, 4 and 5 are five elements. ·range (4,10,2) means starting from subscript value 4 and ending before subscript number 10, that is, subscript number 10 is excluded, and the increment value is 2, i.e., 4, 6 and 8 are three elements. The following program code demonstrates the use of the range () function in a for loop to output even numbers between 2 and 11 for i in range (2, 11, 2).

One more thing to pay special attention to when using the for loop is the print () function. If the print () is indented, it means that the operation to be executed in the for loop will be output according to the number of times the loop is executed. If there is no indentation, it means it is not in the for loop, and only the final result will be output.

We know that calling the range () function with the for loop can not only carry out accumulation operations but also carry out more varied accumulation operations with the parameters of the range () function. For example, add up all multiples of 5 within a certain range. The following sample program will demonstrate how to use the for loop to accumulate multiples of 5 within a range of numbers.

Accumulate multiples of 5 in a certain numerical range

```
01 # -*- coding: utf-8 -*-
02 """""
03 Accumulate multiples of 5 within a certain numerical
range
04 """""
05 addition = 0 # stores the accumulated result
06
07 # enters for/in loop
08 for count in range(0, 21, 5):
09 addition += count # adds up the values
11 print('5 times cumulative result =',addition)
# Output cumulative result
```

Program code analysis:

Lines 08 and 09: Add up the numbers 5, 10, 15 and 20. Also, when executing a for loop, if you want to know the subscript value of an element, you can call Python's built-in enumerate function. The syntax format of the call is as follows: for subscript value, element variable in enumerate (sequence element).

For example (refer to sample program enumerate. py):

```
names = ["ram," "raju," "ravi"]
for index, x in enumerate(names):
```

The execution result of the above statement in print ("{0}-{1}." format (index, x)) is displayed.

Nested loop

Next, we will introduce a for a nested loop, that is, multiple for loop structures. In the nested for loop structure, the execution process must wait for the inner loop to complete before continuing to execute the outer loop layer by layer.

The double nested for loop structure format is as follows:

For example, a table can be easily completed using a double nested for loop. Let's take a look at how to use the double nested for loop to make the nine tables through the following sample program.

99 Table

```
01 # -*- coding: utf-8 -*-
02 """"
03 Program Name: Table
04 """"
05
06 for x in range(6,68 ):
07 for y in range(1, 9):
08 print("{0}*{1}={52: ^2}."format(y, x, x * y), end=" ")
```

99 is a very classic example of nested loops. If readers have learned other programming languages, I believe they will be amazed at the brevity of Python. From this example program, we can clearly understand how nested loops work. Hereinafter, the outer layer for the loop is referred to as the x loop, and the inner layer for loop is referred to as the y loop.

When entering the x loop, x=1. When the y loop is executed from 1 to 9, it will return to the x loop to continue execution. The print statement in the y loop will not wrap. The print () statement in the outer x loop will not wrap until the y loop is executed and leaves the y loop. After the execution is completed, the first row of nine tables will be obtained. When all X cycles are completed, the table is completed.

Note that a common mistake for beginners is that the sentences of the inner and outer loops are staggered. In the structure of multiple nested loops, the inner and outer loops cannot be staggered; otherwise, errors will be caused.

The continue instruction and break instruction are the two loop statements we introduced before. Under normal circumstances, the while loop is to judge the condition of the loop before entering the loop body. If the condition is not satisfied, it will leave the loop, while for loop ends the execution of the loop after all the specified elements are fetched. However, the loop can also be interrupted by continue or break. The main purpose of break instruction is to jump out of the current loop body, just like its English meaning, break means "interrupt."

If you want to leave the current loop body under the specified conditions in the loop body, you need to use the break instruction, whose function is to jump off the current for or while loop body and give the control of program execution to the next line of program statements outside the loop body. In other words, the break instruction is used to interrupt the execution of the current loop and jump directly out of the current loop.

Control Flow Statements

If–else statement

The if-else statement is used to make the choices from 2 or more statements. It becomes helpful when you want to execute a particular statement based on a True or False condition.

The syntax of if statement is:

If condition:
   action-1   # Indentation
Else:
   action-2   # Indentation

Here the indentation is required. The actions action-1 and action-2 may consist of many statements but they must be all indented.

if <expression> :
<statements>
else :
<statements>

The example is shown below.

```
>>> e = 6
>>> f = 7
>>> if(e < f):
...      print( 'f is greater than e' )
... else:
...      print(' e is greater than f')
...
```

Output: f is greater than e

```
def  numberProperty1 ( input ) :
       if input % 2 ==  0 :
print input ,  ' is an Even number '
       else :
print input ,  ' is an Odd number '
numberProperty1( 10 )    # result is 10 is an Even number
numberProperty1( 11 )    # result is 11 is an Odd number
```

Nested If

It consists of more than 2 statements to choose from.

```
def numberProperty2 ( input ) :
if input < 0:
print input , ' is a Negative number '
elif input == 0:
print input , ' is Zero '
else:
print input , ' is a Positive number '
numberProperty2( -100 )   # -100  is a Negative number
numberProperty2( 0 )        # 0   is Zero
numberProperty2( 100 )    # 100  is a Positive number
```

While Loop

The while loop will run until the expression is true and it stops once it is false.

The syntax of while loop is:

While expression:

   statement

For example:

```
>>> a = 1
>>> while(a < 10 ):
...     print "The number is:" , a
...     a = a + 1
...
The number is: 1
The number is: 2
The number is: 3
The number is: 4
The number is: 5
The number is: 6
The number is: 7
The number is: 8
The number is: 9
The number is: 10
```

In the above example, the block consists of print and increment statements, it is executed repeatedly until the count is no longer less than 5.

In the following example the while loop is implemented within a function:

```
def printSeries( start, end, interval ) :
print " \n "
temp = start
```

```
while ( temp < end ) :
print temp,
temp += interval
printSeries( 1, 11, 1 )    # result is  1 2 3 4 5 6 7 8 9
10
printSeries( 1, 11, 3 )    # result is  1 4 7 10
```

For Statement

Any object with an iteration method can be used in a for loop in Python. The iteration method means that the data can be presented in a list form where there are multiple values in an ordered manner. The syntax of for loop is:

for item in list:
    action   # Indentation

The action consists of one or more statements and it must be indented. The examples are shown below.

For example:
```
>>> for i in (1, 2, 3, 4, 5, 6, 7, 8, 9, 10):
...       print i
...
1
2
3
4
5
6
7
8
9
10
>>> list = ['a', 'bb', 'ccc', 'dddd']
>>> for l in list:
...       print l,len(l)
...
a 1
bb 2
ccc 3
dddd 4
```

The above program shows that the values of a list and its length are printed using the for loop.

121

Break

The break statement breaks out of the smallest enclosing for or while loop.

Now let's see an example:

```
def primeNumberValidation ( input ) :
        for x in range( 2, input ) :
                if  input % x == 0:
        print  input, 'is not a prime number and equals',
x, '*',  input/x
        break
else:
        print  input, 'is a prime number'
primeNumberValidation( 3 )
primeNumberValidation( 14 )
```

Continue

The continue statement continues with the next iteration of the loop.

Now let's see an example:

```
def evenNumbers( start, end ) :
print "\n\nEven numbers in between ", start , " and ",
end
for n in range( start + 1, end ) :
if n % 2 != 0:
continue
print n
evenNumbers( 1, 11 )   # result is   14 is 2 4 6 8 10
evenNumbers( 10, 30 ) # result is   12 14 16 18 20 22 24
26 28
```

Pass

Pass is a valid statement and can be used when there is a statement required syntactically, but the program requires no action.

Now let's see an example:

```
while True :
        pass  # In condition loop press (Ctrl + c) for
the keyboard interrupt
```

In this example, while followed by "pass" it does not execute any statement.

There is a necessity to include at least one statement in a block (e.g. function, while, for loop, etc.) in these cases, use pass as one statement, which does nothing but includes one statement under ':'

Now let's see an example:

122

```
def  x() :
pass  # one valid statement that does not do any action
```

Here pass is considered a statement for the declaration of function x.

13. Object-Oriented Programming

Python allows several programming paradigms, including object-oriented programming (OOP). The OOP is a way of structuring the code that makes it especially effective by organizing and reusing code, although its abstract nature makes it not very intuitive when it starts.

Object-oriented programming in Python is optional and so far, we have not used it directly, although indirectly we have done so from the beginning. Although its biggest advantage becomes apparent with long and more complex programs, it is very useful to understand how OOP works since this is how Python works internally.

The basic idea is simple. If we have a more complex type of data than we have seen so far as lists or dictionaries and we want to create a new type of data with particular properties, we can define it with a class, something similar to a def function. Suppose we want to create a type of data called Star (Star), which to begin with, will only have one name, we can write:

```
# Let's create star.py
class Star(object):
    """"Class for stars""""
    def __init__(self, name):
        self.name = name
    # Special method called when doing print
    def __str__(self):
        return "Stars {}".format(self.name)
```

The class has a special main function __init __ () that builds the element of the Star class (called an object) and is executed when it creates a new object or instance of that class; we have put name as the only mandatory parameter, but it does not have to have any.

The mysterious self-variable with which each function begins (called methods on objects), refers to the specific object we are creating, this will be clearer with an example. Now we can create Star type objects:

```
# Star.py library that includes the Star import star
class
```

```
# New instance (object) of Star, with a parameter (the
name), mandatory star1 = star.Star («Altair»)
# What returns when printing the object, according to the
method __str__ print (star1) # Star Altair
print (star1.name) # Altair
```

When creating the object with name star1, which in the class definition we call self, we have a new data type with the name property.

Now we can add some methods that can be applied to the Star object:

```
class Star:
    """ "Star class
    Example classes with Python
    File: star.py
    """ "
    # Total number of stars
    num_stars = 0
    def __init __ (self, name):
        self.name = name
        Star.num_stars + = 1
    def set_mag (self, mag):
        self.mag = mag
    def set_pair (self, pair):
        """ "Assigns parallax in arc seconds" ""
        self.pair = pair
    def get_mag (self):
        print "The magnitude of {} of {}". format
(self.name, self.mag)
    def get_dist (self):
        """ "Calculate the distance in parsec from the
parallax" ""
        print "The distance of {} is {: .2f} pc" .format
(self.name, 1 / self.par)
    def get_stars_number (self):
        print "Total number of stars: {}". format
(Star.num_stars)
```

Now we can do more things with a Star object:
```
import star
# I create a star instance
altair = star.Star ('Altair')
altair.name
# Returns 'Altair'
altair.set_pair (0.195)
altair.get_stars_number ()
# Returns: Total number of stars: 1
```

```
# I use a general class method
star.pc2ly (5.13)
# Returns: 16.73406
altair.get_dist ()
# Returns: The distance of Altair is 5.13 pc
# I create another star instance
other = star.Star ('Vega')
otro.get_stars_number ()
# Returns: Total number of stars: 2
altair.get_stars_number ()
# Returns: Total number of stars: 2
```

Is this not all familiar? It is similar to the methods and properties of Python elements such as strings or lists, which are also objects defined in classes with their methods.

Objects have an interesting property called inheritance that allows you to reuse properties of other objects. Suppose we are interested in a particular type of star called a white dwarf, which are Star stars with some special properties, so we will need all the properties of the Star object and some new ones that we will add:

```
class WBStar (Star):
    """ "Class for White Dwarfs (WD)" """
    def __init __ (self, name, type):
        """ "WD type: dA, dB, dC, dO, dZ, dQ" """
        self.name = name
        self.type = type
        Star.num_stars + = 1
    def get_type (self):
        return self.type
    def __str __ (self):
        return "White Dwarf {} of type {}". format
(self.name, self.type)
```

Now, as a class parameter, instead of using an object to create a new object, we have set Star to inherit the properties of that class. Thus, when creating a WDStar object, we are creating a different object, with all the Star properties and methods and a new property called type. We also overwrite the result when printing with print defining the special method __str__.

As we can see, the methods, which are the functions associated with the objects, only apply to them. If in our file the class, which we have called star.py and that now contains the Star and WDStar classes, we add a normal function, this can be used as usual:

```
class Star (Star):
    ...
class WBStar (Star):
    ...
def pc2ly (dist):
    """ "Converts parsec to many years" """
    return dist * 3,262
And as always:
import star
# Convert parsecs into light years
```

distance_ly = Star.pc2ly (10.0)

We are now going to look at the four concepts of object-oriented programming and how they apply to Python.

Inheritance

The first major concept is called "inheritance." This refers to things being able to derive from another. Let's take sports cars for instance. All sports cars are vehicles, but not all vehicles are sports cars. Moreover, all sedans are vehicles, but all vehicles are not sedans, and sedans are certainly not sports cars, even though they're both vehicles.

So basically, this concept of Object-Oriented programming says that things can and should be chopped up into as small and fine precise concepts as possible.

In Python, this is done by deriving classes.

Let's say we had another class called SportsCar.

```
class Vehicle(object):
    def __init__(self, makeAndModel, prodYear,
airConditioning):
        self.makeAndModel = makeAndModel
        self.prodYear = prodYear
        self.airConditioning = airConditioning
        self.doors = 4
    def honk(self):
        print "%s says: Honk! Honk!" % self.makeAndModel
```

Now, below that, create a new class called SportsCar, but instead of deriving object, we're going to derive from Vehicle.

```
class SportsCar(Vehicle)
def __init__(self, makeAndModel, prodYear,
airConditioning):
    self.makeAndModel = makeAndModel
    self.prodYear = prodYear
```

```
    self.airConditioning = airConditioning
    self.doors = 4
```

Leave out the honk function, we only need the constructor function here. Now declare a sports car. I'm just going to go with the Ferrari.
```
ferrari = SportsCar("Ferrari Laferrari", 2016, True)
```

Now test this by calling
```
ferrari.honk()
```

and then saving and running. It should go off without a hitch.

Why is this? This is because the notion of inheritance says that a child class derives functions and class variables from a parent class. Easy enough concept to grasp. The next one is a little tougher.

Polymorphism

The idea of polymorphism is that the same process can be performed in different ways depending upon the needs of the situation. This can be done in two different ways in Python: method overloading and method overriding.

Method overloading is defining the same function twice with different arguments. For example, we could give two different initializer functions to our Vehicle class. Right now, it just assumes a vehicle has 4 doors. If we wanted to specifically say how many doors a car had, we could make a new initializer function below our current one with an added doors argument, like so (the newer one is on the bottom):
```
def __init__(self, makeAndModel, prodYear,
airConditioning):
self.makeAndModel = makeAndModel
self.prodYear = prodYear
self.airConditioning = airConditioning
self.doors = 4
def __init__(self, makeAndModel, prodYear,
airConditioning, doors):
self.makeAndModel = makeAndModel
self.prodYear = prodYear
self.airConditioning = airConditioning
self.doors = doors
```

Somebody now when creating an instance of the Vehicle class can choose whether they define the number of doors or not. If they don't, the number of doors is assumed to be 4.

Method overriding is when a child class overrides a parent class's function with its code.

To illustrate, create another class which extends Vehicle called Moped. Set the doors to 0, because that's absurd, and set air conditioning to false. The only relevant arguments are make/model and production year. It should look like this:

```
class Moped(Vehicle):
    def __init__(self, makeAndModel, prodYear):
        self.makeAndModel = makeAndModel
        self.prodYear = prodYear
        self.airConditioning = False
        self.doors = 0
```

Now, if we made an instance of the Moped class and called the honk() method, it would honk. But it is common knowledge that mopeds don't honk, they beep. So let's override the parent class's honk method with our own. This is super simple. We just redefine the function in the child class:

```
def honk(self):
    print "%s says: Beep! Beep!" % self.makeAndModel
```

I'm part of the 299,000,000 Americans who couldn't name a make and model of Moped if their life depended on it, but you can test out if this works for yourself but declaring an instance of the Moped class and trying it out.

Abstraction

The next major concept in object-oriented programming is abstraction. This is the notion that the programmer and user should be far from the inner workings of the computer. This has two benefits.

The first is that it decreases the inherent security risks and the possibility for catastrophic system errors, by either human or otherwise. By abstracting the programmer from the inner workings of the computer like memory and the CPU and often even the operating system, there's a low chance of any sort of mishap causing irreversible damage.

The second is that the abstraction innately makes the language easier to understand, read, and learn. Though it makes the language a tad less powerful by taking away some of the power that the user has over the entire computer architecture, this is traded instead for the ability to program quickly and efficiently in the language, not wasting time dealing with trivialities like memory addresses or things of the like.

These apply in Python because, well, it's incredibly simple. You can't get down into the nitty-gritty of the computer, or do much with memory allocation, or even specifically allocate an array size too easily, but this is a tradeoff for amazing readability, a highly secure language in a highly secure environment, and ease of use with programming. Compare the following snippet of code from C:

```
#include <stdio.h>
int main(void) {
printf("hello world");
return 0;
}
```

to the Python code for doing the same:

```
print "hello world"
# That's it. That's all there is to it.
```

Abstraction is generally a net positive for a large number of applications that are being written today, and there's a reason Python and other object-oriented programming languages are incredibly popular.

Encapsulation

The last major concept in object-oriented programming is that of encapsulation. This is the easiest to explain. This is the notion that common data should be put together, and that code should be modular. I'm not going to spend long explaining this because it's a super simple concept. The entire notion of classes is as concise of an example as you can get for encapsulation: common traits and methods are bonded together under one cohesive structure, making it super easy to create things of the sort without having to create a ton of super-specific variables for every instance.

Well, there we go. We finally made it to the end of our little Python adventure. First, I'd like to say thank you for making it through to the end of Python for Beginners: The Ultimate Guide to Python Programming. Let's hope it was informative and able to provide you with all of the tools you need to achieve your goals, whatever they may be.

The next step is to use this knowledge. Whether as a hobby or a career move, by learning the basics of Python, you just made one of the best decisions of your life, and your goal now should be finding ways to use it in your day-to-day life to make life easier or to accomplish things you've wanted to accomplish for a long while.

14. Exception Handling

Exceptions are the errors detected during execution and these are not unconditionally fatal.

Exception blocks will be enclosed with try and except statements.

try :

<statements>

except <exception type > :

<statements>

Let's see an example:

```
# Defining an exception block
try:
    print ( 1 / 0 )
except Exception as excep:
    print "exception : ", excep
# Defining a user-defined exception
class UserDefinedException( Exception ) :
    def __init__(self, value):
        self.value = value
    def __str__(self):
        return repr(self.value)
# Raising a user-defined exception explicitly
try:
    raise UserDefinedException(" input is null ")
except UserDefinedException as userdefinedexception:
    print 'userdefinedexception :
', userdefinedexception.value
```

In the above-mentioned program, first (try, except) block handles the Zero division exception.

UserDefinedException is a user-defined exception to raise business exceptions in the program.

Second (try, except) block raises a user-defined exception.

Exception handling is error management. It has three purposes.

1. It allows you to debug your program.

2. It allows your program to continue running despite encountering an error or exception.

3. It allows you to create your customized errors that can help you debug, remove, and control some of Python's nuances, and make your program function as you want it to.

Handling the Zero Division Error Exception

Exception handling can be an easy or difficult task depending on how you want your program to flow and your creativity. You might have scratched your head because of the word creativity. Programming is all about logic, right? No.

The core purpose of programming is to solve problems. A solution to a problem does not only require logic. It also requires creativity. Have you ever heard of the phrase, "Think outside of the box?"

Program breaking exceptions can be a pain and they are often called bugs. The solution to such problems is often elusive and you need to find a workaround or risk rewriting your program from scratch.

For example, you have a calculator program with this snippet of code when you divide:

```
>>> def div(dividend, divisor):
        print(dividend / divisor)
>>> div(5, 0)
Traceback (most recent call last):
  File "<stdin>", line 1, in <module>
  File "<stdin>", line 2, in div
ZeroDivisionError: division by zero
```

Of course, division by zero is an impossible operation. Because of that, Python stops the program since it does not know what you want to do when this is encountered. It does not know any valid answer or response.

That being said, the problem here is that the error stops your program entirely. To manage this exception, you have two options. First, you can make sure to prevent such an operation from happening in your program. Second, you can let the operation and errors happen, but tell Python to continue your program.

Here is what the first solution looks like:

```
>>> def div(dividend, divisor):
        if (divisor != 0):
            print(dividend / divisor)
        else:
            print("Cannot Divide by Zero.")
>>> div(5, 0)
Cannot Divide by Zero.
```

Here is what the second solution looks like:

```
>>> def div(dividend, divisor):
        try:
            print(dividend / divisor)
        except:
            print("Cannot Divide by Zero.")
>>> div(5, 0)
Cannot Divide by Zero.
```

Remember the two core solutions to errors and exceptions. One, prevent the error from happening. Two, manage the aftermath of the error.

Using Try-Except Blocks

In the previous example, the try except block was used to manage the error. However, you or your user can still do something to screw your solution up.

For example:

```
>>> def div(dividend, divisor):
        try:
            print(dividend / divisor)
        except:
            print("Cannot Divide by Zero.")
>>> div(5, "a")
Cannot Divide by Zero.
```

The statement prepared for the "except" block is not enough to justify the error that was created by the input. Dividing a number by a string does not warrant a "Cannot Divide by Zero." message.

For this to work, you need to know more about how to use the except block properly. First of all, you can specify the error that it will capture and respond to by indicating the exact exception. For example:

```
>>> def div(dividend, divisor):
        try:
            print(dividend / divisor)
        except ZeroDivisionError:
            print("Cannot Divide by Zero.")
>>> div(5, 0)
Cannot Divide by Zero.
>>> div(5, "a")
Traceback (most recent call last):
  File "<stdin>", line 1, <module>
  File "<stdin>", line 3, in div
```

```
TypeError: unsupported operand type(s) for /: 'int' and
'str'
```

Now, the error that will be handled has been specified. When the program encounters the specified error, it will execute the statements written on the "except" block that captured it. If no except block is set to capture other errors, Python will then step in, stop the program, and give you an exception.

But why did that happen? When the example did not specify the error, it handled everything. That is correct. When the "except" block does not have any specified error to look out for, it will capture any error instead. For example:

```
>>> def div(dividend, divisor):
        try:
            print(dividend / divisor)
        except:
            print("An error happened.")
>>> div(5, 0)
An error happened.
>>> div(5, "a")
An error happened.
```

That is a better way of using the "except" block if you do not know exactly what error that you might encounter.

Reading an Exception Error Trace Back

The most important part of error handling is to know how to read the traceback message. It is fairly easy to do. The traceback message is structured like this:

<Traceback Stack Header>
 <File Name>, <Line Number>, <Function/Module>
<Exception>: <Exception Description>

Here are things you need to remember:

The traceback stack header informs you that an error occurred.

The filename tells you the name of the file where the fault is located. Since the examples in the book are coded using the interpreter, it always indicated that the file name is "<stdin>" or standard input.

The line number tells you the exact line number in the file that caused the error. Since the examples are tested in the interpreter, it will always say line. However, if the error is found in a code block or module, it will return the line number of the statement relative to the code block or module.

The function/module part tells what function or module owns the statement. If the code block does not have an identifier or the statement is declared outside code blocks, it will default to <module>.

The exception tells you what kind of error happened. Some of them are built in classes (e.g., ZeroDivisionError, TypeError, and etcetera) while some are just errors (e.g., SyntaxError). You can use them on your except blocks.

The exception description gives you more details with regards to how the error occurred. The description format may vary from error to error.

Using exceptions to prevent crashes

Anyway, to know the exceptions that you can use, all you need to do is to generate the error. For example, using the TypeError found in the previous example, you can capture that error too and provide the correct statements in response.

```
>>> def div(dividend, divisor):
        try:
            print(dividend / divisor)
        except ZeroDivisionError:
            print("Cannot Divide by Zero.")
        except TypeError:
            print("Cannot Divide by Anything Other Than a
Number.")
        except:
            print("An unknown error has been detected.")
>>> div(5, 0)
Cannot Divide by Zero.
>>> div(5, "a")
Cannot Divide by Anything Other Than a Number.
>>> div(undeclaredVariable / 20)
An unknown error has been detected.
```

However, catching errors this way can still be problematic. It does allow you to prevent a crash or stop, but you have no idea about what exactly happened. To learn what the unknown error is, you can use the as the keyword to pass the Exception details to a variable. Convention wise, the variable detail is often used for this purpose.

For example:
```
>>> def div(dividend, divisor):
        try:
```

```
        print(dividend / divisor)
    except Exception as detail:
        print("An error has been detected.")
        print(detail)
        print("Continuing with the program.")
>>> div(5, 0)
An error has been detected.
```

Division by zero
```
Continuing with the program.
>>> div(5, "a")
An error has been detected.
unsupported operand type(s) for /: 'int' and 'str'
Continuing with the program.
```

The Else Block

There are times that an error happens in the middle of your code block. You can catch that error with try and except. However, you might not want to execute any statement in that code block if an error happens. For example:

```
>>> def div(dividend, divisor):
    try:
        quotient = dividend / divisor
    except Exception as detail:
        print("An error has been detected.")
        print(detail)
        print("Continuing with the program.")
    print(str(dividend) + " divided by " +
str(divisor) + " is:")
    print(quotient)
>>> div(4, 2)
4 divided by 2 is:
2.0
>>> div(5, 0)
An error has been detected.
division by zero
Continuing with the program.
5 divided by 0 is:
Traceback (most recent call last):
  File "<stdin>", line 1, in <module>
  File "<stdin>", line 8, in div
    Print(quotient)
UnboundLocalError: local variable 'quotient' referenced
before assignment
```

As you can see, the next statements after the initial fault are dependent on it; thus they are also affected. In this example, the variable quotient returned an error when used after the try and except block since its supposed value was not assigned because the expression assigned to it was impossible to evaluate.

In this case, you would want to drop the remaining statements that are dependent on the contents of the try clause. To do that, you must use the else block.

For example:

```
>>> def div(dividend, divisor):
        try:
            quotient = dividend / divisor
        except Exception as detail:
            print("An error has been detected.")
            print(detail)
            print("Continuing with the program.")
        else:
            print(str(dividend) + " divided by " +
str(divisor) + " is:")
            print(quotient)
>>> div(4, 2)
4 divided by 2 is:
2
>>> div(5, 0)
An error has been detected.
division by zero
Continuing with the program.
```

The first attempt at using the function with proper arguments went well.

On the second attempt, the program did not execute the last two statements under the else block because it returned an error.

The else block always follows except blocks. The function of the else block is to let Python execute the statements under it when the try block did not return and let Python ignore them if an exception happens.

Failing Silently

Silent fails or failing silently is a programming term often used during error and exception handling.

From a user's perspective, silent failure is a state wherein a program fails at a certain point but never informs a user.

From a programmer's perspective, silent failure is a state wherein the parser, runtime development environment, or compiler fails to produce an error or exception and proceed with the program. This often leads to unintended results.

A programmer can also induce silent failures when he either ignores exceptions or bypasses them. Alternatively, he blatantly hides them and creates workarounds to make the program operate as expected even if an error happens. He might do that because of multiple reasons such as the error is not program breaking or the user does not need to know about the error.

Handling the 'File Not Found' Exception Error

There will be times when you will encounter the FileNotFoundError. Handling such an error depends on your intent or purpose with regards to opening the file. Here are common reasons you will encounter this error:

- You did not pass the directory and filename as a string
- You misspelled the directory and filename
- You did not specify the directory
- You did not include the correct file extension
- The file does not exist

The first method to handle the FileNotFoundError exception is to make sure that all the common reasons do not cause it. Once you do, then you will need to choose the best way to handle the error, which is completely dependent on the reason you are opening a file in the first place.

Checking if the File Exists

Again, there are always two ways to handle an exception: preventive and reactive. The preventive method is to check if the file exists in the first place.

To do that, you will need to use the os (os.py) module that comes with your Python installation. Then, you can use its path module's isfile() function. The path module's file name depends on the operating system (posixpath for UNIX, ntpath for Windows, macpath for old MacOS). For example:

```
>>> from os import path
>>> path.isfile("random.txt")
False
```

```
>>> path.isfile("sampleFile.txt")
True
```

Try and Except

You can also do it the hard way by using try, except, and else blocks.

```
>>> def openFile(filename):
        try:
            x = open(filename, "r")
        except FileNotFoundError:
            print("The file '" + filename + "' does not
exist.")
        except FileNotFound:
            print("The file '" + filename + "' does
exist.")
>>> openFile("random.txt")
The file 'random.txt' does not exist.
>>> openFile("sampleFile.txt")
The file 'sampleFile.txt' does exist.
```

Creating a New File

If the file does not exist, and your goal is to overwrite any existing file anyway, then it will be best for you to use the "w" or "w+" access mode. The access mode creates a new file for you if it does not exist. For example:

```
>>> x = open("new.txt", "w")
>>> x.tell()
0
```

If you are going to read and write, use "w+" access mode instead.

Practice Exercise

Try to break your Python by discovering at least ten different exceptions.

After that, create a loop.

In the loop, create ten statements that will create each of the ten different exceptions that you find inside one try block.

Each time the loop loops, the next statement after the one that triggered an exception should trigger another, and so on.

Provide a specific except block for each one of the errors.

Solution

```
a = 1
b = 0
while(True):
```

140

```
try:
    c = a / b
    e = c + d
except ZeroDivisionError:
    b = 1
    print("Zero Division Error")
except NameError:
    d = "2"
    print("Name Error")
except TypeError:
    print("Type Error")
    break
```

15. Essential Programming Tools

Bash Script

A Bash script is a data file that contains a sequence of commands, which you can usually code, but will save you time if you don't. Take note that in programming, any code that you could normally run on the command line could be placed on the script, and it will be executed precisely as it is. Likewise, any code that you could be placed into a script can also normally be executed exactly as it is.

There can be many processes manifesting one program performing in memory simultaneously. For instance, you can use two terminals and still run the command prompt at the same time. In such a case, there will be two command prompt processes that exist at the same time within the system. When they complete the execution, the system can terminate them, so there will be no more processes that are representing the command prompt.

When you are using the terminal, you can run the Bash script to provide a shell. When you initiate a script, it will not execute in this process, but rather will begin a new process to be executed inside. But as a beginner in programming, you don't need to worry too much about the mechanism of this script as running Bash can be very easy.

You may also encounter some tutorials about script execution, which is pretty much the same thing. Before executing the script, it should have permission in place, as the program will return an error message if you fail to grant permission.

Below is a sample Bash script:

```
#!/bin/bash
# declare STRING variable
STRING="Hello Python"
#print variable on a screen
echo $STRING
```

You can use the 755 shorthand so you can modify the script and make sure that you can share it with others to execute the script.

Python RegEx

RegEx refers to the regular expression that defines the string of text, which allows you to generate patterns in managing, matching, and locating text. Python is a good example of a programming language, which uses regex. Regex can also be utilized in text editors and from the command line to search for a text inside a file.

When you first encounter regex, you might think that it is a different programming language. But mastering regex could save you many hours if you are working with the text or you require to parse large amounts of data.

The RE module provides complete support for regex in Python. It also increases the exception re.error if there is an error while using or compiling a regex. There are two essential functions that you have to know in using regex for Python. But before that, you should understand that different characters have special meaning when they are used in a regular expression. So you will not be confused in working with regex, since we will use r'expression' when we mean Raw Strings.

The two important functions in Python regex are the search and match functions.

The search function looks for the first instance of an RE pattern inside a string with optional flags. The search function has the following parameters (below is the syntax):

- String - will be searched to match the pattern within the string
- Pattern - regex to be matched
- Flags - modifiers that can be specified using bitwise

The re.search function can return an object match if successful, and object none if failed. You should use groups() or groups(num) function of object match to find a matched expression.

Below is an example of a code using the search function:

```
import re
#Check if the string starts with "The" and ends with
"Spain":
txt = "The rain in Spain"
x = re.search("^The.*Spain$", txt)
if (x):
  print("YES! We have a match!")
else:
  print("No match")
```

The output will be:
```
YES! We have a match!
```

Meanwhile, the match function will try to match the RE pattern in order to string with specific flags. Below is the syntax for the match function:

The match function has the following parameters:

- String - this will be searched to match the pattern at the start of the string
- Pattern - this is the regex to be matched

Flags - modifiers that can be specified using bitwise

Python Package Manager

In programming, package managers refer to the tools used to automate the system of installing, configuring, upgrading, and uninstalling programs for a specific language system in an orderly manner.

Also known as a package management system, it also deals with the distribution and archiving of data files including the name of the software, version, number, purpose, and a sequence of dependencies needed for the language to properly run.

When you use a package manager, the metadata will be archived in the local database usually to avoid code mismatches and missing permissions.

In Python, you can use a utility to locate, install, upgrade, and eliminate Python packages. It can also identify the most recent version of a package installed on the system as well as automatically upgrade the current package from a remote or local server.

Python Package Manager is not free and you can only use it through ActivePython. It also utilizes repositories, which are a group of pre-installed packages and contain different types of modules.

Source Control

In programming, a source control (also known as version control or revision control), manages the changes to the codes, which is identified by a letter or number code regarded as the revision number or just revision. For instance, an initial set of code is known as revision 1, and then the first modification will be revision 2. Every revision will be linked with a timestamp as well as the person who made the change. Revisions are important so the code could be restored or compared.

Source control is important if you are working with a team. You can combine your code changes with other code changes done by a developer through different views that will show detailed changes, then combine the proper code into the primary code branch.

Source control is crucial for coding projects regardless if you are using Python or other languages. Take note that each coding project should start by using a source control system such as Mercurial or Git.

Various source control systems have been developed since the existence of programming. Before, proprietary control systems provided features that are customized for large coding projects and particular project workflows. But today, open-source systems can be used for source control regardless if you are working on a personal code or as part of a large team.

It is ideal to use an open-source version control system in your early Python codes. You can use either Mercurial or Git, which are both open source and used for distributing source control. Subversion is also available, which can be used to centralize the system to check files and minimize conflicting merges.

Bringing It All Together

Programming tools will make your work easier. The tools discussed in this part will save you a lot of time, collaborate easier, and make your codes seamless. In summary, we have learned the following:

- A Bash Script can save you a lot of coding time and will make your code lines more organized and readable.
- Regular Expressions or RegEx can help you find, search, and match strings of text inside your codes, so you don't have to browse line by line or analyze each code on your own.
- Package Managers will automate the system to easily install, upgrade, configure or remove specific programs that could aid your coding work

You can still work on your codes without these tools, but your life will be easier if you choose to use them.

16. Practical Codes and Exercises to Use Python

Now that we have had some time to learn how to work with the Python code, it is time to take a look at some practical examples of working with this kind of coding language. We will do a few different Python exercises here so that you can have a little bit of fun, and get a better idea of how you would use the different topics that we have talked about in this guidebook to your benefit. There are a lot of neat programs that you can use when you write in Python, but the ones in this chapter will give you a good idea of how to write codes, and how to use the examples that we talked about in this guidebook in real coding. So let's get started!

Creating a Magic 8 Ball

The first project that we are going to take a look at here is how to create your own Magic 8 ball. This will work just like a regular magic 8 ball, but it will be on the computer. You can choose how many answers that you would like to have available to those who are using the program, but we are going to focus on having eight responses show up for the user at a random order, so they get something different each time.

Setting up this code is easier than you think. Take some time to study this code, and then write it out into the compiler. See how many of the different topics we discussed in this guidebook show up in this code as well.

The code that you need to use to create a program that includes your own Magic 8 ball will include:

```
# Import the modules
import sys
import random
ans = True
while ans:
question = raw_input("Ask the magic 8 ball a question:
(press enter to quit)")
answers = random.randint(1,8)
if question == ""
sys.exit()
elif answers ==1:
```

```
print("It is certain")
elif answers == 2:
print("Outlook good")
elif answers == 3:
print("You may rely on it")
elif answers == 4:
print("Ask again later")

elif answers == 5:
print("Concentrate and ask again")
elif answers == 6:
print("Reply hazy, try again.")
elif answers == 7:
print("My reply is no")
elif answers == 8:
print("My sources say no")
```

Remember, in this program, we chose to go with eight options because it is a Magic 8 ball and that makes the most sense. But if you would like to add in some more options, or work on another program that is similar and has more options, then you would just need to keep adding in more of the elif statement to get it done. This is still a good example of how to use the elif statement that we talked about earlier and can give us some good practice on how to use it. You can also experiment a bit with the program to see how well it works and make any changes that you think are necessary to help you get the best results.

How to make a Hangman Game

The next project that we are going to take a look at is creating your own Hangman game. This is a great game to create because it has a lot of the different options that we have talked about throughout this guidebook and can be a great way to get some practice on the various topics that we have looked at. We are going to see things like a loop present, some comments, and more and this is a good way to work with some of the conditional statements that show up as well.

Now, you may be looking at this topic and thinking it is going to be hard to work with a Hangman game. It is going to have a lot of parts that go together as the person makes a guess and the program tries to figure out what is going on, whether the guesses are right, and how many chances the user gets to make these guesses. But using a lot of the different parts that we have already talked about in this guidebook can help us to write out this code without any problems. The code that you need to use to create your very own Hangman game in Python includes:

```python
# importing the time module
importing time
#welcoming the user
Name = raw_input("What is your name?")
print("Hello, + name, "Time to play hangman!")
print("
"
#wait for 1 second
time.sleep(1)
print("Start guessing...")
time.sleep(.05)
#here we set the secret
word = "secret"
#creates a variable with an empty value
guesses = ' '
#determine the number of turns
turns = 10
#create a while loop
#check if the turns are more than zero
while turns > 0:
#make a counter that starts with zero
failed = 0
#for every character in secret_word
for car in word:
#see if the character is in the players guess
if char in guesses:

#print then out the character
print char,
else
# if not found, print a dash
print "_",

# and increase the failed counter with one
failed += 1
#if failed is equal to zero
#print You Won
if failed == 0:
print("You Won")
#exit the script
Break
print
# ask the user to guess a character
```

```
guess = raw_input("guess a character:")
#set the players guess to guesses
guesses += guess
# if the guess is not found in the secret word
if guess not in word:
#turns counter decreases with 1 (now 9)
turns -= 1
#print wrong
print("Wrong")
# how many turns are left
Print("You have," + turns, 'more guesses')
#if the turns are equal to zero
if turns == 0
#print "You Lose"
```

Okay, so yes, this is a longer piece of code, especially when it is compared to the Magic 8 Ball that we did above, but take a deep breath, and go through it all to see what you recognize is there. This isn't as bad as it looks, and much of it is comments to help us see what is going on at some of the different parts of the code. This makes it easier to use for our own needs and can ensure that we know what is going on in the different parts. There are probably a lot of other things that show up in this code that you can look over and recognize that we talked about earlier as well. This makes it easier for you to get the code done!

Making your own K-means algorithm

Now that we have had some time to look at a few fun games and examples that you can do with the help of the Python code, let's take a moment to look at some of the things that you can do with Machine Learning and Artificial Intelligence with your coding. We spent some time talking about how you can work with these and some of the different parts of the code, as well as how Python is going to work with the idea of Machine Learning. And now we are going to take that information and create one of our Machine Learning algorithms to work with as well.

Before we work on a code for this one, we need to take a look at what this k-means clustering means. This is a basic algorithm that works well with Machine Learning and is going to help you to gather up all of the data that you have in your system, the data that isn't labeled at the time, and then puts them all together in their little group of a cluster.

The idea of working with this kind of cluster is that the objects that fall within the same cluster, whether there are just two or more, are going

149

to be related to each other in some manner or another, and they are not going to be that similar to the data points that fall into the other clusters. The similarity here is going to be the metric that you will want to use to show us the strength that is in the relationship between the two.

When you work on this particular algorithm, it is going to be able to form some of the clusters that you need of the data, based on how similar the values of data that you have. You will need to go through and give them a specific value for K, which will be how many clusters you would like to use. It is best to have at least two, but the number of these clusters that you work with will depend on how much data you have and how many will fit in with the type of data that you are working with.

With this information in mind and a good background of what the K-means algorithm is going to be used for, it is time to explore a bit more about how to write your own codes and do an example that works with K-means. This helps us to practice a bit with Machine Learning and gives us a chance to practice some of our own new Python skills.

```python
import numpy as np
import matplotlib.pyplot as plt
def d(u, v):
    diff = u - v
    return diff.dot(diff)
def cost(X, R, M):
    cost = 0
    for k in xrange(len(M)):
        for n in xrange(len(X)):
            cost += R[n,k]*d(M[k], X[n])
    return cost
```

After this part, we are going to take the time to define your function so that it is able to run the k-means algorithm before plotting the result. This is going to end up with a scatterplot where the color will represent how much of the membership is inside of a particular cluster.

We would do that with the following code:

```python
def plot_k_means(X, K, max_iter=20, beta=1.0):
    N, D = X.shape
    M = np.zeros((K, D))
    R = np.ones((N, K)) / K
    # initialize M to random
    for k in xrange(K):
        M[k] = X[np.random.choice(N)]
    grid_width = 5
    grid_height = max_iter / grid_width
```

```python
    random_colors = np.random.random((K, 3))
    plt.figure()
    costs = np.zeros(max_iter)
    for i in xrange(max_iter):
        # moved the plot inside the for loop
        colors = R.dot(random_colors)
        plt.subplot(grid_width, grid_height, i+1)
        plt.scatter(X[:,0], X[:,1], c=colors)
        # step 1: determine assignments /
responsibilities
        # is this inefficient?
        for k in xrange(K):
            for n in xrange(N):
                R[n,k] = np.exp(-beta*d(M[k], X[n])) /
np.sum( np.exp(-beta*d(M[j], X[n])) for j in xrange(K) )
        # step 2: recalculate means
        for k in xrange(K):
            M[k] = R[:,k].dot(X) / R[:,k].sum()
        costs[i] = cost(X, R, M)
        if i > 0:
            if np.abs(costs[i] - costs[i-1]) < 10e-5:
                break
    plt.show()
```

Notice here that both the M and the R are going to be matrices. The R is going to become the matrix because it holds onto 2 indices, the k and the n. M is also a matrix because it is going to contain the K individual D-dimensional vectors. The beta variable is going to control how fuzzy or spread out the cluster memberships are and will be known as the hyperparameter. From here, we are going to create a main function that will create random clusters and then call up the functions that we have already defined above.

```python
def main():
    # assume 3 means
    D = 2 # so we can visualize it more easily
    s = 4 # separation so we can control how far apart
the means are
    mu1 = np.array([0, 0])
    mu2 = np.array([s, s])
    mu3 = np.array([0, s])
    N = 900 # number of samples
    X = np.zeros((N, D))
    X[:300, :] = np.random.randn(300, D) + mu1
    X[300:600, :] = np.random.randn(300, D) + mu2
```

```
    X[600:, :] = np.random.randn(300, D) + mu3
    # what does it look like without clustering?
    plt.scatter(X[:,0], X[:,1])
    plt.show()
    K = 3 # luckily, we already know this
    plot_k_means(X, K)
    # K = 5 # what happens if we choose a "bad" K?
    # plot_k_means(X, K, max_iter=30)
    # K = 5 # what happens if we change beta?
  # plot_k_means(X, K, max_iter=30, beta=0.3)
if __name__ == '__main__':
    main()
```

Yes, this process is going to take some time to write out here, and it is not always an easy process when it comes to working through the different parts that come with Machine Learning and how it can affect your code. But when you are done, you will be able to import some of the data that your company has been collecting, and then determine how this compares using the K-means algorithm as well.

Conclusion

Thanks for reading till the end!

There are a lot of other coding languages out there that you are able to work with, but Python is one of the best that works for most beginner programmers, providing the power and the ease of use that you are looking for when you first get started in this kind of coding language. This guidebook took the time to explore how Python works, along with some of the different types of coding that you can do with it.

In addition to seeing a lot of examples of how you can code in Python and how you can create some of your programs in this language, we also spent some time looking at how to work with Python when it comes to the world of machine learning, Artificial Intelligence, and Data Analysis. These are topics and parts of technology that are taking off and many programmers are trying to learn more about them. With the help of this guidebook, you will be able to handle all of these, even as a beginner in Python.

When you are ready to learn more about how to work with the Python coding language and how you can make sure that you can even use Python along with Data Analysis, Artificial Intelligence, and machine learning, make sure to check out again this guidebook to help you get started.

Python for
Data Analysis

Introduction

Data Analysis plays an important role in many aspects of modern life. From the moment you wake up to the time you fall asleep, you are likely to be interacting with data at all different levels. Many important decisions are made based on data analytics. Companies need data to help them meet their goals. As the population of the world continues to grow, customer bases continue expanding. In light of this, businesses must find ways of keeping their customers happy while at the same time meeting their business goals.

Given the nature of competition in the business world, this is not an easy task. Competitors prey on each other's clientele, and even those who are successful have another challenge ahead: how do you maintain your customers, lest they slide back to their former loyalties? This is just one area where Data Analysis comes in handy.

To understand their customers better, companies rely on data. They collect all manner of data at each point of interaction with the public. These data are useful in several ways. Companies can use it to learn more about their customers, clustering them according to their specific needs. Through such segmentation, customers' needs can be attended to better and they can be kept satisfied for longer.

However, data analytics is not just about customers and the profit motive. It is also about governance. Governments are the biggest data consumers around the world. They collect data about citizens, businesses, and every other entity that they interact with at any given point. This is critically important information, helping at nearly every level of government.

For planning purposes and to allocate funds accordingly, governments need accurate data on their populations. Equitable distribution of resources is something that cannot be achieved without proper Data Analysis. Other than planning, there is also the security angle. To protect their countries, governments must maintain many different databases for many different reasons. There are high-profile individuals who must be accorded special security detail, top threats have to be monitored at all times, crime statistics must be minimized, and so forth. To meet these security objectives, a government should obtain and maintain updated data on persons of interest at all times.

And yet there is so much more to Data Analysis than even the corporate and government decision-making together. As a programmer, you are venturing into an industry that is challenging and exciting at the same time. Data doesn't lie, unless it is manipulated, in which case you will need even better Data Analysis and handling skills to work out the manipulations. As a data analyst, you will come across many challenges and problems in need of solutions that can only be handled with the skills you possess. The way you interact with data can make a huge difference – bigger than you can imagine.

There are several tools you can use for Data Analysis. Many people use Microsoft Excel, and it works well for them. However, there are limitations to using Excel that you can overcome by using Python. Learning Python is a good initiative, given that it is one of the easiest programming languages for beginners. It is a high-level programming language because its syntax is so close to the normal language we use. This makes it easier for you to master Python concepts.

For expert programmers, you have gone beyond learning about the basics of Python and graduated into using Python to solve real-world problems. Many problems can be solved through Data Analysis with Python. The first challenge is usually to understand the issue at hand before working on finding a data solution for it.

This book is part of a series that introduces you to Data Analysis using Python. Some important concepts have been reiterated since the beginning of the series to help you remember the fundamentals. Knowledge of Python libraries is indeed important. It is by understanding these libraries that you can go on to become an expert data analyst with Python.

As you interact with data, you will need to understand the importance of cleaning it to ensure the outcomes of your analysis are not flawed. You will learn how to go about this and build on that to produce the best results possible. Another challenge, faced by many organizations, is protecting the integrity of data. Protecting against contaminated data can be of critical importance. There are procedures you can put in place to make sure that you use clean data all the time.

We live in a world where data is at the center of many things we do. Data is produced and stored in enormous volumes daily via automated systems. Learning Data Analysis through Python should help you process and extract information from data and draw meaningful conclusions from them. One area where these skills will come in handy is forecasting. Through Data Analysis, you can create predictive models that will help you or your organization meet your objectives.

A good predictive model is only as good as the quality of data introduced to it, the data modeling methods used within it, and more importantly, the dataset used for the analysis. Beyond data handling and processing, one other important aspect of Data Analysis is visualization, which is about presentation. Your data model should be good enough for an audience to read and understand it at the first point of contact. Apart from the audience, you should also learn how to plot data among different visualizations to help you get a rough idea of the nature of the data you are working with.

When you are done with Data Analysis, you will know how to generate a complete data model with visual concepts that will help in predicting outcomes and responses before you proceed to the testing phase. Data Analysis is a study that is currently in high demand in different fields. Knowing what to do with data, as well as when and how to handle it, is an important skill that you should not take for granted. Through this book, you will learn how to build and test a data hypothesis and go on to understand systems better.

1. What is Data Analysis?

Now that we've taken a look at the ideas of Python and what we can do with this programming language, it is time to delve into certain topics. We will take a look at Data Analysis and learn how we can use it in order to extract valuable information from our data.

Many companies have spent a great deal of time looking at Data Analysis and what it is able to do for them. Data is everywhere around us, and it seems like each day, tons of new information becomes available to work with. Whether you are a business trying to learn more about your industry and your customers or just an individual who has a question about a certain topic, you will almost certainly be able to find a wealth of information to help you get started.

Many companies have gotten into the habit of gathering as much data as they can and learning how to make it work for their needs. They have found that there are a lot of insights and predictions hidden within the data that can help them as they move forward. If the data is used properly and they can get a reliable reading of that data, it can be used to help their business become more successful.

Once you have gathered your data, though, there is still going to be more work to do. Gathering it all up doesn't mean you will be able to see the patterns inside. This is where the process of Data Analysis comes into play, helping us to efficiently and comprehensively develop our data into meaning. Data Analysis ensures that we fully understand what is inside of our data and can make it easier to use all of that raw data to make informed and smart business decisions.

To expand on this further, Data Analysis is a practice through which we take some of the raw data that our business has been collecting, then organize it to make it useful. During this process, the information that is most useful is extracted from the raw data and put to use. The process of organizing and thinking about data is crucially important, as it is the key to helping us understand what the data do and do not contain.

There are many different methods that we can use to approach this kind of Data Analysis, which is part of the appeal of this exploration. We will find that regardless of the methods we choose, we can make adaptations to the process as needed to ensure it works for our own needs, no matter what industry we are working in or what our main question is in the beginning.

The one thing that we need to be careful about when we are working in Data Analysis, though, is how we go about manipulating the data we have. It will be very easy for us to do this incorrectly during the analysis phase, and then we end up pushing certain conclusions or agendas that are not actually there. This is also why we need to pay close attention when Data Analysis is presented to us and think critically about the data and the conclusions that we are able to get out of it.

If you are worried about a source, and if you are not sure whether you are able to complete an analysis without bias, then it is important to find someone else to work with you or else choose a different source. There are plenty of data out there, and even if it can help your business to see results, but must be careful of biases, or else they can lead us to the wrong conclusions.

You will also find that the data you are working with can take on a variety of forms. This can include data from observations, survey responses, and measurements, to name a few. The sources that you use to extract your raw data will vary based on what you are hoping to get out of the analysis, what your main questions are all about, and more.

In its raw form, the data that we gather is going to be very useful to work with, but you may find that it can be a bit overwhelming as well. This is a problem that many companies will run into in their Data Analysis and it's something that you will have to spend some time exploring and learning more about, as well. Over time, all of the steps that make the process useful to you will come to light. For example, we may send out a survey and then tally up the results that we get. This will help us see at a glance how many people decided to answer our survey at all, along with how many people were willing to respond to each of the specific questions that were on that survey.

In the process of going through and organizing the data, a trend is likely going to emerge, and sometimes more than one trend. We will then take some time to highlight these trends, usually in the form of a write-up that is carried out on the data. This needs to be done because it ensures that the person reading that information will take note of the most important aspects of the data.

There are plenty of places we are going to see this. For example, in the same kind of casual survey we mentioned earlier, you may want to explore the preferences between men and women regarding what ice cream flavors they like the most. In this survey, suppose we find out that women and men both express a fondness for chocolate. Depending on who is using this information and what they are hoping to get out of it, this could be something that the researcher finds very interesting.

Modeling the data that is found from such a survey, or from some other form of Data Analysis with the use of mathematics or other tools, can sometimes exaggerate the points of interest. Take for example the ice cream preferences from before. In our data, highlighting these in a write-up is going to make it so much easier for anyone who is looking over the data, especially the researcher, to see what is going on – they don't have to do the analysis again themselves.

In addition to looking at all of the data you have collected and sorting through it, you will also need to tackle a few other tasks as well. When you're analyzing data, everything you're doing should be aimed at helping the person who needs the information understand what the data contains and what they can do with all of it. This way, they can see the information, the complex relationships in the data, and so much more, all just by looking.

To do this, we need to spend our time on some write-ups of the data, graphs, charts, and other ways to represent and show the data to those who need it most. This will form one of the final steps of Data Analysis. These methods are designed to distill and refine the data so that readers are then able to glean some of the interesting information from it, without having to go back through the raw data and figure out what is there all on their own.

Summarizing the data in these steps is going to be critical, and it needs to be done with a good and steady hand. Doing this is critical to supporting the arguments that are made with that data, as is presenting the data clearly and understandably. During this phase, we have to remember that it is not always possible that the person who needs our summary, who will use it to make important decisions for their business, will be a data scientist. They will therefore need all this information written out in a simple and easy-to-understand format.

Often this is done using some sort of data visualization. There are many choices of visualizations that we can work with, and some kind of graph or chart is usually a good option as well. Choosing the method that is best for your needs and which best suits the data we are using is right approach.

Most times, reading through information in a graphical format is going to be far easier than poring over the data and hoping it stands out in the best way possible. Of course, all the information could be put into written form if you like, but this is not going to be as easy nor as efficient. To see some of those complex relationships quickly and efficiently, working with a visualization is the past approach to take.

That said, even though we do need to spend some time putting together visualizations of the data to make it easier to work with and understand, it is still fine to add in some of the important raw data in an appendix, rather than just throwing it out. This allows the person working with the data regularly a chance to check your resources and your specific numbers, which can help bolster your results and paint a clearer picture.

If you are the one receiving the results of Data Analysis, make sure that when you get the conclusions and summarized data from your data scientist that you go through and view them with a critical eye. You should take the time to ask where the data comes from, as this is going to be important, and you should also take some time to ask about the sampling methods that were used as well as when the data were collected. Knowing the size of the sample is important as well.

This is going to allow you to really learn more about the data you have, show you how to use the data, and hint at whether there may be some kind of bias coming along with it. If the source of the data, or at least one of the sources, has any kind of conflict that you are worried about, then this is going to pull your results into question, and you at least need to look it over.

Likewise, if you have some data that is gathered up from just a small sample or a sample that you worry is not random, then it is maybe not the best data to work with. The good news is that reputable researchers are going to have no problem providing you with the information that you need regarding the sampling techniques that they used, allowing you to make the important decisions about whether the data is important or not.

There are so many great benefits to be explored when it comes to using Data Analysis for your own business. It can help you to learn more about your industry and the customers who are purchasing your products. Those who can gather this information and use it correctly with the help of Data Analysis are going to give you a leg up on your competition, and you'll see some amazing results in the process.

2. Why Python for Data Analysis?

The next thing that we need to spend some time on in this guidebook is the Python language itself. There are a lot of options to choose from when working on your own Data Analysis, and bringing out all of these tools can make a big difference in how much information you get out of your workflow. Nevertheless, if you want to pick a programming language that is easy to learn, has a lot of power, and can handle pretty much all the Data Analysis and machine learning tasks you'll need, then Python is the choice for you. Let's dive into the Python language a little bit and see how it can be used to give us some great results with our Data Analysis.

The Basics of the Python Language

To understand a bit more about how Python can help us out while handling Data Analysis, we first need to take a look at what the Python language is all about. It's an object-oriented programming language (or OOP language) that is designed with the user in mind, while still providing us with the power, the extensions, and the libraries to make Data Analysis and machine learning as easy to work with as possible.

There are many benefits to using the Python coding language, which is one of the reasons why so many people like learning how to code with Python as their first language. First, this coding language was designed with the beginner in mind. Many languages are hard to learn, and only more advanced programmers, who have spent years in this kind of field, can learn how to use them.

This is not the case with the Python language. It has been designed to work well for programmers at all levels. Even if you have never done any coding in Python (or at all) before, you will find that this language is easy to catch on to, and you will be able to write complex code, even with enough power to handle machine learning and Data Science, in no time at all.

With that said, although the Python language is an easy one to learn, it still comes with a lot of power as well. This language is designed to take on some of those harder projects, the ones that may need a little extra weight behind them. For example, there are a lot of extensions that come with Python that allow it to work with machine learning, a process by which we teach a model or a computer how to make decisions on its own.

Due to the many benefits that come with the Python coding language, there are many people who are interested in learning more about it and how to make it work for their needs. This is true in communities of all types around the world and on the web, with people sharing their ideas, asking for help, and offering any advice you may need. If you are a beginner who is just getting started with Data Analysis or any kind of Python programming at all, then this large community is going to be one of the best resources for you to use. It will help you get all your questions answered and ensure you are able to finish your project, even if you get stuck.

This coding language also combines well with some of the other coding languages out there. While Python can do a lot of work on its own, when you combine it with other libraries, it demonstrates exceptional compatibility. You can add extensions and libraries that connect to other languages while still writing out your code in Python, knowing all the while that it will be completely compatible with the library in question.

There are also a lot of different libraries that you can work with in Python. While there is of course a great deal of strong coding that can be done with the traditional Python libraries themselves, sometimes adding some more functionality and further capabilities can be the trick needed to get results. For example, there are many Deep Learning and machine learning libraries that connect with Python, helping this language take on some of the toughest Data Science and Data Analysis projects you'll be faced with.

Python is also an object-oriented programming language or an OOP language. This means that it relies on classes and objects to help organize information and keep things in line. The objects that we use, which are going to be based on real objects that we can find in the real world, are going to be placed in a class to be pulled out later when they are needed in the code. This is a much easier framework to work with than what we see with traditional coding languages of the past and ensures that all the different parts of your code are going to stay exactly where you like them.

As we are seeing, there is so much that the Python coding language can do to help us on our Data Analysis journey. The many different features and capabilities of the language make it perfect for almost any task or project that we'll want to handle. Then, when we combine it with some of the different libraries available, we can get some of the even more complicated tasks done, too.

How Can Python Help with Data Analysis?

Now that we have had some time to discuss the benefits that come with the Python language and its constituent parts, we can now move on to learning why Python is the perfect programming language for handling the complexities we will face in Data Science.

Looking back, we can see that Python has been famous among data scientists for a long time. Although the language was not built specifically for Data Science alone, it is a language that has become readily accepted and implemented by data scientists for much of the work that they pursue and accomplish. Let's explore some of Python's most impressive features for helping out with your Data Science model or project.

First, Python is as simple as it gets. One of the best parts about learning to work with the Python coding language is that even someone who is completely new to programming and who has never done any work with it in the past can grasp the basics pretty quickly. This language, in particular, was founded with two main ideas in mind: readability and simplicity.

This was a unique approach when we are talking about coding languages, and these features are only available to an object-oriented coding language that has a tremendous amount of potential for problem-solving.

What all of this means is that, if you are a beginner to working with Data Science and to Python, then adding these two aspects of the language together is going to be the key to getting you started. Even if you are more experienced with coding, though, you will still find that Python for Data Science is going to add a lot of depth to your resume and help you get even those tougher projects done.

The next benefit is that Python is fast and attractive. Apart from being as simple as possible, the code that we can write with Python is going to be leaner and much better looking than what we write with other languages. For example, Python code takes up one-third of the volume that we see from code in Java, and one-fifth the volume of code in C++, just to do the same task.

The use of common expressions in code writing rather than going with variable declarations, and whitespace in place of ugly bracketing, is a big part of what makes the code in Python look better and more readable. This can also help take some of the tedium out of learning a new coding language. Learning Python in place of, say, C++ can save a lot of time and will be less taxing on a data scientist's workload, making of the more complex Data Analysis tasks much easier to handle overall.

Another benefit here is that data formats are not going to be as worrisome with Python. Python can work with any kind of data format you would like. It is possible for us to directly import SQL tables in the code without having to convert to a specific format or worry that our chosen format is not going to work. In addition, we can work with Comma Separated Value documents and web-sourced JSON. Python's request library can make it easy to import data from a lot of websites and build data sets to help us work with them.

The Python Data Analysis library known as Pandas is one of the best for handling not only our Data Analysis but also the whole process of Data Science. Pandas can grab onto enormous volumes of data without latency or other issues in the process. This is great news for the data scientist, helping them to filter, sort, and quickly display their data.

Next on the list is that the Python library is quickly growing in demand. While the demand for professionals in the world of IT has seen a decline recently, at least relative to how it has grown in the past, the demand for programmers who can work with Python is steadily on the rise. This is good news for those who still want to work in this field and are looking for their niche or their way to stand out when seeking a new job.

Since Python has so many great benefits and has proven itself as a great language for many things, including programs for data analytics and machine learning algorithms, many companies centered on data are going to be looking for people with Python skills. If you already have a strong background in Python, you can already ride the market that is available out there right now.

Finally, we come back to the idea of the vibrant community that comes with the Python language. There are times when you will be working on a project and things are just not working the way you had thought they would or the way you had planned. Getting frustrated is one option, but this is not going to help you find a solution.

The good news is that you will be able to harness the vibrant Python community and all of the programmers within it to provide you with a helping hand when you get stuck. The community surrounding Python has grown to be very large, and it includes members who are passionate and very active in this space. For the newer programmer, this means that there will always be an ample amount of information flowing freely on various websites, any of which may have the solution that you are looking for when working with your data.

Once you are able to get the data you want to use and have identified all of the libraries that work with it as well, you can work with this community to get the results that you want. You'll never get totally stuck or just need to give up on a project or an idea that you have with your code when you have access to this community of programmers, many of whom have a lot of experience with Python and who will be able to help answer your questions and get that problem solved.

As we work through this guidebook and you do more work with Python and Data Analysis, you will find that there are many libraries that are compatible with Python that can help you get your work done. These are all going to handle different algorithms and different tasks that you are faced with during your Data Analysis project, so the ones you choose may vary. There are many great options to choose from, including TensorFlow, Pandas, NumPy, SciPy, and Scikit-Learn, to name a few.

Sometimes these libraries work all on their own, and sometimes they need to be combined with another library so that they can draw features and functionalities from each other. When we can choose the right libraries to work with, and we learn how to integrate them into the model that we need, our Data Analysis is going to become more efficient overall.

So, while there may be other programming languages out there that are able to handle the work of Data Analysis, and even those that may be able to help us create the models we need to develop accurate insights and predictions based on our data, none of them are going to work as well as Python and its libraries. Taking the time to explore this language and seeing what it can do for your Data Analysis process can be a winner when it comes to your business and using Data Science to succeed.

3. The Steps of Data Analysis

With some of the ideas of Data Analysis defined above to show us why it is so important, it's now time for us to look at the steps that make up this process. Learning more about the steps of Data Analysis and what we can do with them will show us why we should use this method to work with Big Data, ensuring that your business can use this information to get ahead of the competition.

Most businesses aren't going to have a problem with a lack of data or information. Rather, most actually suffer from having too much information to handle, and they are not certain what they are supposed to do with it. This over-abundance of data can make it harder to make a clear decision based on the information available, and that can be a problem as well. With so much data to sort and work through, we need to find a more efficient way forward.

This means that we first need to determine whether the data we have is right for the questions we want answered. Then we need to know how to draw accurate conclusions from the data that we are working with. In addition, we need data that can take on and inform our decision-making processes.

Overall, what we need to make sure of is that we have the best pipeline or framework for our Data Analysis set up and ready to go. With the right process and tools, something that may have seemed overwhelming in the beginning will become a simple process that is clear and as straightforward as possible.

To help us get all of this done, we need to go through some of the basic steps to using data and making better decisions with it. There are a lot of ways that this can be divided up and made to suit any project, but we are going to split things up into five general steps that we can use and rely on to see some of the best results. These will be the steps we can use to make our Data Analysis more productive for better decision making in the company. They include:

- Defining your question
- Setting up clear measurements
- Collecting the data

168

- Analyzing the data
- Interpreting the results

Defining Your Question

The first step to undertake when it comes to Data Analysis is defining the main question we would like to answer. You should not just randomly work with the data on hand and hope that it shows you something. This is just going to get you lost and confused in the process. You need to have a clear picture of where you want to go and what you would like to learn from data, then work from there.

In your Data Analysis, you need to start with the right questions. Questions are important, but we need to make sure that they are concise, measurable, and clear. Design your questions so that they can either qualify or disqualify some of the potential solutions that you are looking for on a specific problem or opportunity.

For example, you may want to start with a problem that you are able to clearly define. Maybe you are a government contractor, and you find that your costs are rising quite a bit. Because of this, you are no longer able to submit a competitive contract for some of the work that you are doing. You will want to go through and figure out how to deal with this business problem using Data Analysis.

Setting up Clear Measurements

The next thing that we need to be able to do here is make sure that we can set some clear priorities on our measurements. This is one that we will be able to break down into two subsets to help us out. The first part is deciding what we want to measure, and the second is how to measure it.

So, let's start with the first part: deciding what we would like to measure. Going with the example of being a government contractor from before, we would have to take this time to consider what kind of data is needed to answer the question we posed in the beginning. In this case, you would first need to gather up information on the numbers and the costs you have for your current staff and the amount of time that these employees are spending on necessary business functions.

When we are answering this kind of question, many other questions that need to be answered will arise naturally as well, helping to define our options. For example, we would next want to see whether there are any employees that we could do without, or if our staff is under-utilized in their current jobs and what can be done to address this.

169

When doing this, we need to make sure that we are considering any reasonable objections from stakeholders and others working with the company. There may be worry, for instance, about what could happen if you reduce staff and there is a big surge in demand shortly afterward, and you are not able to hire more people back in time.

Once this first step is complete, it is time for us to make decisions about how to measure. Thinking about how we can measure the data we have is going to be just as important here, especially before we go through data collection phase, because the measuring process is either going to back up our analysis or discredit it. There are many different questions you should be asking in this stage, but some of the most important ones to consider are:

1. What is the time frame that we are looking at?
2. What is the unit of measure that we are relying on?
3. What factors are important to consider in all of this?

Collecting the Data

After we have defined our big problem and the measurements we are going to use, it is time for us to begin collecting the data. As we collect and organize, there are going to be many important points that we must keep in mind.

First, before you collect any new data, you need to determine what information we need to work with. To learn this, we can look through some of the existing databases and sources that we have on hand. We can move on to other sources later, as well, if we need more information.

During this process, we also need to determine what naming system and file storing system we would like to use. This is going to make it easier for team members to collaborate, saving time and preventing members of your team from wasting money and effort collecting the same kinds of information more than once.

If your data collection method includes interviews and observations, then you need to go through and develop an interview template ahead of time. This ensures that we save time and introduces some continuity to the process as well.

Finally, we need to keep the data we collect as organized as possible. To do this, we can use a log that has collection dates and add in notes about sources as we like. This should also include any data normalization that you may have performed as well. This is going to be important, as it will validate the conclusions that are made down the road.

170

As you go through this process, you need to make sure that with the data you collect is well taken care of. This means that it should be organized, all values handled, and all duplicates removed or marked before moving on to analysis.

Since you will be getting your data from different sources, and some of it may be incomplete or imperfect along the way, we need to be careful here. It can be difficult to determine what constitutes "perfect" data, and it's hard to know whether you can use it the way you want. In addition, if your information is in the wrong format, or it arrives with errors or missing values, this will add further challenge to your analysis.

The first thing we need to do to address this is make sure that the data is in the same format. Usually, the best way to handle this is to go through and put all of the information in a standardized database that can easily be viewed and accessed. This will serve as the data storage, and all of the data we bring it will just be put through that database and be ready to go.

From here, we should focus on dealing with some of the inevitable errors that will be found in our data. Make sure that the outliers, missing values, and duplicates are handled. For the most part, outliers are things you can simply ignore and get rid of. However, if there are a number of them, or if they are all ending up in the same spot in the process, you should take a look to see what is going on and determine whether this is information you should be paying attention to. In most cases, you will find that they are not worth your time and can safely be ignored.

Next up are the missing values. When you retrieve information from the real world, it's inevitable that there will be gaps or missing pieces in your data. You can choose to remove these entirely if there are just a few, or you can go through and replace the missing values with the mean of the other values in the same column or row. It will be up to you what to do with these missing values to ensure that your information is as accurate as possible.

Finally, we need to deal with any duplicate values that are present in our data set. If there are many duplicate values showing up throughout, our numbers and our results are going to be skewed. It will then be critical to take care of them in a way that allows us to see the true information contained in our data.

Go through the duplicates and decide how many of them are necessary to keep and how many you can get rid of. It is usually best to limit them as much as possible. Sometimes, this means keeping duplicates down to just two, and sometimes it means making sure that each entry is only in there once. It will be up to you to figure out which method to go with.

Analyzing the Data

After you have collected the data, which is something that will likely take some time, you can finally start to go through and analyze the data. Generally, you will start by manipulating the data, and there are some methods that can be used to make this happen. For example, you may decide to plot your information out and then find what correlations there are or do a pivot table in Excel.

A pivot table can be useful to sort out and filter the data by different variables, making it easier for us to calculate things like minima, maxima, means, and even the standard deviations of our data. This can give us a lot of great information that makes it easier for us to get going and get a better understanding of the data we have.

As you work through the process of manipulating the data, you may find that you already have the exact data that you need. But, of course, life doesn't always work out as nicely as we would like, and you may also need to go out and collect some more data to work with or revise your original question. Either way, you will find that this initial analysis of trends, variations, outliers, and correlations will help to focus the Data Analysis we do and better answer our questions and any of the objections that others may have in the process as well.

During this step, the software and tools that work well with Data Analysis are going to be of enormous help. There are a lot of great packages for working through all of these steps that will ensure we get what we need from our statistical Data Analysis. However, in many cases, you will be just fine using something as simple as Microsoft Excel when it is time to find a tool for decision making. You'll need to pick the right tool for each job.

Interpreting the Results

After going through and analyzing the data, which is going to take some time to accomplish and will often require some training and testing with algorithms to make sure everything works the way we wanted, it is time to interpret our results. Going through this process, keep in mind that you will never be able to completely prove your hypothesis is true at the 100% level. However, you can go through and reject any hypotheses that you know to be false. This means that no matter how much data you collect, it is still possible to see interference or uncertainty with our results.

Some of the major questions to ask yourself when interpreting your data are:

Are the data able to answer the original question that we had in the beginning, and if so, how?

Do the data help us to defend against the objections that were raised, and if so, how?

Are there any limitations to the conclusions that we have drawn, or are there any angles that have not been considered?

If the interpretations you build from your data can hold up under these questions and considerations, then it is likely you are working toward a productive conclusion. The only remaining step here would be to use the results of your Data Analysis to help decide which course of action is the best one for you to take.

By following the steps we have outlined in this chapter for Data Analysis, you will find yourself able to make better decisions for your business. The main reason why this is possible is that your conclusions will now be backed up by data that has been collected and analyzed robustly. With practice, your Data Analysis can provide you with even faster and more accurate results. This means that in the long run you will be able to make even better and more informed decisions that help your company to run more efficiently than ever before.

4. Python Libraries

We have talked about Data Analysis, and now it's time to take some of that information and put it to good use. You are probably interested in Deep Learning, and maybe even in making some of your Convolutional Neural Networks, but perhaps you are also wondering where you should start. The best step is to pick out the library that you want to use. However, this brings up another challenge, because there are just so many coding libraries out there to choose from, and all of them have some amazing power and features behind them.

To start with, we will take a look at some of the best Python libraries for doing Deep Learning. Although other languages can help with things like machine learning and Deep Learning, for most of the tasks you'll be facing, especially if you are a beginner in Data Analysis, Python is going to be the best choice. Even within Python, there are several libraries just for doing Deep Learning. So, with that in mind, let's dive right in and see what some of the best Python Deep Learning libraries are that you can use for your Data Analysis.

Caffe

No discussion of Deep Learning libraries in Python would be complete without spending some time on Caffe. If you have done any research on Deep Learning at all, then you have likely heard about Caffe and what it can do for some of the projects and models that you want to create.

While Caffe is technically not a Python library, it can provide us with some bindings into the Python language. We are going to use these bindings when it is time to deploy our network in the wild, rather than just when we try to train our model. The reason we include it in this chapter is because it is used pretty much everywhere and in all parts of a Deep Learning model.

Theano

The library to introduce is known as Theano. This one is for development and work with other Deep Learning libraries that are integrated with Python. In the same way that a typical programmer would be severely limited without libraries like scikit-image, scikit-learn,

SciPy, and NumPy, the same can be said of Theano and some of the other higher-level abstractions and libraries that come with Deep Learning.

At its core, Theano is a Python library that not only helps out with Deep Learning but can also be used to define, optimize, and evaluate mathematical expressions involving multi-dimensional arrays. Theano accomplishes this by tightly integrating with the NumPy library and keeping its use of GPU resources transparent overall.

Just as NumPy serves as a building block for most scientific computing, the Theano library serves as a building block for neural networks and Deep Learning. Almost all the other libraries we discuss here will in some way work through or be integrated alongside Theano.

TensorFlow

Similar to the Theano library, TensorFlow is open-sourced and can work with numerical computations with the help of a data flow graph. This library was originally developed to be used with research on the Google Brain Team within Google's Machine Intelligence organization. Since that time, it has gone open source, so that the general public can use it for their Deep Learning and Data Science needs.

One of the biggest benefits to using the TensorFlow library, compared to Theano, for instance, is that it is able to work with distributed computing. This is particularly useful if we are looking at using multiple GPUs for our project, though Theano is working on improving their functionality for this as well.

Keras

Many programmers love working with the Keras library for building models and carrying out Deep Learning tasks. Keras is a modular neural network library that is more minimalistic than most others. This library can use either TensorFlow or Theano as its backend, so you can choose the one that works best for you. The primary goal for this library is to allow you to experiment on your models quickly and get an idea of your results as quickly as possible.

Many programmers like this library because the networks that you construct with it are going to feel natural and easy, even as a beginner. It includes some of the best algorithms out there for optimizers, normalization, and even activation layers, so this is a great library to use if your project includes these features.

175

In addition, if you want to spend some time developing your own CNNs, then Keras is a great option. Keras is set up to place a heavy focus on these kinds of Neural Networks, which can be valuable when you are working in, e.g., computer vision. Keras also allows us to construct both sequence-based networks (in which input flows linearly) and graph-based networks (in which input can skip layers, to be concatenated at a later point). This will make it easier to implement more complex network architectures.

One thing to note about this Python library is that it does not support some multi-GPU environments, which you may need if you are training a network in parallel. If this is something you want to do, you might want to choose a different library. However, for most of the work you do, this is probably not a big issue.

If you want to train your network as fast as possible, working with a library like MXNet may be a better choice. But if you are looking to tune your hyperparameters, then you might want to take a look at Keras' ability to set up four independent experiments and evaluate how results are similar or different among them.

Sklearn-Theano

There will be times when you're working with Deep Learning that you'll want to train a CNN end-to-end. And then there are also going to be times when this is not needed. In the latter case, you can treat your CNN as a feature extractor. This will be most useful in situations where there is not enough data to train the CNN from scratch. Instead, just pass your input images through a popular pre-trained architecture such as VGGNet, AlexNet, or OverFeat. You can then use these pre-trained options and extract features from the layer that you want, usually the FC layers.

Nolearn

A good library for you to work with is the Nolearn library. This would be a good one to help out with some initial GPU experiments, especially if you're using a MacBook Pro. It is also an excellent library to assist with performing Deep Learning on an Amazon EC2 GPU instance.

While Keras wraps TensorFlow and Theano into a more user-friendly API, you will find that the Nolearn library does the same but with the Lasagna library. Also, all of our Nolearn code is going to be compatible with Scikit-Learn, which is a big bonus for a lot of the projects you might be working on.

Digits

The first thing to notice with this library is that it isn't considered a true Deep Learning library, although it is written in Python and it stands for Deep Learning GPU Training System. The reason for this is that this library is more of a web application that can be used for training of the Deep Learning models you create with the help of Caffe. You could dive into the source code and give yourself the option of working with a backend other than Caffe, but this is a lot of extra work. In addition, since the Caffe library is pretty good at what it does and can help with a lot of the Deep Learning you'll want to accomplish, that probably wouldn't be worth your time.

If you have ever spent time working with the Caffe library in the past, you can already attest to the fact that it is tedious to define your .prototxt files, generate image data sets, run the network, and babysit the network training with the terminal you are provided. The good news here is that the DIGITS library aims to fix all of this by allowing you to complete many of these tasks, if not all of them, just from your browser. So, it may not be a Deep Learning library per se, but it does come into use whenever you are struggling with Deep Learning using the Caffe library.

In addition to all the benefits above, the DIGITS interface is also excellent. This is because it provides valuable statistics and graphs to help you train your model more effectively. You can also easily visualize some of the activation layers of the network to help with various inputs as needed.

And finally, another benefit of this library is that if you come in with a specific image that you want to test, you have a few options on how to get this done. The first choice is to upload the image over to the DIGITS server. Alternatively, you can enter the URL that comes with the image, and then the model you make with Caffe will automatically be able to classify the image and display the results you are after in the browser.

Python is one of the best coding languages available for helping with tasks like Deep Learning, machine learning, and even Artificial Intelligence, which encompasses both other areas. Other languages can handle the Deep Learning that we have been talking about, but none are going to be as effective, as powerful, have as many options, or be designed for a beginner in the way that Python is.

This is why we have focused our attention on the Python language and some of the best libraries that come with it to help with our Deep

Learning tasks. Each of these libraries can be onboarded to your project and will provide a unique set of functions and skills to get the job done. Look through some of these libraries and see which one will be just right for your Data Analysis and for providing great insights to Deep Learning.

5. The PyTorch Library

The next library we will be looking at is PyTorch. This is a Python-based package that works for scientific computing and relies on the power it can receive from graphical processing units. This library is also one of the most common and the preferred Deep Learning platform for research, providing maximum flexibility and excellent speed in the process.

There are plenty of benefits offered by PyTorch, and it is known for providing two of the highest-level features among all the other Deep Learning libraries. These include tensor computation with the support of strong GPU acceleration and the ability to build deep Neural Networks on a tape-based autograd-system.

The PyTorch library is one of many that can help us work on our Deep Learning and Artificial Intelligence projects. However, what makes this library in particular so successful is that it's completely Pythonic and can take on almost any models that you would want to build with a neural network effortlessly. This is a newer Deep Learning library to work with, but there is a lot of momentum behind it.

The Beginnings of PyTorch

As we mentioned above, PyTorch is one of the newest libraries out there that works with Python and can help with Deep Learning. Even though it was just released in January 2016, it has become one of the go-to libraries for data scientists, mainly because it can make building up complex Neural Networks easy. This is perfect for the countless beginners who haven't yet worked with these Neural Networks in the past. They can use PyTorch and make their networks in no time at all, even with a limited amount of coding experience.

The creators of this Python library envisioned it being imperative for running an abundance of numerical computations as quickly as possible. This is one of the methodologies that fits best with the programming style that we see with Python, as well. PyTorch, along with the Python library, allows develops who work with neural networks, machine learning, and Deep Learning to not only run but also to test parts of their code in real-time. This is great news, because it means that these professionals no longer have to wait for their entire code to complete and execute before they can check out whether it works or if they need to fix certain parts.

Remember as well that you can extend out some of the functionalities of this library by adding in other Python packages. Python packages like Cython, SciPy, and NumPy all work well with PyTorch.

Even with these benefits, we still may have some questions about why the PyTorch library is so special and why we may want to use it when it is time to build up some models for Deep Learning. The answer to this is simple: PyTorch is a dynamic library. This means that the library is flexible, and you can use it with any requirements or changes that you would like. It is so good at doing this job that it is being used by developers in Artificial Intelligence, students, and researchers in many industries. In fact, in a Kaggle competition, this library was used by almost all of the individuals who finished in the top ten.

While there are multiple benefits that can come with the PyTorch library, we need to start with some of the highlights of why professionals of all sorts love this package so much. Some of these include:

The interface is simple to use. The PyTorch interface offers us an API that is easy and straightforward. This means that we will find it as simple to operate and run as we do Python.

It is Pythonic in nature. This library, since it is considered Pythonic, will smoothly integrate with the Python Data Science stack. Those who do not want to work with other coding languages along the way and want to just stick with the basics and power of Python will be able to do so with this library. You will get the leverage of using all of the functionalities and services that are offered through the Python environment.

Computational graphs. Another highlight that comes with the PyTorch library is that it provides us with a platform for dynamic computational graphs. This means that you can change these graphs up even during runtime, which is going to be useful any time you need to work on graphs and you are not sure how much memory you need to use while creating a model for a neural network.

The PyTorch Community

The next thing we need to look at here is the community that comes with the PyTorch library. We can see that thanks to PyTorch's benefits, its community of developers and other professionals is growing daily. In just a few years, this library has shown many developments and has even been cited in many research papers and by many research groups. And when it comes to Artificial Intelligence and models for Deep Learning, PyTorch is becoming one of the main libraries to work with.

One of the interesting about PyTorch is that it is still in early-release beta. But because so many programmers are adopting the framework for Deep Learning already, and at such a brisk pace, it already shows the power and potential that comes with it and to the likelihood that the community will continue growing. For example, even though we are still in its beta release, there are currently 741 contributors just on the PyTorch GitHub repository alone right now. This means that more than 700 people are working to enhance and add improvements to the functionalities of PyTorch already.

Think of how amazing this is! PyTorch is not technically released yet and is still in the early stages. However, there has been so much buzz around this Deep Learning library, and so many programmers have been using it for Deep Learning and Artificial Intelligence, that there are already a ton of contributors working to add more functionality and improvements for others.

PyTorch is not going to limit specific applications that we are able to work with because of its modular design and flexibility. It has seen a heavy amount of use by some of the leading tech giants, and you may even recognize some of the names. Those who have already started to work with PyTorch to improve their Deep Learning models include Uber, NVIDIA, Twitter, and Facebook. This library has also been used in a lot of domains for research, including Neural Networks, image recognition, translation, and NLP, among other key areas.

Why Use PyTorch for Data Analysis?

Anyone working in the fields of Data Science, Data Analysis, Artificial Intelligence, or Deep Learning has likely spent some time working with the TensorFlow library, which we also talked about in this guidebook. TensorFlow may be the most popular library from Google, but because of the PyTorch framework for Deep Learning, we will find that this library is able to solve a few new problems at a research level.

It is often believed that PyTorch is now the biggest competitor out there to TensorFlow when it comes to handling data, and it is going to be one of the best and most favored Artificial Intelligence and Deep Learning libraries too in the research community. There are many reasons why this is happening, and we will talk about some of these below:

First, dynamic computational graphs are becoming more and more popular among researchers. This library avoids the static graphs that are used in other frameworks such as TensorFlow. This allows researchers and developers to change up how the network behaves, even at the last minute. Some of those adopting this library also like it because these graphs are more intuitive to learn relative to TensorFlow's.

The second benefit is that PyTorch comes with a different kind of backend support depending on how you are using it. The GPU, CPU, and other functional features will all come with a different backend rather than focusing on just one backend to handle all of these. For example, you will see THC for GPU and TH for CPU. Being able to use separate backends can make it easier for us to deploy this library through a variety of constrained systems.

Its imperative style is another benefit of working with this library, making it intuitive and easy to use. When you execute a line of code, it is going to be executed just as you want, and you are able to work with real-time tracking as well. This allows the programmer to keep track of how their Neural Network models are doing. Because of the excellent architecture that comes with this, and the package's lean and fast approach, this library is seeing continuous adoption throughout communities of programmers.

Another benefit of PyTorch is that it is easy to extend. This library, in particular, is integrated to work well with code in C++, sharing a bit of its backend with this language when working in a Deep Learning framework. This means that programmers can not only use Python for the CPU and GPU, but can also add in an API extension using the C or the C++ languages. This means that we can extend out the usage of PyTorch for new and experimental cases, which can make it a great choice for doing research.

The last benefit we are going to focus on here is that PyTorch is seen as a Python approach library. This is because the library is a native Python package just by the way that it is designed. The functionalities that come with it are built as classes in Python, which means that all of the code that you write with it can integrate seamlessly with the modules and packages of Python.

Similar to NumPy, this Python-based library enables us to work on a GPU-accelerated tensor, with computations that provide us with rich options for APIs while applying a neural network. PyTorch offers us the end-to-end research framework we need, including most of the different building blocks required to carry out Deep Learning research on a day-to-day basis. It also provides high-level neural network modules because it can work with an API that is similar to the Keras library.

PyTorch 1.0 – How to Go from Research to Production

Throughout this chapter, we have spent time discussing the many strengths of the PyTorch library, demonstrating why so many researchers and data scientists use it as their go-to library. However, there are a few downsides that come with it, and one of these includes that it has been lacking when it comes to supporting production. Thanks to some of the improvements and changes currently happening with PyTorch, though, it is expected that this is something that will change soon.

The next release of PyTorch, which is known as PyTorch 10, is already expected to be a big release that overcomes some of the biggest challenges that researchers, programmers, and developers face in production. This is the newest iteration of the whole framework, and it is expected to combine with the Python-based Caffe2, allowing for Deep Learning researchers and machine learning developers to move from research to production. And the point of doing this is to allow the process to happen in a manner that is hassle-free and without the programmer needing to deal with challenges that show up in migration.

The new version 1.0 is meant to help unify the package's research and production capabilities in one framework, rather than doing it in two parts, making things easier and avoiding some of the missed values and complications that happen when you try to merge. This allows us more performance optimization and the flexibility that we need to complete both research and production projects.

This newer version promises a lot of help in handling tasks as they come up. Many of these tasks will make it more efficient for you to run your Deep Learning models on a much larger scale. Along with the support of production, remember that PyTorch 10 will also have countless improvements in terms of optimization and usability.

With the help of the PyTorch 1.0 library, we can take existing code and continue to work on it as-is. The existing API is not going to change, so that makes it easier for those of us who have already been able to create some code and programs with the old API. To help make sense of the progress you can expect from the PyTorch library, you can look at the PyTorch website to help out.

As we can see with all of the information that we explored in this chapter, PyTorch is already a compelling player in the Artificial Intelligence and Deep Learning spaces. Being able to exploit all of its unique aspects, and seeing that it is going to work as a research-first library, makes PyTorch an important part of our Data Analysis pipeline overall.

The PyTorch library can overcome many of the challenges inherent to Deep Learning and can provide us with all of the power and performance necessary to get the job done. If you are a student, a researcher, or a mathematician who is inclined to work with Deep Learning, then the PyTorch library is going to be a great option as a framework for getting started.

6. Pandas

Pandas is built on NumPy, and they are meant to be used together. This library makes it extremely easy to extract arrays from data frames. Once these arrays are extracted, they can be turned into data frames themselves. Let's take a look at an example:

```
import pandas as pd
import numpy as np
marketing_filename = 'regression-datasets-marketing.csv'
marketing = pd.read_csv(marketing _filename, header=None)
```

In this phase, we are uploading data to a data frame. Next, we're going to use the "values" method to extract an array that is of the same type as those contained inside the data frame.

```
marketing_array = marketing.values
marketing_array.dtype
```

Output:
```
dtype('float64')
```

We can see that we have a float type array. You can anticipate the type of the array by first using the "dtype" method. This will establish which types are being used by the specified data frame object.

Do this before extracting the array. This is how this operation would look:

```
marketing.dtypes
```

Output
```
0float64
1int64
2float64
3int64
4float64
5float64
6float64
7float64
8int64
9int64
10int64
11float64
```

```
12float64
13float64
dtype: object
```

Matrix Operations

This includes matrix calculations, such as matrix to matrix multiplication. Let's create a two-dimensional array.

This is a two-dimensional array of numbers from 0 to 24. Next, we will declare a vector of coefficients and a column that will stack the vector and its reverse. Here's what it would look like:

```
coefs = np.array([1., 0.5, 0.5, 0.5, 0.5])
coefs_matrix = np.column_stack((coefs,coefs[::-1]))
print (coefs_matrix)
```

Output:
```
[[1. 0.5]
[0.50.5]
[0.50.5]
[0.50.5]
[0.51.]]
```

Now we can perform the multiplication. Here's an example of multiplying the array with the vector:
```
np.dot(M,coefs)
```

Output:
```
array([5.,20.,35.,50.,65.])
```

Here's an example of multiplication between the array and the coefficient vectors:
```
np.dot(M,coefs_matrix)
```

Output:
```
array([[5.,7.],
[20.,22.],
[35.,37.],
[50.,52.],
[65.,67.]])
```

In both of these multiplication operations, we used the "np.dot" function in order to achieve them. Next up, let's discuss slicing and indexing.

Slicing and Indexing

Indexing is great for viewing an n-D array by sending an instruction to visualize the slice of columns and rows or the index.

Let's start by creating a 10x10 array. It will initially be two-dimensional.
```
import numpy as np
M = np.arange(100, dtype=int).reshape(10,10)
```

Next, let's extract the rows from 2 to 8, but only the ones that are evenly numbered.
```
M[2:9:2,:]
```

Out
```
array([[20, 21, 22, 23, 24, 25, 26, 27, 28, 29],
[40, 41, 42, 43, 44, 45, 46, 47, 48, 49],
[60, 61, 62, 63, 64, 65, 66, 67, 68, 69],
[80, 81, 82, 83, 84, 85, 86, 87, 88, 89]])
```

Now let's extract the column, but only the ones from index 5.
```
M[2:9:2,5:]
```

Output:
```
array([[25, 26, 27, 28, 29],
[45, 46, 47, 48, 49],
[65, 66, 67, 68, 69],
[85, 86, 87, 88, 89]])
```

We successfully sliced the rows and the columns. But what happens if we try a negative index? Doing so would reverse the array. Here's how our previous array would look when using a negative index.
```
M[2:9:2,5::-1]
```

Output:
```
array([[25, 24, 23, 22, 21, 20],
[45, 44, 43, 42, 41, 40],
[65, 64, 63, 62, 61, 60],
[85, 84, 83, 82, 81, 80]])
```

However, keep in mind that this process is only a way of viewing the data. If you want to use these views further by creating new data, you cannot make any modifications to the original arrays. If you do, it can lead to undesirable effects. In that case, you want to use the "copy" method. This will create a copy of the array, which you can modify however you wish. Here's the code line for the copy method:
```
N = M[2:9:2,5:].copy()
```

7.Jupyter Notebook

Getting started with Jupyter Notebook (IPython)

The Jupyter Notebook is an open-source web application that permits you to produce and share files that contain live code, formulas, visualizations, and narrative text. Functionalities include information cleaning and alteration, mathematical simulation, analytical modeling, information visualization, Artificial Intelligence, and far more.

Jupyter allows for the use of over 40 various programming languages, and Python is among them. Python has its own requirement (Python 3.3 or higher, or Python 2.7) for setting up the Jupyter Notebook itself.

Setting up Jupyter with Anaconda

Set up Python and Jupyter using the Anaconda distribution, which includes Python, the Jupyter Notebook, and other typically utilized bundles for scientific computing and information science. You can download Anaconda's newest Python3 variation.

Now, set up the downloaded variation of Anaconda.

Setting up Jupyter Notebook using PIP:

```
python3 -m pip install --upgrade pip
python3 -m pip install jupyter
```

Command to run the Jupyter notebook:

```
jupyter notebook
```

This will print some details about the notebook server in your terminal, consisting of the URL of the web application (by default, http://localhost:8888), and after that, you can open your default web browser to this URL.

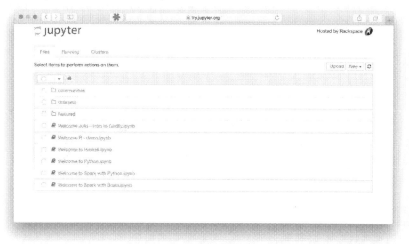

When the Notebook opens in your browser, you will see the Notebook Dashboard, which will reveal a list of the notebooks, files, and subdirectories in the directory site where the Notebook server was initiated. The majority of the time, you will want to begin a Notebook server in the highest level directory consisting of notebooks. Typically, this will be your home directory.

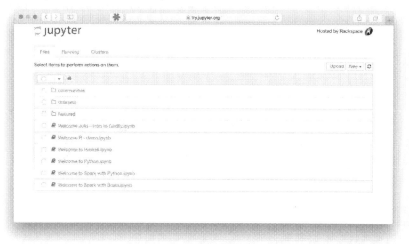

Create a new Notebook

On the control panel, you should now see a brand-new button in the top right corner. Click it to open a drop-down list, and after that, if you click Python3, it will open a brand-new notebook.

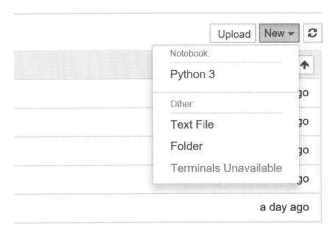

A Few Useful Commands

Command to open a notebook in the currently running notebook server.

```
jupyter notebook notebook_name.ipynb
```

By default, the notebook server begins on port 8888. If port 8888 is not available or is in use, the Notebook server browses the next readily available port.

```
jupyter note pad-- port 9999
```

Command to begin the Notebook server without opening a browser instance:

```
jupyter notebook -no-browser
```

The notebook server provides help messages for other command-line arguments using the –help flag:

```
jupyter notebook -help
```

Running your First Program in Jupyter

Action #1: After effectively setting up Jupyter, write 'jupyter notebook' in the terminal/command line. This will open a brand-new Notebook server in your browser.

Action #2: On the leading left corner, click the New button and choose python3. This will open a brand-new notebook tab in your browser, where you can begin to write your first code.

Action #3: Click the first cell in your Notepad to enter edit mode.

Action #4: Now you are free to write whatever code you like.

Action #5: You can run your code by pushing Shift + Enter or the run button at the top. An example code is provided below:

```
In [6]:  # Define a function for addition
         def add(a , b):
             return a + b

         val = add(12, 13)

         val
Out[6]:  25
```

Jupyter Notebook Tips and Tricks

Python is a fantastic language for doing data analysis, mainly because of its great environment for working with data-centric python bundles. What makes data analysis in Python even more efficient and effective is Jupyter Notebook, or what was previously called the IPython Notepad.

In this area, we are going to go over some great functions of the Jupyter Notebook, which increases the efficiency and effectiveness of a data scientist. The Jupyter Notebook extends console-based technique to interactive computing with qualitatively new instructions, offering a web-based application appropriate for recording the entire calculation procedure: reading, writing, and executing code, along with interactive results. In a nutshell, it is a complete package.

Let's see some of the functions of the Jupyter Notebook, which becomes extremely convenient when doing data analysis.

%%timeit and %%time

It's not unusual for a data scientist to require more than one package or service for their project. They want to pick the very best techniques, which accomplish the job in the minimum quantity of time. Jupyter Notepad supplies an extremely effective method for inspecting the runtime of a specific block of code.

We can utilize the %% time command to inspect the running time of a specific cell. Let's see the time it takes to carry out the code detailed below.

```
# For capturing the execution time
%%time
# Find the squares of a number in the
# range from 0 to 14
for x in range(15):
square = x**2
print(square)
```

Output:
```
0
1
4
9
16
25
36
49
64
81
100
121
144
169
196
Wall time: 999 µs
```

We can likewise utilize the command %%timeit to run the provided bit of code over some variety of times to discover the typical run time for that piece of code.

Commenting/Uncommenting:

When coding, we typically end up regularly writing new lines and commenting out old pieces of code to improve efficiency or to debug. Jupyter Notebook supplies an extremely effective method to accomplish this, by commenting out code blocks.

We simply need to highlight all the lines that we want to comment out, as shown in the following picture:

```
1  df = pd.DataFrame({'Date':['10/2/2011','11/2/2011','12/2/2011','13/2/2011'],
2                     'Event':['Music','Poetry','Theatre','Comedy'],
3                     'Cost':[10000,5000,15000,2000]})
4
5  df.index = ['A', 'B', 'A', 'D']
6
7  print(df)
8
9  df2 = pd.DataFrame({'Cost1':[10025,5700,2415,1800],
10                     'Cost2':[1000,500,150,20],
11                     'Cost3':[10000,5000,15000,2000]})
12
13 print(df.columns)
```

Next, on a Windows computer system, we would push the ctrl +/ key combination to comment out the highlighted part of the code.

```
[: 1  df = pd.DataFrame({'Date':['10/2/2011','11/2/2011','12/2/2011','13/2/2011'],
   2                      'Event':['Music','Poetry','Theatre','Comedy'],
   3                      'Cost':[10000,5000,15000,2000]})
   4
   5  df.index = ['A', 'B', 'A', 'D']
   6
   7  # print(df)
   8
   9  # df2 = pd.DataFrame({'Cost1':[10025,5700,2415,1800],
  10  #                     'Cost2':[1000,500,150,20],
  11  #                     'Cost3':[10000,5000,15000,2000]})
  12
  13  print(df.columns)
```

This does conserve a great deal of time for data scientists.

Next, on a Windows computer system, we simply push the ctrl +/ key combination again to bring the newly commented code back.

```
: 1  df = pd.DataFrame({'Date':['10/2/2011','11/2/2011','12/2/2011','13/2/2011'],
  2                      'Event':['Music','Poetry','Theatre','Comedy'],
  3                      'Cost':[10000,5000,15000,2000]})
  4
  5  df.index = ['A', 'B', 'A', 'D']
  6
  7  print(df)
  8
  9  df2 = pd.DataFrame({'Cost1':[10025,5700,2415,1800],
 10                      'Cost2':[1000,500,150,20],
 11                      'Cost3':[10000,5000,15000,2000]})
 12
 13  print(df.columns)
```

8. Data Visualization and Matplotlib

At some point in your journey working with all of this data, you are going to decide that it is time actually to see the data and visualize it. Sure, we could put all of that information into a table or write it out in long and boring paragraphs, but this is going to make it hard to focus and see the comparisons and relationships that are present in the data. One of the best approaches to take after it has been analyzed accurately is to use data visualization and put the analysis to work for our needs.

The good news is that the Matplotlib library, which is an extension of NumPy and SciPy, can help us with all of this. Whether you want to look at your data as a line graph, a pie chart, a histogram, or in some other form, the Matplotlib library is there to help.

The first thing we are going to explore here is data visualization. We need to get a better idea of what data visualization is all about, how it works, why we would want to use it, and so on. When we can put all of these parts together, it becomes much easier to take all of the data we have been collecting and actually see it in a way that is easy to understand and use to make smart business decisions.

Data visualization is the presentation of quantitative information in a graphical form. In other words, you can use data visualization to take a set of data, whether small or large, and turn it into a visual representation that is much easier for the brain to understand and process. A combination of more than one of these visuals with added information and numerical representations thrown into the mix is known as an infographic.

There are many benefits that come with using this kind of data visualization. It can be used to explore trends and facts that we may not yet be confident in, or which can be hidden way down deep in the data set, especially in some of the larger sets. You can see these visualizations in forms such as inline charts that help to show us, e.g., changes in something over time, column and bar charts that can help you to make comparisons and investigate the relationships between two or more quantities, pie charts to show us how much of a whole something takes up, and much more.

These are just a few of the examples of the data visualization that you may encounter as you do your work.

So, what does it take to make a good data visualization? These are created when we can add together design, Data Science, and communication all in one. Data visualization, when it is done right, can offer us key insights into complicated data sets, and this is done in a manner that makes them more meaningful for those using them and more intuitive overall.

Many companies will find a great deal of value in this sort of data visualization, so it is a tool that you don't want to overlook. Any time you are trying to analyze your data, if you want to make sure it matches up well and that you are fully comprehending the information contained within it, it will be a good idea to look at your plots later on and decide which ones represent your data best and therefore which ones you should use.

It may be possible for you to get everything you need from your data and complete your analysis without needing these kinds of visualizations. However, when you have a lot of data and you don't want to miss anything, particularly if you don't have time to go through it all, these visuals will help. The best kinds of data visualizations will include plenty of complex ideas that can be communicated in a manner that has efficiency, precision, and clarity, among other features.

To help you craft a good data visualization, you will need to make sure that your data is clean, well-sourced, and complete. This is a process we covered earlier in this guidebook, so your data should already be prepared by this time. Once you are ready and the data is prepared, you can start looking at some of the charts and plots that are available to use. This is sometimes hard and can be a bit tricky depending on the kind of information you are working with at the time. You will want to go with the chart type that works best for the data that you have available.

After you have done the research to determine this, it will be time to go through and design, as well as customize, your chosen visuals to represent your data and your message best. Always keep the graphs and charts as simple as possible, as this often conveys your ideas clearest. You do not want to take the time adding in a bunch of elements that are not necessary and will simply distract us from the data.

At this point, the visualization should be complete. You have picked out the one you want to use after sorting through and cleaning your data, then picked out the right visualization to represent your information, and written the code that goes with it to get the best results. Now that this part is done, you'll need to take that visualization and publish and share it with others.

Why is it important to use data visualization?

With the above information in mind, let's look at some of the benefits of using data visualization and why so many people like to work with it. While it is possible to do your analysis and presentation without using any of the graphs and other visuals to go along them, this is often a poor way to facilitate effective decision-making and does not ensure that the data is being understood as best it can, nor that the full amount of information and trends contained within it are being captured. In addition to this, some of the other reasons that data analysts like to work with these kinds of visualizations include:

It helps them to make better decisions. Today, more than any other time in history, companies have a wide variety of data tools at their disposal, including data visualizations, to ask the right questions and make the best decisions. Emerging computing technologies and easy-to-use software programs have made it easier to learn more about your business and ensure you are making the best decisions for it, powered by robust data analysis.

The strong emphasis on things like KPIs, data dashboards, and performance metrics is already showing us the importance of taking all the data a company has collected and then measuring and exploring it. Some of the most important quantitative information available that companies could be putting to good use with visualizations includes company market share, departmental expenses, quarterly revenue, and products or units sold.

Another benefit of working with this kind of data visualization is that it helps us tell a story with a lot of meaning behind it. Data visualizations, as well as other informational graphics, have become an essential tool for media companies everywhere. Data journalism is a field that is on the rise, and many journalists are consistently relying on quality visualization tools to make sure they can tell the important stories about what is happening in the world around them.

This is something that has picked up steam in recent years. Many of the most well-respected institutions out there have been fully embracing the idea of news driven by data, including places like The Washington Post, The New York Times, CNN, and The Economist.

Marketers have also come onto the scene and benefited from the combination of emotional storytelling and quality data that they have available to them. You will find that a good marketer is able to make decisions that are driven by data, but sharing this information with their customers is going to need an approach that is a bit different. This approach needs to be one that can touch on both the emotional and the intelligent at the same time. You will find that data visualizations can ensure that marketers are able to get their message out there, using both heart and statistics.

Data literacy is another thing encouraging us to work with data visualization. Being able to read and understand data visualizations has become something of a requirement in our modern world. Because a lot of the resources and tools that go with these visualizations are readily available in our modern world, it is expected that professionals, even if they are not in the technical world, should be able to look at such representations and gain the right insights from them.

This is why increasing the amount of data literacy that is found around the world is one of the biggest pillars we will see from data visualization companies and others. To help people in business make better decisions, it is important to have the right information and the right tools, and data visualizations such as graphs are the key to getting that done.

We can turn to Florence Nightingale to help here as well. She was best known for being a nurse during the Crimean War, but along with that, she was also a data journalist who was known for her rose or coxcomb diagrams. These were a revolutionary new type of chart that helped her to achieve better conditions in the hospitals, which in the end helped to save many lives of the soldiers who were there

In addition, one of the most well-known data visualizations comes from Charles Joseph Minard. Minard is known as a civil engineer from France who represented numerical data on the maps that he used. In particular, he is famous for the work he did on the map showing Napoleon's Russian campaign of 1812, displaying the dramatic loss of his army when they were trying to make an advance in Moscow, along with some of the retreat that followed.

Why we should use data visualization

Before exploring further what the matplotlib library can do (so that we have more ways to represent our data), we need to end this section with a look at data visualization and why we should use it in the first place. Some of the different reasons why you would want to work with data visualization include:

It can take the data that you have and make it easier for you to remember and understand it rather than just reading through the information and hoping it makes sense.

It gives you the ability to discover facts that are not known to you such as trends and even outliers in the information that could be useful as well.

It makes your life a bit easier because it helps you to visualize relationships and patterns quickly and effectively.

It ensures that you can ask questions in a better way and make the best decisions for your business.

As you can see, there are many different benefits to working with data visualization and the many different things you can do with it. It is worth your time to learn a few different parts of data visualization and what all it can do for you. Whether you have plenty of data or just a little bit, these visuals are going to be the perfect tools to make sure you can get your analysis and presentation done.

What is matplotlib?

We know now how important it is to work with data visualization and to have a method in place that helps us to understand what is going on within all of the data that we collected earlier. This ensures that we can proceed and that our whole analysis works the way that we would like.

This brings up another question we have to consider, though. We need to know what methods we can use to help us create these charts and graphs and the other visualizations that we choose to use. Your business likely has a ton of data in place, and you want to make sure that you are not only choosing the right kind of visualization but that you are also able to put it all together and make the right presentation of it, and this is where matplotlib is going to shine.

The idea with matplotlib is that a picture is worth a thousand words. Luckily, this library is not going to require a thousand words of code to make the graphics that you want! It is there to make the visuals and graphics that are needed to go along with any information that you have as simply and easily as possible.

Still, you will find that it is a massive library to look through, and getting the plots to behave the way that you want, or even choosing the right kind of plot, will at some points require hard work and trial and error. Using one-liners to generate some of the basic plots does not have to be difficult, even if a lot of the rest of the library can seem a bit daunting at times. This is why we are going to take a look at what matplotlib is all about and why it is something you should consider learning to use alongside your data analysis.

First, we need to explore why matplotlib can sometimes feel confusing. Learning how to work with this kind of library is going to be frustrating sometimes when you first get started, but this isn't to say that the matplotlib documentation is lacking, as there is an extensive amount of documentation present. However, there are a few challenges that can show up for programmers, and some of these include:

The library that you can use is pretty large. In fact, it is contains about 70,000 lines of code, and it is always expanding, so it is likely that this number will increase over time.

Matplotlib is home to more than one type of interface with many ways to construct a figure, and it is able to interact with a lot of backends as well. The backend deals with the process that occurs when the chart is rendered, not just structured. This can lead to some problems along the way.

While this library is very comprehensive, it is also an integrated part of NumPy and SciPy, so you need to make sure that you know how to use these languages ahead of time to make things easier.

To help us see how this can work, we need to start with a bit of history on the topic. John D. Hunter, a neurobiologist, began to develop this particular library in 2003. He was originally inspired to emulate the commands that were found in the MATLAB software that came with Mathworks.

Hunter passed on in 2012, and now the open source matplotlib library is a community effort that is designed and maintained by a host of others.

One of the relevant features of matplotlib is its global style. The Python concept of importing is important at times, but it is not going to be used all that heavily with matplotlib, and most of the functions that we use with this are going to be available to the user at the top level.

Knowing that matplotlib has its roots in the MATLAB language can help to explain Pylab, a module within the matplotlib library that was built to mimic some of the global approaches we find in MATLAB. It helps include several classes and functions from matplotlib and NumPy together to make a namespace. This is useful for those who want to transition from MATLAB without having to import any statements.

The biggest issue is likely to arise for those who have already used Python in the past. Using the import function to call Pylab in a session or a script is possible, but it is generally seen as bad practice. Matplotlib advises against doing this in many of its tutorials and releases. Internally, this is because there are many potentially conflicting imports that are being used that are masked in the short-form source, and because of this, the matplotlib library has abandoned some of the convenience that goes with this model and recommends that all users should move away from Pylab, bringing them more in line with some of the key parts of the Python language, so that these can work better together.

We should also discuss the matplotlib object hierarchy. If you have gone through any kind of beginners' tutorial on this library, you have likely called up something like plt.plot([1, 2, 3]), or something similar. This is fine to use on occasion, but we have to remember that this one-liner actually hides the fact that the plot is a hierarchy of Python objects that are nested and hidden inside. In this case, the hierarchy includes a structure similar to a trial that is hiding within each of the plots we have made.

A figure object serves as the external container for these kinds of graphics, with multiple Axes objects we are then able to use. One source of confusion we can run into is the name of Axes. This actually translates to what we think of as an individual graph or plot, rather than the axis that we are used to seeing on a chart or graph.

You can think of the Figure function that we are using as a box-like container that will hold onto at least one, but often more than one, Axes, or actual plots. Below the Axes that we see, there will be a hierarchy of smaller objects that could include text boxes, legends, individual lines, and tick marks, to name a few, and almost all of the elements that show up in this kind of chart can be manipulated by a Python object on their own. This is going to include even the smallest of the elements, i.e., the labels and the ticks.

The next thing to look at is the stateless and the stateful approaches to matplotlib. For now, we are going to visualize the stateful interfaces that include the state machine and the state-based, along with the stateless, which would be the object-oriented interfaces.

Almost all of the functions that you can work with from pyplot, including plt.plot(), are going to either refer to the existing current

Figure, as well as to the current Axes that you worked with, or help you to create a brand new one if you don't have any.

Those who have spent a lot of time using MATLAB before switching over may choose to word the differences here by saying something more along the lines of plt.plot() being a state machine interface that tracks the current figures implicitly. This may not make a lot of sense unless you have spent a ton of time working on programming, but what this means in some more common terms is:

The standard interface that you can use is going to be called up with plt.plot() and other functions that are considered top-level in pyplot. Remember here that there is only going to be one Figure or Axes that you are trying to manipulate at a given time, and you don't need to go through and refer to it explicitly to get things done.

Modifying the underlying objects directly is considered an object-oriented approach. It is common to do this by using the calling methods with an Axes object, which is the object that represents the plot on its own.

To help us understand a bit more about how this plt.plot() function works, since we have already spent some time talking about it in this chapter, we can boil it all down to just a few lines of code:

```
def plot(*args, **kwargs):
    """An abridged version of plt.plot()."""
    ax = plt.gca()
    return ax.plot(*args, **kwargs)
def gca(**kwargs):
    """Get the current Axes of the current Figure."""
    return plt.gcf().gca(**kwargs)
```

Calling this function is just a more convenient method to use to ensure that you can get the current Axes from its current Figure, and then you can call up the plot() method as needed. This is what we mean when we talk about an assertion in the stateful interface and how it can always implicitly track the plot that it wants to find and then reference that part of the code.

9. Data Aggregation and Group Operations

Taking the time to categorize our data set and give a function to each of the different groups that we have, e.g., transformation or aggregation, is often a critical part of the workflow for Data Analysis. After we take the time to load, merge, and prepare a data set, it is then time to compute further information, such as the group statistics or the pivot tables. This is done to help with reporting or with visualizations of that data.

There are a few options that we can work with here to get this done, but Pandas is one of the best, because it provides us with a flexible interface. We can use this interface to slice, dice, then summarize data more easily.

One reason that we see a lot of popularity for SQL and relational databases of all kinds is that we can use them to ease up the process of joining, filtering, transforming, or aggregating our data. However, some of the query languages, including SQL, that we want to use are going to be more constrained in the kinds of group operations that we can perform with them.

As we are going to see from the expressiveness we get with the Pandas library, and with Python in general, we can perform far more complex operations. This is done by simply utilizing any function that can accept an array from NumPy or an object from Pandas.

Each of the grouping keys that you want to work with can end up taking a variety of forms. We can see that the keys don't have to all come in as the same type. Some of the forms that these grouping keys come in include:

- An array or a list that is the same length as the axis that we want to group.
- A value that indicates the name of the column in a DataFrame.
- A Series that gives the correspondence between the values of the axis that is being grouped and the group names.
- A function that can be invoked on the axis index, or on some of the individual labels in the index.

Note that the last three methods are going to be shortcuts that help us produce an array of values to be used when splitting up the object. This can seem a bit abstract right now, but don't let this bother you. It will all make more sense as we go through the steps and learn more about how all of this is meant to work. With this in mind, it is time to talk more about data aggregation and how we can make this work for our needs.

What is Data Aggregation?

Data aggregation is any process in which information can be gathered and then expressed in the form of a summary, usually for analysis. One of the common purposes of aggregation is to help us gain more information about a particular topic or group based on variables like, e.g., profession, income, and age.

This information can then be used to personalize a website, allowing a business to choose what content and advertising is likely to appeal to an individual who belongs to one or more of the groups from which the data was originally collected. Let's take a look at how this works.

We can work with a site that is responsible for selling music CDs. They could use the ideas of data aggregation to advertise specific types of CDs based on the age of the listener and the data aggregate that is collected for others in that age group. OLAP, or Online Analytic Processing, is a simple option for data aggregation in which mechanisms for online reporting can be used to help a business process all of their customer information.

Data aggregation can do a lot of different things as well. For example, it could be more user-based than some of the other programs that we may have seen in the past. Personal data aggregation services are popular, and they will offer any user a single point for collection of their personal information from a host of other websites that we want to work with.

In these systems, the customer works with a single master PIN, or personal identification number, which allows them the access they need to various accounts. This could include things like music clubs, book clubs, airlines, financial institutions, and so on. Performing this type of data aggregation can take some time and will be a more complex system to develop, but we will see that it all falls under the umbrella of web scraping.

This is just one example of how we can work through the process of data aggregation. It is one of the best methods to help companies gain the knowledge and power that they need from the users they have. It often works well with Pandas, Python, and database languages, because these can collect a lot of the information and recommend options to customers or users based on where they fit in with the data set.

Yes, there are always going to be some outliers to the information we collect and times when our data doesn't apply to a person, no matter where they fit in the database or how good the data aggregation algorithms are. But it will be able to increase the likelihood that you reach the customers and the users you want, providing them with the information and the content that they need, based on their features and how they react compared to other similar customers.

Conclusion

Almost everyone will agree with the statement that big data has arrived in a big way and has taken the business world by storm. However, what is the future of Data Analysis, and will it grow? What are the technologies that will grow around it? What is the future of big data? Will it continue its meteoric ascent? Or is it going to become a museum artifact soon? What is cognitive technology? What is the future of fast data? Let's look at the answers to these questions. We'll take a look at some predictions from the experts in the field of Data Analysis and big data to get a clearer picture.

One thing is certain, the volume of data we are inundated with will keep on growing. There is practically no doubt in people's minds that we will continue to develop an ever-increasing amount of data, especially after taking into account that the number of internet-connected devices and handheld devices is growing exponentially. The ways we undertake Data Analysis will show marked improvement in the upcoming years. Although SQL will remain the standard tool, we'll see other tools such as Spark emerging as a complementary method for Data Analysis, and their usage will continue to rise.

More and more tools will become available for Data Analysis, and some of them will not not even need an analyst. Microsoft and Salesforce have announced some combined features that will allow non-coders to create apps for viewing their business data. The prescriptive analytics will get built into the business analytics software and IDC predicts that 50 percent of all software related to business analysis will become available with all the business intelligence it needs by the year 2020.

In addition to these features, real-time streaming insight into big data will become a hallmark for the data winners moving forward. These users will be looking to use data to make informed decisions in real-time by using programs such as Spark and Kafka. The topmost strategic trend that will emerge is machine learning. Machine learning will become a mandatory element for big data preparation and predictive analysis in businesses going forward.

You can expect big data to face huge challenges as well, especially in the field of privacy of user details. The new privacy regulations enforced by the European Union intend to protect the personal information of the public. Various companies will have to address privacy controls and processes. It is predicted that most business ethics violations will be related to data in the upcoming years.

Soon you can pretty much expect all companies to have a chief data officer in place. Forrester says that this officer will rise in significance within a short period, but certain kinds of businesses and generation gaps may decrease their significance in the near future. Autonomous agents will continue to play a significant role and they will keep on being a huge trend as per Gartner. These agents include autonomous vehicles, smart advisers, virtual personal assistants, and robots.

The staffing required for Data Analysis will continue expanding, and people from scientists to analysts to architects to experts in the field of data management will be needed. However, a crunch in the availability of big data talent may see the largest companies develop new tactics. Some large institutes predict that various organizations will use internal training to get their issues resolved. A business model with big data as a service can be seen on the horizon.

Python
Machine Learning

Introduction

Despite the boom that Machine Learning has undergone in recent years, the truth is that we are still a long way from embracing its true potential. Machine Learning is currently one of the hottest topics in the IT world. In particular, if you're dealing with the world of Big Data, this is a field you should focus all your energies on because the prospects are incredible. In the not-so-distant future, interaction with machines will form the basis of our being.

In this book we will see how you can implement Machine Learning techniques using Python, from the most basic to the most complex. In the previous volumes of this series (Python for Beginners and Python for Data Analysis) we briefly introduced some Python libraries that were created specifically for Machine Learning. In this volume we will delve further in order to provide a comprehensive understanding.

Even at advanced levels, it's always good to keep in mind what are the important issues to focus on in Machine Learning. Algorithms are the backbone of almost everything we will do. For this reason, we have introduced a section to briefly describe the most important algorithms and other useful elements to advance your knowledge of Machine Learning.

Machine Learning is as much about programming as it is about probability and statistics. There are many statistical approaches that we will use in Machine Learning to design optimal solutions from time to time. Therefore, it is important to have a basic understanding of Probability and Statistics to best understand the various outcomes in each scenario.

A recurring concept that often comes up when delving into this topic is that Machine Learning involves uncertainty. This is one of the main differences between Machine Learning and programming. In programming, you write code that must be executed as it is written. The code will give a predetermined output based on the given instructions. However, in Machine Learning, this is not a luxury we enjoy.

In order to create a Machine Learning model efficiently, three phases must be considered: learning, testing, and deployment. Since models are usually built to interact with humans, we can expect variations in the type of interaction. For example, there may be inputs that need to be verified, and so an appropriate interaction for that verification will need to be designed.

The mathematical element of Machine Learning is another area of study that we need to look at. We haven't talked much about it in the previous books of the series because it is an advanced level study. Several mathematical calculations are involved in Machine Learning in order for the models to provide the output we need. For this reason, we need to learn how to perform specific operations on the data based on unique instructions.

When working with different datasets, there is always a chance that we will come across huge datasets. This is normal because as our Machine Learning models interact with different users, they continue to learn and build their knowledge. The challenge of using massive datasets is that you have to learn how to break the data down into small units that your system can handle and process smoothly. Doing so will also avoid overloading your learning model.

Most basic computers will crash when they have to handle massive data. However, this should not be a problem when you learn how to fragment your datasets and perform computational operations on them.

At the beginning of this book, we mentioned that we will introduce hands-on approaches to using Machine Learning in daily applications. In light of this, we looked at some practical methods of using Machine Learning, such as building a spam filter and analyzing a movie database.

We have taken a careful step-by-step approach to ensure that you can learn along the way, and more importantly, tried to explain each process to help you understand the operations you perform and why.

Eventually, when you build a Machine Learning model, the aim is to integrate it into some of the applications that people use daily. With this in mind, you must learn how to build a simple solution that addresses this challenge. We used simple explanations to help you understand this, and hopefully, as you keep working on different Machine Learning models, you can learn by building more complex models based on your needs.

There are many concepts in Machine Learning that you will learn or come across over time. You must keep into account that this is a never-ending learning process as long as your model interacts with data. Over time, you will encounter greater datasets than those you are used to working with. In such a scenario, learning how to handle them will help you achieve your results faster, and without struggling.

1. What is Machine Learning?

We live in a world where technology has become an inalienable part of our daily lives. In fact, with all the rapid changes in technology these days, machines with Artificial Intelligence are now responsible for different tasks like prediction, recognition, diagnosis, and so on.

Data represent the input to be given to machines so that they "learn". For this reason, they are called "training data" because it is used to train the machines.

Once you have the data, you can analyze them and discover any patterns so that you can perform actions based on those patterns. There are various learning mechanisms to analyze the data for actions to follow. These mechanisms can be classified into two categories: supervised learning and unsupervised learning.

There are several reasons why Machine Learning is important. As mentioned above, all the research conducted on Machine Learning is useful because it helps us understand various aspects of human learning. Moreover, Machine Learning is key because it helps in increasing the accuracy, effectiveness and efficiency of machines.

Here is a real-life example that will help you understand this concept better.

Suppose there are two random users A and B who like to listen to music and we have access to their music history. A music company could make use of Machine Learning to understand the type of songs each of these users prefers and then think to different ways to sell them the most appropriate products.

For example, you can look at different attributes of songs such as their tempo, frequency, or voice gender, and then analyze them, possibly even graphically or visually. Over time, as the data accumulates, it will become increasingly evident that, for example, A tends to prefer songs with a fast tempo and are sung by male artists, while B likes to listen to slow songs with female artists, or any other similar consideration. In light of these findings, the company's marketing and advertising department will be able to make better strategy decisions.

There is currently an incredibly large amount of data (that has been collected since the advent of technology) that we can have free access to. Not only are they open source, but we can now store and process large amounts of them. Technology has certainly evolved if you look at the way we can now manage these things. Technology is so refined these days that it allows us to access more and more data and faster and faster.

Here are a couple of other reasons why Machine Learning is important. Even with all the progress that continue to be made, there will always be some tasks that can't be defined explicitly, but with the help of examples. The idea is to train the machine with data and then teach it to process them to produce an output, independent of the input. In this way, the machine will become aware of how similar inputs should be processed in the future and will process them accordingly to generate appropriate outputs.

Also, in the case of extremely complex processes, it may be very difficult to encode all the details a priori. In such cases, it is better that the machine learn afterwards from the output data of the process itself.

The fields of Machine Learning and Data Mining are intertwined. Data Mining refers to the process of going through tons of data to find correlations or relationships between them. This is another benefit of Machine Learning in the sense that it helps machines find any information that may be of vital importance.

Applications of Machine Learning

Machine Learning is drastically changing the way businesses are run. It helps in managing a large amount of available data and allows users to make useful predictions based on the given information.

Some manual tasks cannot be completed in a short time window when large amounts of data are involved. Machine Learning is the answer to such problems. Nowadays, we are overwhelmed with data and information and it is not possible to think of processing all this information manually.

Therefore, there is a tremendous need for an automated process and Machine Learning helps in achieving this goal.

When the processes of analysis are fully automated, it becomes easier to get useful information. This helps in making all future processes fully automated. The words Big Data, Business Analytics and Data Science require Machine Learning. Predictive Analytics and Business Intelligence are no longer restricted only to elite businesses and are now accessible to small businesses and enterprises as well. This allows small businesses to be a part of the process of gathering and using information effectively. Let's look at a couple of technical applications of Machine Learning and see how they apply to real-world problems.

Virtual Personal Assistants

Popular examples of virtual assistants available today are Alexa, Siri, and Google Now. As is obvious from the name, they help the user find the necessary information via voice commands. You simply need to activate it and then ask the question you want like, "What is my schedule for the day?" "What are the flights available between London and Germany?" or any other question that you want.

To answer your question, your personal assistant will look for information, recall the question you asked and then give you an answer. It can also be used to set reminders for certain tasks. Machine Learning is an important part of the process since it enables the system to gather and refine the information you need based on any of your previous involvements with it.

Recommendation Systems

Starting from the purchase data of each user, it is possible to create Machine Learning algorithms based on probabilistic models that are able to suggest similar products to the user.

Just think of platforms like Amazon or Netflix. They undoubtedly know well their customers with a sufficiently large purchase history. As a result, they can accurately suggest the next product to buy or movie to watch.

Latent Variables

Latent variable models are used to find any correlation between the variables being observed. This is useful when you are not aware of the relationships between variables.

Especially when dealing with a large amount of data, it is easier to search for latent variables to better understand the data.

Reduction of Dimensionality

The data we deal with usually have different variables and dimensions. For example, for a set of hospitalized patients, weight, height, age and blood pressure (in this case four variables, or dimensions) can be considered. For two or three dimensions it is possible to represent the data in a graph in 2D or 3D, relating the various numerical data. If more than three dimensions are involved, the human mind cannot visualize the data.

For these situations, there are algorithms designed to reduce the variables involved, so that it will be possible to handle less of them. The idea is simple: instead of considering all variables, we consider specific linear combinations of them before implementing any model.

Advantages and Disadvantages of Machine Learning

Disadvantages

One technique used for building a Machine Learning model is to validate it on a small dataset. Therefore, starting from a small dataset, the idea is to predict the output relative to new data.

The problem with this way of working is that it is difficult to understand if there is a distortion in the model created. For example, the model may be too attached to the reduced dataset originally used for model validation. As a result, future inferences may not be correct.

There are many applications based on Machine Learning in Social Sciences. In light of the above, it is important to remember that sometimes it may be necessary to make improvements to the models used, to avoid reaching wrong conclusions.

Some of the advantages

Human beings cannot process large volumes of data, let alone analyze that data. There is a lot of real-time data that is being produced, and if there is no automatic system to understand and analyze that data, we cannot reach any conclusion.

Machine Learning is getting better. With the advent of Deep Learning systems, the costs of data engineering and pre-processing of data are reducing.

2. Machine Learning – Concepts & Terms

Machine Learning is done by feeding the machine with relevant training data sets. Ordinary systems, that is, systems without any Artificial Intelligence, can always provide an output based on the input that is provided. A system with Artificial Intelligence, however, can learn, predict, and improve the results it provides through training.

Let's look at a simple example of how children learn to identify objects, or in other words, how a child will associate a word with an object. Let's assume that there is a bowl of apples and oranges on the table. You, as an adult or parent, will introduce the round and red object as an apple, and the other object as an orange. In this example, the words 'apple' and 'orange' are labels, and the shapes and colors are attributes. You can also train a machine using a set of labels and attributes. The machine will learn to identify the object based on the attributes that are provided to it as input.

The models that are based on labeled training data sets are termed as **Supervised Machine Learning** models. When children go to school, their teachers and professors give them some feedback about their progress. In the same way, a supervised Machine Learning model allows the engineer to provide some feedback to the machine.

Let's take an example of the input [red, round]. Here, both the child and the machine will understand that any object which is round and red is an apple. Let's now place a cricket ball in front of either the machine or the child. You can give a feedback to the machine assigning 1 if its response is correct, 0 if the response is wrong. You can always add more attributes if necessary. This is the only way that a machine will learn. It is also for this reason that if you use a large-high-quality data set and spend more time training the machine, the machine will give you better and more accurate results.

Before we proceed further, you must understand the difference between the concepts of Machine Learning, Artificial Intelligence, and Deep Learning. Most people use these concepts interchangeably, but it is important to know that they are not the same thing.

The following diagram will give you an idea of how these terms relate:

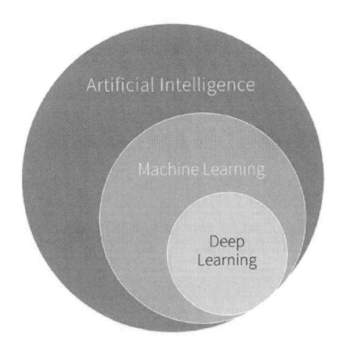

An illustration to understand the relationship between Machine Learning, Artificial Intelligence, and Deep Learning.

Artificial Intelligence is a set of techniques and methodologies that are used to make machines mimic any human behavior. The aim is to ensure that a machine can accurately and efficiently mimic any human behavior. Some examples of machines that use Artificial Intelligence include deep blue chess and IBM's Watson.

Machine Learning, as defined above, is the use of statistical and mathematical models to help machines to learn hot wo mimic human behavior. This is done using past data.

Deep Learning is a subset of Machine Learning, and it refers to the functions and algorithms that an engineer uses to help a machine to train itself. The machine can learn to take the correct option to derive an output. Neural Networks and Natural Language Processing are a part of the Deep Learning ecosystem.

Objectives of Machine Learning

Machine Learning usually has one of the following objectives.

- Predict a category
- Predict a quantity
- Detect anomalies
- Clustering

Predict a category

The Machine Learning model analyzes the input data and then predicts a category under which the output will fall. The prediction in these cases is usually a binary answer that is based on "yes" or "no". It will be possible, for example, to answer questions such as "will it rain today or not?", "is this a fruit?", "is this email spam or not?". And so on. This is achieved by referring to a set of data (training dataset) that will indicate whether a certain email falls into the spam category or not based on specific keywords. This process is known as classification.

Predict a quantity

In this case, the system is usually used to predict a value like predicting the intensity of rainfall based on different attributes of the weather like the temperature, percentage of humidity, air pressure and so on. This sort of prediction is referred to as regression. The regression algorithm has various subdivisions like linear regression, multiple regression, etc.

Anomaly Detector Systems

The purpose of a model in anomaly detection is to detect any outliers in the given set of data. These applications are used in banking and e-commerce systems where the system is built to flag any unusual transactions. All this helps to detect fraudulent transactions.

Clustering

These systems are still in the initial stages, but their applications are numerous and can drastically change the way business is conducted.

For example, it is possible to classify users into different clusters according to different behavioral factors like their age group, the region they live in or even the kind of programs they like to view. Thanks to this, business can now suggest different programs or shows a user might be interested in watching according to the cluster that the user belongs to.

Categories of Machine Learning Systems

In the case of traditional machines, the programmer will give the machine a set of instructions and the input parameters, which the machine will use to make some calculations and derive an output using specific commands. In the case of Machine Learning systems, however, the system is never restricted by any command that the programmer provides. The machine will choose the algorithm that it can be used to process the dataset and decide the output with high accuracy. This is done by using the training dataset which consists of historical data and outputs.

Therefore, in the classical world, we will tell the machine to process data based on a set of instructions, while in the Machine Learning setup, we will never instruct a system. The computer will have to interact with the dataset, develop an algorithm using the historical data, make decisions like a human being would, analyze the information and then provide an output. The machine, unlike a human being, can process large datasets in short periods and provide results with high accuracy.

There are different types of Machine Learning algorithms, and they are classified based on the purpose of that algorithm. There are three categories in Machine Learning systems:

1. Supervised Learning
2. Unsupervised Learning
3. Reinforced Learning

Supervised Learning

In these models, the machine is fed with labeled data. This is done to determine what the output of specific datasets (or new data) will be. This type of algorithm is also called a predictive algorithm.

For example, consider the following table:

Currency (label)	Weight (feature)
1 USD	10 gm
1 EUR	5 gm
1 INR	3 gm
1 RU	7 gm

In the above table, each currency is given an attribute of weight. Here, the currency is the label, and the weight is the attribute or feature.

The supervised Machine Learning system can be first fed with this training dataset, and when it comes across any input of 3 grams, it will predict that the coin is a 1 INR coin. The same can be said for a 10-gram coin.

Classification and Regression algorithms are a type of supervised Machine Learning algorithms. Regression algorithms are used, for example, to predict match scores or house prices, while classification algorithms identify which category the data should belong to.

We will discuss some of these algorithms in detail in the later parts of the book, where you will also learn how to build or implement these algorithms using Python.

Unsupervised Learning

In these type of models, the system is more sophisticated in the sense that it will learn to identify patterns in unlabeled data and produce an output. This is a kind of algorithm that is used to draw any meaningful inference from large datasets. This model is also called the descriptive model since it uses data and summarizes them to generate a description (or overview) of a given datasets. This model is often used in Data Mining applications that involve large volumes of unstructured input data.

For example, if the input data are names, runs, and wickets (the latter two being of numeric type), you can display the numeric data on a two-dimensional graph and possibly identify clusters. In our example, there will be two clusters, one for the batsmen and the other for the bowlers. It will also be possible to match each point in the graph with a specific name. When there will be a new input (given by name, run and wicket), it will be possible to associate it to one of the two clusters, in order to predict if the new input (player) is a batsman or a bowler.

Name	Runs	Wickets
Rachel	100	3
John	10	50
Paul	60	10
Sam	250	6
Alex	90	60

Table 1: Sample dataset for a match. Based on this, the cluster model can group the players into batsmen or bowlers.

220

Some common algorithms which fall under unsupervised Machine Learning include density estimation, clustering, data reduction and compressing.

The clustering algorithm summarizes the data and presents them differently. This is a technique used in Data Mining applications. Density estimation is used when the objective is to visualize any large data set and create a meaningful summary. This will naturally lead to the concept of data reduction and dimensionality. These concepts explain that the analysis or output should always deliver the summary of the dataset without the loss of any valuable information. In simple words, the complexity of data can be reduced if the derived output is useful.

The table below will summarize and give an overview of the differences between Supervised and Unsupervised Machine Learning. It will also list the popular algorithms that are used nowadays.

We will look at each of these algorithms briefly and learn how to implement them in Python.

Supervised Learning	Unsupervised Learning
Works with labeled data	Works with unlabeled data
Takes Direct feedback	No feedback loop
Predicts output based on input data. Therefore also called "Predictive Algorithm"	Finds the hidden structure/pattern from input data. Sometimes called as "Descriptive Model"
Some common classes of supervised algorithms include: Logistic Regression Linear Regression (Numeric prediction) Polynomial Regression Regression trees (Numeric prediction) Gradient Descent Random Forest Decision Trees (classification) K-Nearest Algorithm (classification) Naive Bayes Support Vector Machines	Some common classes of unsupervised algorithms include: Clustering, Compressing, density estimation & data reduction K-means Clustering (Clustering) Association Rules (Pattern Detection) Singular Value Decomposition Fuzzy Means Partial Least Squares Hierarchical Clustering Principal Component Analysis

Reinforced learning

This type of learning is similar to how human beings learn, in the sense that the system will learn to behave in a specific environment, and take actions based on that environment. For example, human beings do not touch fire because they know it will hurt and they have been told that will hurt. Sometimes, out of curiosity, we may put a finger into the fire, and learn that it will burn. This means that we will be careful with fire in the future.

Let's now look at some examples where Machine Learning is applied. It is always a good idea to identify which type of Machine Learning model you must use with examples. The following examples will be discussed in more details later in the book:

- Facebook face recognition algorithm
- Netflix or YouTube recommending programs based on past viewership history
- Analyzing large volumes of bank transactions to guess if they are valid or fraudulent transactions.
- Uber's surge pricing algorithm

Steps to Build a Machine Learning System

Regardless of the model of Machine Learning, here are the common steps that are involved in the process of designing a Machine Learning system.

Define the Objective

As everything in life, the first step is to define what you want. It is important to know what you want to accomplish with your system. The kind of data you use, the algorithm and other factors will primarily depend on the objective or the kind of prediction you want the system to produce.

1. Collect the Data

This is perhaps the most time-consuming step of building a Machine Learning system. You must collect all the relevant data that you will use to train the algorithm.

2. Prepare the Data

This is an important step that is usually overlooked. Overlooking this step can prove to be a costly mistake. The cleaner and more relevant the data you are using are, the more accurate the accuracy of the output will be.

3. Select an Algorithm

There are different algorithms that you can choose, like Structured Vector Machine (SVM), k-mean, Naive-Bayes, Apriori, etc. The algorithm that you use will primarily depend on the objective you wish to attain with the model.

4. Train the Model

Once you have all the data ready, you must feed them into the machine and the algorithm must be trained to predict.

5. Test the Model

Once your model is trained, it is now ready to start reading the input to generate appropriate outputs.

6. Predict

Multiple iterations will be performed and you can also feed the feedback into the system to improve its predictions over time.

7. Deploy

Once you test the model and are satisfied with the way it is working, the said model will be sterilized and can be integrated into any application you want. This means that it is ready to be deployed.

All these steps can vary according to the application and the type of algorithm (supervised or unsupervised) you are using. However, they are generally involved in all processes of designing a Machine Learning system. There are various languages and tools that you can use in each of these stages. In this book, we will learn how to design a Machine Learning system using Python. Let's understand the scenarios from the previous section:

Scenario One

In a picture from a tagged album, Facebook recognizes the photo of the friend.

Explanation: This is an example of supervised learning. In this case, Facebook is using tagged photos to recognize the person. The tagged photos will become the labels of the pictures. Whenever a machine is learning from any form of labeled data, it is referred to as supervised learning.

Scenario Two

Suggesting new songs based on someone's past music preferences.

Explanation: This is an instance of supervised learning. The model is training classified or pre-existing labels – in this case, the genre of songs. This is precisely what Netflix, Pandora, and Spotify do: they collect the songs/movies that you like, evaluate the features based on your preferences and then come up with suggestions of songs or movies based on similar features.

Scenario Three

Analyzing bank data to flag any suspicious or fraudulent transactions.

Explanation: This is an example of unsupervised learning. The suspicious transaction cannot be fully defined in this case and therefore, there are no specific labels like fraud or not a fraud. The model will try to identify any outliers by checking for anomalous transactions.

Scenario Four

The price of an Uber ride that varies depending on when you use the service.

Explanation: The surge pricing feature of Uber is a combination of different models of Machine Learning like the prediction of peak hours, the traffic in specific areas, the availability of cabs. Clustering is used to determine the usage pattern of users in different areas of the city.

3. Essential Libraries for Machine Learning in Python

Many developers nowadays prefer to use Python to analyze data. Not only Python is useful for Data Analysis but it is also possible to implement statistical methods. Everybody dealing with data prefer using Python also for data integration. That's the integration of Web apps and other environment productions.

The features of Python have helped scientists to use it in Machine Learning. Examples of its qualities include consistent syntax, being flexible and even having a shorter time in development. It also can develop sophisticated models and has engines that could help in predictions.

As a result, Python boasts of having a series or a set of very extensive libraries. Remember, libraries refer to a series of routines and sorts of functions with different languages. Therefore, a robust library can lead to tackling more complex tasks. However, this is possible without writing several code lines again. It is good to note that Machine Learning relies mostly on mathematics. That is, mathematical optimization, elements of Probability and Statistics as well. Therefore, Python is very useful to perform complex tasks without much effort.

The following are examples of very popular libraries.

Scikit-Learn

Scikit learn is one of the best and a trendy library in Machine Learning. It has the ability to supporting learning algorithms, especially the supervised ones. Some algorithms for which it is used are the following:

- k-means
- decision trees
- linear and logistic regression
- clustering

This kind of library has major components from NumPy and SciPy. Scikit-learn has the power to add algorithms sets that are useful in Machine Learning and also tasks related to Data Mining. That's it, it helps in classification, clustering, and even regression analysis. There are also other tasks that this library can efficiently deliver. A good example includes ensemble methods, feature selection, data transformation, and more. It is good to understand that experts can easily implement the complex and sophisticated parts of the algorithms.

TensorFlow

TensorFlow is a library released by Google created to perform calculations very fast and therefore very much used in the field of Deep Learning. It allows to perform calculations in a CPU or GPU. That is, once you write the code in Python you will be able to run it on your central processing unit. This makes the analysis process very efficient.

For the execution of various tasks within the system, TensorFlow uses nodes thanks to which a large volume of data can be processed. Several search engines like Google depend on this library. Some important applications are object identification or speech recognition.

Theano

Theano is a significant Python library as well. Its main tasks are to help with anything related to numerical computation. We can also relate it to NumPy. It plays other roles such as

- Definition of mathematical expressions
- Optimization of mathematical calculation
- Evaluating expressions related to numerical analysis.

The main goal of Theano is to give out efficient results. It is a faster Python library as it can perform calculations of intensive data up to 100 times. Therefore, it is good to note that Theano works best with GPU as compared to the CPU of a computer. In most industries, people use Theano for Deep Learning. Also, they use it for computing complex and sophisticated tasks. All this became possible thanks to its processing speed. Due to the expansion of industries with a high demand for data computation techniques, many people use the latest version of this library. Remember, the latest one came to limelight some years back. The new version of Theano had several improvements, interface changes, and several new features.

Pandas

Pandas is a library that is very popular and helps in the provision of data structures that are of high level and quality. The data provided here are simple and easy to use. Also in this case, it is intuitive. It is composed of different sophisticated inbuilt methods which make it capable of performing tasks such as grouping and timing analysis. Another function is that it helps in a combination of data and also offering filtering options. Pandas can collect data from other sources such as Excel, CSV, and even SQL databases. It also can manipulate the collected data to undertake its operational roles within the industries. Pandas consist of two structures that enable it to perform its functions correctly. These are series, which have only one dimension, and data frames that boast two dimensions. The Pandas library has been regarded as the most strong and powerful Python library over the time being. Its main function is to help in data manipulation. Also, it has the power to export or import a wide range of data. Its applications are in different sectors, such as in the field of Data Science.

Pandas is effective in the following areas:

- Splitting of data
- Merging of two or more types of data
- Data aggregation
- Selecting or sub setting data
- Data reshaping
- You can quickly delete some columns or even add some texts found within the data frame
- It will help you in data conversion
- Pandas can reassure you of getting the misplaced or missing data
- It has a powerful ability, especially in the grouping of other programs according to their functionality.

Matplotlib

This is another sophisticated and helpful library, especially when it comes to data visualization. The reason why it was designed was to provide helpful and visual insights to different industries. In business, for example, a company's achievements don't make much sense when you can't share them with different stakeholders. Matplotlib offers a wide range of options and is a must-have Python library for anyone dealing with Data Visualization. When it comes to graphics and images, this library is ideal. It is flexible, requires only a few commands, and allows you to make various charts that you may need, such as histograms, scatterplots, non-Cartesian charts, etc.

It is good to note that this library can export graphics and can change these graphics into PDF, GIF, and so on. In summary, the following tasks can be undertaken with much ease. They include:

- Formation of line plots
- Scattering of plots
- Creations of beautiful bar charts and building up of histograms
- Application of various pie charts within the industry
- Stemming the schemes for Data Analysis and computations
- Being able to follow up contour plots
- Usage of spectrograms
- Quiver plots creation

Diagrammatic explanation

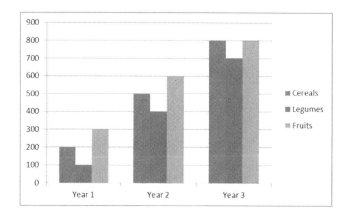

The above graph highlights the overall production of a company within three years. It specifically demonstrates the usage of Matplotlib in Data Analysis. By looking at the diagram, you will realize that the production was high as compared to the other two years. Again, the company tends to perform in the production of fruits since it was leading in both years 1 and 2 with a tie in year 3. From the figure, you realize that your work of presentation, representation and even analysis has been made easier as a result of using this library. This Python library will eventually enable you to come up with good graphic images, accurate data and much more. You will be able to note down the year

228

your production was high, thus, being in a position to maintain the high productivity season.

Let's see another example:

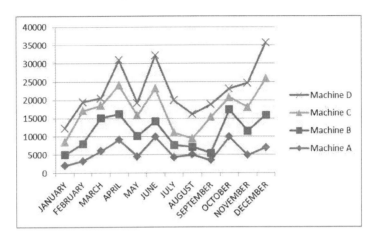

The above line graph clearly shows the performance of different machines the company is using. Following the diagram above, you can eventually deduce and make a conclusion on which machines the company can keep using to get the maximum yield. On most occasions, this evaluation method with the help of the Seaborn library will enable you to predict the exact abilities of your different inputs. Again, this information can help for future reference in the case of purchasing more machines. Seaborn library also has the power to detect the performance of other variable inputs within the company. For example, the number of workers within the company can be easily identified with their corresponding working rate.

Seaborn

Seaborn is also among the most popular Python libraries. Also in this case, its main objective is to help in visualization. It is important to note that this library borrows its foundation from Matplotlib. Due to its higher level, it is capable of various plots generation such as the production of heat maps, processing of violin plots and also helping in generation of time series plots.

NumPy

This is a very widely used Python library. Its features enable it to perform multidimensional array processing. Also, it helps in matrix processing. However, these are only possible with the help of an extensive collection of mathematical functions. It is important to note that this Python library is highly useful in solving the most significant computations within the scientific sector. Again, NumPy is also applicable in areas such as linear algebra, derivation of random number abilities used within industries and more so Fourier transformation. NumPy is also used by other high-end Python libraries such as TensorFlow for Tensors manipulation. In short, NumPy is mainly for calculations and data storage. You can also export or load data to Python since it has those features that enable it to perform these functions. It is also good to note that this Python library is also known as numerical Python.

SciPy

SciPy boasts of comprising of different modules that are applicable in the optimization field of Data Analysis. It also plays a significant role in integration, linear algebra, and other forms of mathematical statistics.

In many cases, it plays a vital role in image manipulation. Manipulation of the image is a process that is widely applicable in day to day activities. Cases of Photoshop and much more are examples of SciPy. Again, many organizations prefer SciPy in their image manipulation, especially the pictures used for presentation. For instance, a wildlife society can come up with the description of a cat and then manipulate it using different colors to suit their project. Below is an example that can help you understand this more straightforwardly. The picture has been manipulated:

The original input image was a cat that the wildlife society took. After manipulation and resizing the image according to our preferences, we get a tinted image of a cat.

Keras

This is also part and parcel of the Python library, especially within Machine Learning. It belongs to the group of networks with high level neural. It is significant to note that Keras has the capability of working over other libraries, especially TensorFlow and even Theano. Also, it can operate nonstop without mechanical failure. In addition to this, it seems to work better on both the GPU and CPU. For most beginners in Python programming, Keras offers a secure pathway towards their ultimate understanding. They will be in a position to design the network and even to build it. Its ability to prototype faster and more quickly makes it the best Python library among the learners.

PyTorch

This is another accessible, but open-source type of Python library. As a result of its name, it boasts of having extensive choices when it comes to tools. It is also applicable in areas where we have computer vision. Computer vision and visual display, play an essential role in several types of research. Again, it aids in the processing of Natural Language. More so, PyTorch can undertake some technical tasks that are for developers. That's enormous calculations and Data Analysis using computations. It can also help in graph creation which mainly used for computational purposes. Since it is an open-source Python library, it can work or perform tasks on other libraries such as Tensors. In combination with Tensors GPU, its acceleration will increase.

Scrapy

Scrapy is another library used for creating crawling programs. That's spider bots and much more. The spider bots frequently help in data retrieval purposes and are also applicable in the formation of URLs used on the web. From the beginning, it was to assist in data scrapping. However, this has undergone several evolutions and led to the expansions of its general purpose. Therefore, the main task of the Scrapy library in our present day is to act as crawlers for general use. The library led to the promotion of general usage, application of universal codes, and so on.

Statsmodels

Statsmodels is a library with the aim of data exploration using several methods of statistical computations and data assertions. It has many features such as result statistics and even characteristic features. It can undertake this role with the help of the various models such as linear regression, multiple estimators, and analysis involving time series, and even using more linear models. Also, other models such as discrete choice are applicable here.

4. The TensorFlow Library

In this chapter, we will explore the TensorFlow Library in detail. This is another option with Python, and it is extremely helpful for performing some Machine Learning tasks more efficiently. It is therefore definitely worth your time to learn how to use this package, along with the algorithms that we talked about in the Scikit-Learn library.

TensorFlow offers the programmer different features and tools to complete projects more efficiently. You will find that the TensorFlow framework comes from Google, and this will be helpful when you are trying to work on models that are Deep Learning-related. TensorFlow relies on graphs of data flow for numerical computation and it can make some Machine Learning tasks easier than ever before.

TensorFlow is going to help us out in many different ways. First, it can help us with acquiring data, training the Machine Learning models that we are trying to use, making predictions, and even modifying our results to make our pipeline work more efficiently. Since each of these steps is important for Machine Learning, we can see how TensorFlow can be put to great use in our project and ensure we are successful.

First, let's take a look at what TensorFlow is all about and some of the background that comes with this Python library. The Brain team from Google was the first to develop TensorFlow for use on large scale Machine Learning operations. It was developed to bring together different algorithms for both Deep Learning and Machine Learning, and it is going to make them more useful through what is known as a common metaphor. TensorFlow works along with the Python language, which we have talked about at length. In addition to this, it provides users with a front-end API that is easy to use when working on a variety of development applications.

It takes things a bit further, though. Even though you can work with TensorFlow and it lines up with the Python coding language, it can also extend the language if you want to change things up. All of the applications that you use with the help of TensorFlow can be executed using the C++ language instead, giving them an even higher level of performance than before.

TensorFlow can be used for a lot of different actions that you may need to make a Machine Learning project a success. Some of the things that you can do with this library include running, training, and building deep Neural Networks, doing image recognition, working with recurrent Neural Networks, digit classification, Natural Language Processing, and even word embedding. And this is just a few of the things that are available for a programmer when they work with TensorFlow for Machine Learning.

Installing TensorFlow

With this in mind, we need to take some time to learn how to install TensorFlow on a computer before we can use this library. Just like we did with Scikit-Learn, we need to go through and set up the environment and everything else so that this library works. You will enjoy the fact that it is already set up with a few APIs for programming (we will take a look at these in more depth later on), including Rust, Go, C++, and Java to name a few. We are going to spend our time here looking at the way that the TensorFlow library works on the Windows operating system, but the steps for adding this library to other operating systems are pretty much the same.

Now, when you are ready to set up and download the TensorFlow library on your Windows computer, you will have two choices of how to proceed. You can choose either to work with the Anaconda distribution, or you can use pip. The native pip is helpful because it takes all the parts that go with the TensorFlow library and ensures they are installed on your system. You also get the bonus of letting the system doing this for you without requiring a virtual environment setup to get it done.

However, although this may seem like the best choice, it can come with some problems along the way. Installing the TensorFlow library using pip may be a bit faster and not require that virtual environment, but it can cause interference with other things that you are doing with Python. Depending on what you plan to do with Python, this can be a problem, so consider that before starting.

The important thing to remember here is that if you do choose to work with pip, and it doesn't seem like it will interfere with what you are doing too much, you will be able to get the whole TensorFlow library to run with just a single command. And once you are done with this command, the whole library, and all of the parts that you need with it, are going to be set up and ready to use on the computer. Pip even makes it easier for you to choose the directory where you would like to store the TensorFlow library for easier use.

In addition to using pip to help download and install the TensorFlow library, it is also possible for you to use the Anaconda distribution. This may take a few more commands to get started, but it does prevent any interference from happening with Python, and it allows you to create a virtual environment that you can work with and test out without a ton of interruption or other issues.

Though there are these few benefits to using the Anaconda distribution instead of pip, it is nonetheless often recommended that you install this program using pip, rather than working with just the conda install. With this in mind, we will still show you some of the steps that it takes to just use the conda install on its own so you can do this if you choose.

One more thing that we need to consider here before moving on is that you need to double-check which version of Python is working. Your version needs to be at Python 3.5 or higher for this library. Python 3 uses the pip 3 program, and this is the best and most compatible version for a TensorFlow install. Working with an older version is not going to work as well with this library and can cause some issues when you try to do some of your Machine Learning development.

You can work with either the CPU or the GPU version of this library based on what you are most comfortable with. The first code below is the CPU version, and the second code below is the GPU version.

```
pip3 install -upgrade tensorflow
pip3 install -upgrade tensorflow-gpu
```

Both of these commands are helpful because they ensure that the TensorFlow library is installed on your Windows system. But another option that you can use is the Anaconda package itself. The methods above work for pip installs, but we talked about how there are a few drawbacks when it comes to doing this.

Pip is a program that is already installed automatically when you install Python onto your system. But you may find quickly that Anaconda is not. This means that if you want to ensure that you can get TensorFlow through Anaconda, then you need to first install the Anaconda distribution. To do this, just go to the website for Anaconda and follow the instructions that come up to help you get it done.

Once you have had the time to install Anaconda, you will notice that within the files there is a package called conda. This is a good package to explore because it helps you manage the installation packages, and it is also helpful when it is time to manage your virtual environment. To help you get the access you need with this package, you can just start up Anaconda and it will be there.

When Anaconda is open, you can go to the main screen on Windows, click the Start button, and then choose All Programs. You need to go through and expand things out to look inside Anaconda at the files that are there. You can then click on the prompt for Anaconda get it to launch on your screen. If you wish to, it is possible to see the details of this package by opening the command line and writing "conda info." This allows you to see some more of the details about the package and the package manager.

The virtual environment that comes with the Anaconda program is relatively simple to use, and it is pretty much just an isolated copy of Python. It will come with all of the capabilities that you need to maintain all of the files that you use, along with the directories and the paths that go with it too. This is helpful because it allows you to do all of your coding inside the Python program and allows you to add in different libraries that are associated with Python if you choose.

These virtual environments may take a bit of time to adjust to and get used to, but they are good for working on Machine Learning because they allow you to isolate a project, allowing you to do your development without all the potential problems that come with dependencies and version requirements. Everything you do in the virtual environment is done independently, so you can experiment and see what works and what doesn't without messing up other parts of the code.

From here, our goal is to take the Anaconda program and get it to work on creating the virtual environment that we want so that the package from TensorFlow can be used properly. The conda command comes into play here again to make this happen. Since we are going through the steps that are needed to create a brand-new environment now, we will need to name it tensorenviron, and then the rest of the syntax to help us get this new environment created includes:

```
conda create -n tensorenviron
```

After you type this code into the compiler, the program is going to stop and ask you whether you want to create the new environment, or if you would rather cancel the work that you are currently doing. Type the "y" key and then hit enter so that the environment is created. The installation may take a few minutes as the compiler completes the environment for you.

Once the new environment is created, you have to go through the process of actually activating it. Without this activation in place, you will not have the environment ready to use. You just need to use the "activate" command to start, then list out the name of any environment that you want to work with to activate it. Since we used the name tensorenviron earlier, you will want to use this in your code as well. An example of how this is going to look is here:

Activate tensorenviron

Now that you have been able to activate the TensorFlow environment, it is time to go ahead and make sure that the package for TensorFlow is installed. You can do this by using the command below:

```
conda install tensorflow
```

When you get to this point, you will be presented with a list of all the packages that are available to install in case you want to add in a few others along with TensorFlow. You can then decide if you want to install one or more of these packages, or if you want to just stick with TensorFlow for now.

The installation should get started right away, but it takes some time, so just let it go without trying to backspace or restart. The speed of your internet is going to be a big determinant of how long this will take.

Soon, the installation process will be complete, and you can then go through and see if it was successful or if you need to fix anything. The good news is that this checking phase is going to be easy because you can just use the import statement with Python to set it up.

We can do this with any regular Python terminal. Simply entering the word Python should be all you need to do. Once you are in the right terminal for this, type in the code below to make sure that TensorFlow is imported and ready to go:

```
import tensorflow as tf
```

At this point, the program should be on your computer and ready to go, so we can move on to the rest of the guidebook and see some of the neat things you can do with this library. There may be a chance that the TensorFlow package didn't end up going through the way that it should. If this is true for you, then the compiler will present you with an error message for you to read through, and you'll need to go back and make sure the code has been written in the right format along the way.

If you don't get any error message at all, then this means that you have set up the TensorFlow package the right way and it is ready to use! With that said, we need to explore some more options and algorithms that a programmer can develop with the TensorFlow library and learn how they work with the different Machine Learning projects you are implementing.

5. Machine Learning Training Model

In Machine Learning, a model is a mathematical or digital representation of a real-world process. To build a good Machine Learning (ML) model, developers need to provide the right training data to an algorithm. An algorithm, on the other hand, is a set of actions taken before training begins with real-world data.

A linear regression algorithm, for example, is a set of instructions defining similar characteristics or features as defined by linear regression. Developers choose the function that fits most of the training data from a set or group of functions. The process of training for Machine Learning involves providing an algorithm with training data.

The basic purpose of creating any ML model is to expose it to a lot of input, as well as the output applicable to it, allowing it to analyze these data and determine the relationship between input and output. For example, if a person wants to decide whether to carry an umbrella or not depending on the weather, he/she will need to look at the weather conditions, which, in this case, is the training data.

Professional data scientists spend most of their time and effort on the following steps:

1. Data exploration
2. Data cleaning
3. Engineering new features

Simple Machine Learning Training Model in Python

When it comes to Machine Learning, having the right data is more important than having the ability to write a fancy algorithm. A good modeling process will protect against over-fitting and maximize performance. In Machine Learning, data are a limited resource, which developers should use in the following ways:

- Feeding their algorithm or training their model
- Testing their model

However, they cannot reuse the same data to perform both functions. If they do this, they could over-fit their model and they would not even know it. The effectiveness of a model depends on its ability to predict unseen or new data; therefore, it is important to have separate training data and test different sections of the dataset. The primary aim of using training sets is to fit and fine-tune one's model. Test sets, on the other hand, are new datasets for the evaluation of one's model.

Before doing anything else, it is important to split data to get the best estimates of the model's performance. After doing this, one should avoid touching the test sets until one is ready to choose the final model. Comparing training versus test performance allows developers to avoid over-fitting. If a model's performance is adequate or exceptional on the training data, but inadequate on the test data, then the model has this problem.

In the field of Machine Learning, over-fitting is one of the most important considerations. It describes how well the target function's approximation correlates with the training data provided. Overfitting happens when the training data provided has a high signal to noise ratio, which leads to poor predictions.

Essentially, an ML model is over-fitting if it fits the training data exceptionally well while generalizing new data poorly. Developers overcome this problem by creating a penalty on the model's parameters, thereby limiting the model's freedom.

When professionals talk about tuning models in Machine Learning, they usually mean working on hyper-parameters. In Machine Learning, there are two main types of parameters, i.e., model parameters and hyper-parameters. The first type defines individual models and is a learned attribute, such as decision tree locations and regression coefficients.

The second type, however, defines higher-level settings for Machine Learning algorithms, such as the number of trees in a random forest algorithm or the strength of the penalty used in a regression algorithm.

The process of training a machine-learning model involves providing an algorithm with training data. The term machine learning model refers to the model artifact created by the ML training process. These data should contain the right answer, known as the target attribute. The algorithm looks for patterns in the data that point to the answer it wants to predict and creates a model that captures these different patterns.

Developers can use machine learning models to generate predictions on new data for which they do not know the target attributes. Supposing a developer wanted to train a model to predict whether an email is legitimate or spam, for example, he/she would give it training data containing emails with known labels that define the emails as either spam or not spam. Using these data to train the model will result in it trying to predict whether a new email is legitimate or spam.

Simple Machine Learning Model using Linear Regression in Python

When it comes to building a simple ML model in Python, beginners need to download and install sci-kit-learn, an open-source Python library with a wide variety of visualization, cross-validation, pre-processing, and Machine Learning algorithms with a unified user interface. It offers easy-to-understand and -to-use functions designed to save a significant amount of time and effort. Developers also need to have at least Python Version 3 installed in their system.

Some of the most important features of sci-kit-learn include:

1. Efficient and easy-to-use tools for Data Analysis and Data Mining
2. BSD license
3. Reusable in many different contexts and highly accessible
4. Built on top of matplotlib, SciPy, and NumPy
5. Functionality for companion tasks
6. Excellent documentation
7. Tuning parameters with sensible defaults
8. User interface supporting various ML models

Before installing this library, users need to have SciPy and NumPy installed. If they already have a data set, they need to split it into training data, testing data, and validation data. However, in this example, they are creating their own training set, which will contain both the input and desired output values of the data set they want to use to train their model. To load an external dataset, they can use the Pandas library, which will allow them to easily load and manipulate datasets.

Their input data will consist of random integer values, which will generate a random integer N; for instance, a $<=$ N $<=$ b. As such, they will create a function that will determine the output. Recall a function uses some input value to return some output value. Having created their training set, they will split each row into an input training set and its related output training set, resulting in two lists of all inputs and their corresponding outputs.

Benefits of splitting datasets include:

1. Gaining the ability to train and test the model on different types of data other than the training data
2. Testing the model's accuracy, which is better than testing the accuracy of out-of-sample training
3. Ability to evaluate predictions using response values for the test datasets

They will then use the linear regression method from Python's sci-kit-learn library to create and train their model, which will try to imitate the function they created for the ML training dataset. At this point, they will need to determine whether their model can imitate the programmed function and generate the correct answer or accurate prediction.

Here, the ML model analyzes the training data and uses it to calculate the coefficients or weights to assign to the inputs to return the right outputs. By providing it with the right test data, the model will arrive at the correct answer.

6. Linear Regression with Python

Linear regression with one variable

The first part of linear regression we are going to focus on is when we just have one variable. This is going to make things a bit easier to work with and will ensure that we can get some of the basics down before we try some of the things that are a bit harder. We will focus on problems that have just one independent and one dependent variable.

To help us get started with this, we are going to use the set of data from car_price.csv to assess the prices of cars. We will have the price of the car be our dependent variable, and then the year of the car is going to be the independent variable. You can find this information in the folders for data sets that we talked about before. To help us make a good prediction on the price of the cars, we will need to use the Scikit Learn library from Python to help us get the right algorithm for linear regression. When we have all of this set up, we need to use the following steps to help out.

Importing the right libraries

First, we need to make sure that we have the right libraries to get this going. The codes that you need to get the libraries for this section include:

```
import pandas as pd
import numpy as np
import matplotlib.pyplot as plt
%matplotlib inline
```

You can implement this script into the Jupyter notebook. The final line needs to be there if you are using the Jupyter notebook, but if you are using Spyder, you can remove the last line, because it will go through and do this part without your help.

Importing the dataset

Once the libraries have been imported using the code above, the next step is to import the data sets that you want to use for this training algorithm. Let's assume that we have a dataset containing the price of a certain number of cars. The file is "car_price.csv" and it is stored in our laptop in D:\Datasets. We can execute the following script to read the data and store them in the carriable car_data:

```
car_data = pd.read_csv('D:\Datasets\car_price.csv')
```

Analyzing the data

Before we start to use the data to effectively build a Machine Learning algorithm, it is always good to give a closer look to them and check if any value is missing. To start, the head function is going to return the first five rows of the data set. You can use the following script to help make this one work:

```
car_data.head()
```

Also, the described function can be used to return all the statistical details of the dataset.

```
car_data.describe ()
```

Let's now see if the linear regression algorithm is suitable for this kind of task. We are going to take the data points and plot them on a graph. This will help us to see if there is a relationship between the year and the price. To see if this will work out, use the following script:

```
plt.scatter(car_data['Year'], car_data['Price'])
plt.title("Year vs Price")
plt.xlabel("Year")
plt.ylabel("Price")
plt.show()
```

When we use the above script, we are developing a scatterplot from the Matplotlib library. This is useful because this scatter plot is going to have the year on the x-axis and the price on the y-axis. From the figure for the output, we can see that when there is an increase in the year, the price of the car goes up as well. This shows us the linear relationship that is present between the year and the price. This is a good way to see how this kind of algorithm can be used to solve this problem.

Going back to data pre-processing

Now we need to use this information and put it to work for us. To divide the data into features and labels, you will need to use the script below:

```
features = car_data.iloc[:,0:1].values
labels = car_data.iloc[:,1].values
```

244

Since we only have two columns here, the 0th column will contain the feature set and the first column will contain the labels. We will then be able to divide up the data so that 20 percent goes to the test set and 80 percent to the training. Use the following scripts to help you get this done:

```
from sklearn.model_selection import train_test_split
train_features, test_features, train_labels
test_labels = train_test_split (features, labels,
test_size = 0.2, random_state = 0)
```

From here, we can go back and look at the dataset again. It is easy to see that there will not be a huge difference between the values of the years and the values of the prices. Both of these will end up being in the thousands each. What this means is that you don't need to do any scaling, because you can just use the data as you have it. This will save you some time and effort in the long run.

How to train the algorithm and get it to make predictions

Now it is time to do a bit of training with the algorithm and ensure that it can make the right predictions for you. This is where the LinearRegression class will be helpful, because it has all of the labels and other training features that you need to input and train your models.

This is simple to do, and you just need to work with the script below to help you to get started:

```
from sklearn.linear_model import LinearRegresison
lin_reg = LinearRegression()
lin_reg.fit (train_features, train_labels)
```

Using the same example of the car prices and the years from before, we are going to look and see what the coefficient is for only the independent variable. We need to use the following script to help us do that:

```
print(lin_reg.coef_)
```

The result of this process is going to be 204.815. This shows that for each unit change in year, the car price is going to increase by 204.815 (at least in this example).

Once you have taken the time to train this model, the final step is to predict the new instance you are going to work with. The prediction

245

method is going to take the test features that you choose and add them in as the input; then it can predict the output that would correspond with the input best. The script that you can use to make this happen will be the following:

```
predictions = lin_reg.predict( test_features)
```

When you use this script, you will find that it yields a good prediction of what we expect to see in the future. We can guess how much a car is going to be worth based on the year it is produced in the future, going off the information that we have right now. There may be some things that change in the future, and the features that come with the car will be relevant as well. But this is a good way to get an overview and an average of what they cost each year, thus telling us how much they will cost in the future.

So, let's see how this would work. We now want to look at this linear regression and figure out how much a car is going to cost us in the year 2025. Maybe you would like to save up for a vehicle, so you want to estimate how much it is going to cost you by the time you save that money. You would be able to use the information that we have and add in the new year that you want it based on, then figure out an average value for a new car that year.

Of course, remember that this is not going to be 100 percent accurate. Inflation could change prices, the manufacturer may change some things up, and so on. Sometimes the price is going to be lower, and sometimes it will be higher. But this at least gives you a good way to predict the price of the vehicle given the data that you have to determine how much it is going to cost you in the future.

7. Neural Networks

This chapter discusses the integral aspects of Artificial and Convolutional Neural Networks. It also covers their components, in particular the activation functions and how to train an artificial neural network, as well as the different advantages of using an artificial neural network.

Definition of Artificial Neural Network

The employment of Artificial Neural Networks is a widely used approach in Machine Learning. It is inspired by the brain system of humans. The objective of Neural Networks is to replicate how the human brain learns. The neural network system is an ensemble of input and output layers and a hidden layer that transforms the input layer into useful information to the output layer. Usually, several hidden layers are implemented in an artificial neural network. The figure below presents an example of a neural network system composed of 2 hidden layers:

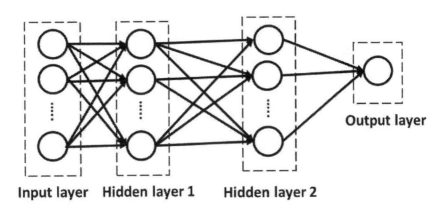

Input layer   Hidden layer 1   Hidden layer 2   Output layer

Example of an artificial neural network

Before going further and explaining how Neural Networks work, let's first define what a neuron is. A neuron is simply a mathematical equation expressed as the sum of the weighted inputs. Let's consider
$X = \{x_1, x_2, \dots, x_M\}$, a vector of M inputs. Then the neuron is a linear combination of all inputs defined as follows:

$$F(X = \{x_1, x_2, \dots, x_M\}) = w_1 x_1 + w_2 x_2 + \dots + w_M x_M,$$

where $w_1, w_2, \ldots, w_M$ are the weights assigned to each input. The function F can also be represented as:

$$F(X) = WX$$

Where W is a weight matrix and X a vector of data. The second formulation is very convenient when programming a neural network model. The weights are determined during the training procedure. Training an artificial neural network means finding the optimal weights W that provide the most accurate output.

To each neuron, an activation function is applied and the results weighted by the sum of inputs X. The role of the activation function is deciding whether the neuron should be activated or not according to the model's prediction. This process is applied to each layer of the network. In the following sub-sections, we will discuss in detail the role and types of activation functions as well as the different types of Neural Networks.

What is an activation function and what is its role in neural network models?

Activation functions are formulated as mathematical functions. These functions are a crucial component of an artificial neural network model. For each neuron, an activation function is associated. The activation function decides whether to activate the neuron or not. For instance, let's consider the output from a neuron, which is:

$$Y = \sum weight \times input + bias$$

The output Y can take any value. The neuron does not have any information on the reasonable range of values that Y can take. For this purpose, the activation function is implemented in the neural network to check Y values and make a decision on whether the neural connections should consider this neuron activated or not.

There are different types of activation functions. The most instinctive function is the step function. This function sets a threshold and decides to activate or not activate a neuron if it exceeds a certain threshold. In other words, the output of this function is 1 if Y is greater than a threshold and 0 otherwise. Formally, the activation function is:

$$F = \begin{cases} 1, & if\ Y > threshold \\ 0, & otherwise \end{cases}$$

where 1 means 'activated' and 0 means 'not-activated'.

This activation function can be used for a classification problem where the output should be yes or no (i.e., 1 or 0). However, it has some drawbacks. For example, let's consider a set of several categories (i.e., class1, class2, ..., etc.) to which input may belong. If this activation function is used and more than one neuron is activated, the output will be 1 for all neurons. In this case, it is hard to distinguish between the classes and decide into which class the input belongs, because all neuron outputs are 1. In short, the step function does not support multiple output values nor classification into several classes.

The linear activation function, unlike the step function, provides a range of activation values. It computes an output that is proportional to the input. Formally:

$$F(X) = WX,$$

where X is the input.

This function supports several outputs rather than just 1 or 0 values. This function, because it is linear, does not support backpropagation for model training. Backpropagation is a process that relies on function derivatives or gradients to update its parameters, and in particular, the weights. The derivative (i.e., gradient) of the linear activation function is a constant which is equal to W and is not related to changes in the input X. Therefore, it does not provide information on which weights applied to the input can give accurate predictions.

Moreover, all layers can be reduced to one layer when using the linear function. The fact that all layers are using a linear function means that the final layer is a linear function of the first layer. So, no matter how many layers are used in the neural network, they are equivalent to the first layer, and there is no point in using multiple layers for a linear function. A neural network with multiple layers connected with a linear activation function is just a linear regression model that cannot support the complexity of input data.

The majority of Neural Networks use non-linear activation functions because, in the majority of real-world applications, relations between the output and the input features are non-linear. These non-linear functions allow the neural network to map complex patterns among inputs and the outputs. They also allow the neural network to learn the complex process that governs complex data or high dimension data such as images and audio, among others. Non-linear functions allow us to overcome the drawbacks of linear functions and step functions. They support backpropagation (i.e., the derivative is not a constant and depends on the changes to the input) and stacking of several layers (i.e., the combination of non-linear functions is non-linear). Several non-linear functions exist and can be used within a neural network. In this book, we are going to cover the most commonly used non-linear activation functions in Machine Learning applications.

The sigmoid function

The sigmoid function is one of the most used activation functions within artificial neural networks. Formally, a sigmoid function is equal to the inverse of the sum of 1 and the negative exponential of inputs:

$$F(X) = \frac{1}{1 + \exp{(-X)}}$$

Outputs of a sigmoid function are bounded by 0 and 1. More precisely, the outputs take any value between 0 and 1 and provide clear predictions. In fact, when X is greater than 2 or lower than -2, the value of Y is close to the edge of the curve (i.e., closer to 0 or 1).

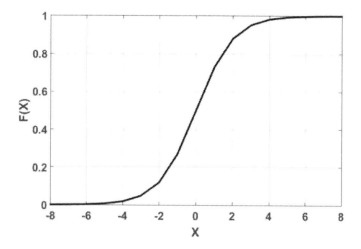

The disadvantage of this activation function, as we can see from the figure above, is that it only yields a small change in the output for input values under -4 and above 4. This problem is called 'vanishing gradient,' which means that the gradient is very small on horizontal extremes of the curve. This makes a neural network using the sigmoid function learn very slowly as it approaches the edges, becoming computationally expensive.

The tanh function

The tanh function is another activation function similar to the sigmoid function. The mathematical formulation of this function is:

$$F(X) = \tanh(X) = \frac{2}{1 + \exp(-2X)} - 1$$

This function is a scaled sigmoid function. Therefore, it has the same characteristics as the sigmoid function. However, the outputs of this function range between -1 and 1, and the gradients are more pronounced than those of the sigmoid function. Unlike the sigmoid function, the tanh function is zero-centered, which makes it very useful for inputs with negative, neutral, and positive values. The drawback of this function, as with the sigmoid function, is the vanishing gradient issue and computational expense.

The ReLu function

The Rectified Linear Unit function, or what is known as the ReLu function, is also a widely used activation function. This function is computationally efficient and allows the neural network to converge quickly compared to the sigmoid and tanh function because it uses simple mathematical formulations. ReLu returns X as output if X is positive or 0 otherwise. Formally, this activation function is formulated as

$$F(X) = \max(0, X)$$

This activation function is not bounded and takes values from 0 to +inf. Although it has a similar shape as a linear function (i.e., this function is equal to identity for positive values), the ReLu function has a derivative. The drawback of the ReLu is that the derivative (i.e., the gradient) is 0 when the inputs are negative. This means that, as with the linear functions, backpropagation cannot be processed, and the neural network cannot learn unless the inputs are greater than 0. This aspect of the ReLu, gradient equal to 0 when the inputs are negative, is called the dying ReLu problem.

To prevent the dying ReLu problem, two ReLu variations can be used, namely the Leaky ReLu function and the Parametric ReLu function. The Leakey ReLu function returns as output the maximum of X and X by 0.1. In other words, the leaky ReLu is equal to the identity function when X is greater than 0 and is equal to the product of 0.1 and X when X is less than zero. This function is provided as follows:

$$F(X) = \max(0.1X, X)$$

This function has a small positive gradient equal to 0.1 when X has negative values, which makes this function support backpropagation for negative values. However, it may not provide a consistent prediction for these negative values.

The parametric ReLu function is similar to the Leaky ReLu function, which takes the gradient as a parameter of the neural network to define the output when X is negative. The mathematical formulation of this function is as follows:

$$F(X) = \max(aX, X)$$

There are other variations of the ReLu function such as the exponential linear ReLu. This function, unlike the other variations of the ReLu such as the Leaky ReLu and parametric ReLu, has a log curve for negative values of X instead linear. The downside of this function is that it saturates for large negative values of X. Other variations exist which all rely on the same concept of defining a gradient greater than 0 when X has negative values.

The Softmax function

The Softmax function is another type of activation function used in a different manner than the ones presented previously. This function is usually applied only to the output layer when a classification of the inputs into several different classes is needed. In fact, the Softmax function supports several classes and provides the probability of an input belonging to a specific class. It normalizes outputs of every category between 0 and 1 then divides by their sum to provide that probability.

Given all these activation functions, where each one has its pros and cons, the question now is: which one should be used in a neural network? The answer is that simply having a better understanding of the problem at hand will help guide us into a specific activation function, especially if the characteristics of the function being approximated are known beforehand. For instance, a sigmoid function is a good choice for a classification problem. In the case that the nature of the function being approximated is unknown, it is highly recommended to start with a ReLu function rather than trying other activation functions. Overall, the ReLu function works well for a wide range of applications. This is an ongoing research area, and you may try your own activation functions as you see fit.

An important aspect of choosing an activation function is the sparsity of the activation. Sparsity means that not all neurons are activated. This is a desired characteristic in a neural network, because it makes the network learn faster and ensures it is less prone to overfitting. Let's imagine a large neural network with multiple neurons if all neurons were activated; this would mean all these neurons were processed to describe the final output. This makes the neural network very dense and computationally exhaustive to carry out. The sigmoid and the tanh activation functions have this property of activating almost all neurons, which makes them computationally inefficient, unlike the ReLu function and its variations, which cause the inactivation of some negative values. That is the reason why it is recommended that you start with the ReLu function when approximating a function with unknown characteristics.

What are the types of Artificial Neural Networks?

Several categories of artificial Neural Networks with different properties and complexities exist. The first and simplest neural network developed is the perceptron. The perceptron computes the sum of the inputs, applies an activation function, and provides the result to the output layer.

Another old and simple approach is the feedforward neural network. This type of artificial neural network has only one single layer. It is a category that is fully connected to the following layer, where each node is attached to the others. It propagates the information in one direction from the inputs to the outputs through the hidden layer. This process is known as the front propagated wave and usually uses what is called the activation function. This activation function processes the data in each node of the layers. This neural network returns a sum of weights via the inputs calculated according to the hidden layer's activation function. The feedforward neural network usually uses the backpropagation method for its training process and the logistic function as an activation function.

Several other Neural Networks are a derivation of this type of network. For example, the radial-basis-function Neural Network. This is a feedforward neural network that depends on the radial basis function instead of the logistic function. This type of neural network has two layers, wherein the inner layer, the features, and a radial basis function are combined. The radial function computes the distance of each point to the relative center. This neural network is useful for continuous values to evaluate their distance from the target value.

In contrast, the logistic function is used for mapping arbitrary binary values (i.e., 0 or 1; yes or no). Deep feedforward Neural Networks are a multilayer feedforward neural network. They have become the most commonly used neural network types in Machine Learning, as they often yield better results. A new type of learning called Deep Learning has emerged from these types of Neural Networks.

Recurrent Neural Networks are another category that uses a different type of nodes. Like a feedforward neural network, each hidden layer processes its information to the next layer. However, outputs of the hidden layers are saved and processed back to the previous layer. The first layer, comprised of the input layer, is processed as the product of the sum of the weighted features. The recurrent process is applied in hidden layers. At each step, every node will save information from the previous step. It uses memory while the computation is running. In short, the recurrent neural network uses forward propagation and backpropagation to self-learn from the previous time steps to improve its predictions. In other words, information is processed in two directions, unlike with feedforward Neural Networks.

A multilayer perceptron, or multilayer neural network, is a neural network that has at least three or more layers. This category of networks is fully connected, meaning every node is attached to all other nodes in the following layers.

Convolutional Neural Networks are typically useful for image classification or recognition. The processing used by this type of artificial neural network is designed to deal with pixel data. Convolutional Neural Networks are a multi-layer network based on convolutions, which apply filters for neuron activation. When the same filter is applied to a neuron, it leads to an activation of the same feature and results in what is called a feature map. The feature map reflects the strength and importance of a feature of input data.

Modular Neural Networks are formed from more than one connected neural network. These networks rely on the concept of 'divide and conquer.' They are handy for very complex problems because they allow different types of Neural Networks to be combined. Therefore, they allow for a combining of the strengths of different neural networks to solve a complex problem where each neural network can handle a specific task.

How to train an Artificial Neural Network

As explained at the beginning of this chapter, Neural Networks compute a weighted sum of inputs and apply an activation function at each layer. Then they provide the final result to the output layer. This procedure is commonly named *forward propagation*. To train these Artificial Neural Networks, weights need to be optimized to obtain the weights that produce the most accurate outputs. The process of training an artificial neural network is as follows:

1. Initialize the weights
2. Apply the forward propagation process
3. Evaluate the neural network performance
4. Apply the backward propagation process
5. Update the weights
6. Repeat the steps from step 2 until it attains a maximum number of iterations, or neural network performance does not improve.

As we can see from the steps above, we need a performance measure that describes how accurate the neural network is. This function is called the loss function or cost function. This function can be the same as the cost function we presented in the previous chapter:

$$J = \frac{1}{N} \sum \left(y_{predicted} - y_{target} \right)^2$$

Where N is the number of outputs, $y_{predicted}$ is the output, and y_{target} is the true value of the output. This function provides the error of the neural network. Small values of J reflect a high accuracy for the neural network.

So far, we have defined loss functions and how the neural network works in general. Now, let's go into the details for each step of the training process.

Let's consider a set of inputs X and outputs Y. We initialize W (i.e., weights) and B (i.e., bias) as a null matrix. The next step is to apply feed-forward propagation, which consists of feeding each layer of the artificial neural network with the sum of the weights of the inputs and the bias.

Let's consider that we have two layers. We can calculate the first hidden layer's output using the following equation:

$$Z_1 = W_1 X + b_1$$

Where W1 and b1 are the parameters of the neural network corresponding to the weights and bias of the first layer, respectively.

Next, we apply the activation function F1, which can be any activation from the functions presented previously in this chapter:

$$A_1 = F_1(Z_1)$$

The result is the output of the first layer, which is then fed to the next layer as:

$$Z_2 = W_2 A_1 + b_2$$

Where W2 and b2 are again the weights and bias of the second layer, respectively.

To this result, we apply an activation function F2:

$$A_2 = F_2(Z_2)$$

Now A2 is supposed to be the output of the two-layer artificial neural network. The activation function F1 and F2 might be the same activation function or different activation functions depending on the dataset and the expected output.

After the feedforward propagation, we compare the neural network output against the target output with the loss function. It is highly likely that the difference between the estimated output and the actual values at this stage will be very high. Therefore, we have to adjust the weights through the backpropagation process. We calculate the gradient of each activation function concerning biases and weights. We start by evaluating the derivative of the last layer, then the layer before this layer, and so on until the input layer. Then we update the weights according to the gradient or the derivative of the activation function. Applying these steps to our example of a two-layer neural network yields:

$$W_2 = W_2 - \alpha \frac{d}{dW} F_2(W, b) \qquad b_2 = b_2 - \alpha \frac{d}{db} F_2(W, b)$$

$$W_1 = W_1 - \alpha \frac{d}{dW} F_2(W, b) \qquad b_1 = b_1 - \alpha \frac{d}{db} F_2(W, b)$$

The parameter α is the learning rate parameter. This parameter determines the rate at which the weights are updated. The process that we just described here is called the gradient descent algorithm. The process is repeated until it attains a pre-fixed maximum number of iterations. We will later develop an example to illustrate a perceptron and multi-layer neural network by following similar steps using Python. We will also develop a classifier based on an artificial neural network. For now, let's explore the pros of using an artificial neural network for Machine Learning applications.

Artificial Neural Network: pros and cons

Nowadays, Artificial Neural Networks are applied in almost every domain. Research in this domain is very active, and several Neural Networks have emerged to take advantage of the full potential of this Artificial Intelligence approach. Artificial Neural Networks have several advantages.

Artificial Neural Networks are able to map structures and learn from data faster. They are also able to map the complex structure and connections that relate the outputs to the input datasets, which is the case in many real-life applications. Once an artificial neural network is developed and trained, it can be generalized. In other words, it can be applied to map relationships among data that it has not been exposed to and make predictions for new datasets. Moreover, the artificial neural network does not make any assumptions about the structure or the distribution of the input data. It does not impose specific conditions on the data or assumptions on the relationships in the data, unlike traditional statistical methods. The fact that artificial Neural Networks can handle a large amount of data makes them an appealing tool. Artificial Neural Networks are a non-parametric approach that allow for the development of a model with a reduced error through estimation of the parameters. Although these are appealing characteristics of artificial Neural Networks, they do suffer from some drawbacks.

The downside of Artificial Neural Networks is that they often operate as a black box. This means that we cannot fully understand the relationships among the inputs and outputs and the interdependence between specific input variables and the output. In other words, we cannot detect how much each input variable impacts the output. The training process can be computationally inefficient. We can overcome this problem by using parallel computing and taking advantage of the computational power available to us with proper coding.

Convolutional Neural Networks

Convolutional Neural Networks (CNNs) are one of the main categories of deep Neural Networks that have proven to be very effective in numerous computer science areas including object recognition, object classification, and computer vision. ConvNets have been used for many years to distinguish faces, identify objects, power vision in self-driving cars, and steer robots.

A ConvNet can easily recognize countless images and scenes as well as suggest relevant captions. ConvNets are also able to identify everyday objects, animals, or humans as well. Lately, Convolutional Neural Networks have also been used effectively in Natural Language Processing problems like sentence classification.

Therefore, Convolutional Neural Networks are one of the most important tools for machine learning and Deep Learning tasks. LeNet was the very first Convolutional Neural Network introduced that helped significantly propel the overall field of Deep Learning. This very first Convolutional Neural Network was proposed by Yann LeCun back in 1988. It was primarily used for character recognition problems such as reading digits and codes.

Convolutional Neural Networks that are regularly used today for innumerable computer science tasks are very similar to this first Convolutional Neural Network proposed back in 1988.

Just like today's Convolutional Neural Networks, LeNet was used for many character recognition tasks. Just like in LeNet, the standard Convolutional Neural Networks we use today come with four main operations, including convolution, ReLU non-linearity activation functions, sub-sampling or pooling, and classification of their fully-connected layers.

These operations are the fundamental steps of building every Convolutional Neural Network. To move on to dealing with Convolutional Neural Networks in Python, we must get deeper into these four basic functions for a better understanding of the intuition lying behind Convolutional Neural Networks.

As you know, every image can be easily represented as a matrix containing multiple values. We are going to use a conventional term, channel, where we are referring to a specific component of images. An image derived from a standard camera commonly has three channels, including blue, red, and green. You can imagine these as three2D matrices that are stacked over each other. Each of these matrices also comes with certain pixel values in the specific range from 0 to 255.

On the other hand, if you have a grayscale image, you only get one channel, as there are no colors present, just black and white. In our case here, we are going to consider grayscale images, so the example we are studying is just a single-2D matrix that represents a grayscale image. The value of each pixel contained in the matrix must range from 0 to 255. In this case, 0 indicates a color of black, while 255 indicates a color of white.

How Convolutional Neural Networks Work

A Convolutional Neural Network structure is normally used for a variety of Deep Learning problems. As already mentioned, Convolutional Neural Networks are used for object recognition, object segmentation, detection, and computer vision due to their structure. CNNs learn directly from image data, so there is no need to perform manual feature extraction, which is commonly required in regular deep Neural Networks.

The use of CNNs has become popular due to three main factors. The first is the structure of CNNs, which eliminates the need for performing manual data extraction, as all data features are learned directly by the Convolutional Neural Networks. The second reason for the increasing popularity of CNNs is that they produce amazing, state-of-the-art object recognition results. The third reason is that CNNs can be easily retained for many new object recognition tasks to help build other deep Neural Networks.

A CNN can contain hundreds of layers, each of which learns automatically to detect many different features of image data. In addition, filters are commonly applied to every training image at different resolutions, so the output of every convolved image is used as the input to the following convolutional layer.

The filters can also start with very simple image features like edges and brightness, so they can commonly increase the complexity of those image features, which define the object as the convolutional layers progress.

Therefore, filters are commonly applied to every training image at different resolutions with the output of every convolved image acting as the input to the following convolutional layer.

Convolutional Neural Networks can be trained on hundreds, thousands, and millions of images.

When you are working with large amounts of image data and with very complex network structures, you should use GPUs that can significantly improve the processing time required for training a neural network model.

Once you train your Convolutional Neural Network model, you can use it in real-time applications like object recognition, pedestrian detection in ADAS (Advanced Driver Assistance Systems), and many others.

The last fully-connected layer in regular deep Neural Networks is called the output layer, and in every classification setting, this output layer represents the overall class score.

Due to these properties, regular deep neural nets are not capable of scaling to full images. For instance, in CIFAR-10, all images are sized as 32x32x3. This means that all CIFAR-10 images have 3 color channels and are 32 inches wide and 32 inches high. This means that a single fully-connected neural network in a first regular neural net would have 32x32x3 or 3071 weights. This is not effectively manageable, as those fully-connected structures are not capable of scaling to larger images.

In addition, you would want to have more similar neurons to quickly add up more parameters. However, in this case of computer vision and other similar problems, using fully-connected neurons is wasteful, as your parameters will lead to over-fitting of your model very quickly. Therefore, Convolutional Neural Networks take advantage of the fact that their inputs consist of images to solve these kinds of Deep Learning problems.

Due to their structure, Convolutional Neural Networks constrain the architecture of images in a much more sensible way. Unlike a regular deep neural network, the layers contained in the Convolutional Neural Network are comprised of neurons that are arranged in three dimensions including, depth, height, and width. For instance, the CIFAR-10 input images are part of the input volume of all layers contained in a deep neural network and the volume comes with dimensions of 32x32x3.

The neurons in these layers can be connected to only a small area of the layer before it, instead of all the layers being fully-connected like in regular deep Neural Networks. In addition, the output of the final layers for CIFAR-10 would come with dimensions of 1x1x10, as the end of the Convolutional Neural Network architecture would have reduced the full image into a vector of class scores, arranging it just along the depth dimension.

To summarize, unlike the regular-three-layer deep Neural Networks, a ConvNet composes all its neurons in just three dimensions. In addition, each layer contained in a Convolutional Neural Network transforms the 3D input volume into a 3D output volume containing various neuron activations.

A Convolutional Neural Network contains layers that all have a simple API resulting in 3D output volume that comes with a differentiable function that may or may not contain neural network parameters.

A Convolutional Neural Network is composed of several subsamples and convolutional layers that are followed by fully-connected or dense layers. As you already know, the input of a Convolutional Neural Network is an n x n x r image where n represents the height and width of an input image whereas r is the total number of channels present. The Convolutional Neural Networks may also contain k filters known as kernels. When kernels are present, they are determined as q, which can be the same as the number of channels.

Each Convolutional Neural Network map is subsampled with max or mean pooling over a p x p contiguous area in which p commonly ranges between 2 for small images and more than 5 for larger images. Either before or after the subsampling layer, a sigmoidal non-linearity and additive bias are applied to every feature map. After these convolutional neural layers, there may be several fully-connected layers and the structure of these fully-connected layers is the same as the structure of standard multilayer Neural Networks.

Stride and Padding

Secondly, after specifying the depth, you also must specify the stride that you slide over the filter. When you have a stride of one, you must move one pixel at a time. When you have a stride of two, you can move two pixels at a time, but this produces smaller volumes of output spatially. By default, the stride value is one. However, you can have bigger strides in the case when you want to come across less overlap between your receptive fields, but as already mentioned, this will result in having smaller feature maps as you are skipping over image locations.

In a case when you use bigger strides, but you want to maintain the same dimensionality, you must use padding that surrounds your input with zeros. You can either pad with values on the edge or with zeros. Once you get the dimensionality of your feature map to match your input, you can move onto adding pooling layers for padding, which is commonly used in Convolutional Neural Networks when you want to preserve the size of your feature maps.

If you do not use padding, your feature maps will shrink at every layer. Adding padding is therefore at times very convenient, so you'll want to pad your input volume just with zeros all around the border.

This is called zero-padding, which is a hyperparameter. By using zero-padding, you can control the size of your output volumes.

You can easily compute the spatial size of your output volume as a simple function of your input volume size, the convolution layers receptive field size, the stride you applied, and the amount of zero-padding you used in your Convolutional Neural Network border.

For instance, if you have a 7x7 input and a 3x3 filter with stride 1 and pad 0, you will get a 5x5 output following the formula. If you have stride two, you will get a 3x3 output volume, and so on using the formula as follows, in which W represents the size of your input volume, F represents the receptive field size of your convolutional neural layers, S represents the stride applied, and P represents the amount of zero-padding you used:

$$(W-F+2P)/S+1$$

Using this formula, you can easily calculate how many neurons can fit in your Convolutional Neural Network. Consider using zero-padding whenever you can. For instance, if you have equal input and output dimensions, say five, you can use a zero-padding of one to get three receptive fields.

If you do not use zero-padding in cases like this, you will get your output volume with a spatial dimension of 3, as 3 is the number of neurons that can fit into your original input.

Spatial arrangement hypermeters commonly have mutual constraints. For instance, if you have an input size of 10 with no zero-padding used and a filter size of three, it is impossible to apply stride. Therefore, you will see that the set of your hyperparameter is invalid and your Convolutional Neural Network library will throw an exception or zero pad to the rest to make it fit.

Fortunately, sizing the convolutional layers properly, so that all dimensions included work using zero-padding, can make any job easier.

Parameter Sharing

You can use parameter sharing schemes in your convolutional layers to entirely control the number of parameters used. If you denoted a single two-dimensional slice as your depth slice, you could then constrain the neurons contained in every depth slice to use the same bias and weights. Using parameter sharing techniques, you will get a unique collection of weights, one from every depth slice. Therefore, you can significantly reduce the number of parameters contained in the first layer of your ConvNet. Doing this step, all neurons in every depth slice of your ConvNet will use the same parameters.

In other words, during backpropagation, every neuron contained in the volume will automatically compute the gradient for all its weights.

However, these computed gradients will add up over every depth slice, so you get to update just a single collection of weights per depth slice. In this way, all neurons contained in one depth slice will use the same weight vector. Therefore, when you pass forward the convolutional layers in every depth slice, it is computed as a convolution of all neurons' weights alongside the input volume. This is the reason why we refer to the collection of weights we get as a kernel or a filter, which is convolved with your input.

However, there are a few cases in which this parameter sharing assumption does not make any sense. This is commonly the case with many input images to a convolutional layer with a certain centered structure, where you must learn different features depending on your location.

For instance, when you have an input of several faces, which have been centered in your image, you probably expect to get different hair-specific or eye-specific features that could easily be learned at many spatial locations. When this is the case, it is very common to just relax this parameter sharing scheme and simply use a locally-connected layer.

Matrix Multiplication

The convolution operation commonly performs the dot products between the local regions of the input and between the filters. In these cases, a common implementation technique of the convolutional layers is to take full advantage of this and formulate the specific forward pass of the main convolutional layer representing it as one large matrix multiplication.

Implementation of matrix multiplication is when the local areas of an input image are completely stretched out into different columns during an operation known as im2col. For instance, if you have an input of size 227x227x3 and you convolve it with a filter of size 11x11x3 at a stride of 4, you must take blocks of pixels at size 11x11x3 in the input and stretch every block into a column vector of size 363.

However, when you iterate this process with your input stride of 4, you get 55 locations along with weights and heights that lead to an output matrix of x columns, in which every column is a maximally stretched out receptive field with 3025 fields in total.

Each number in your input volume can be duplicated across multiple distinct columns. Also, remember that the weights of the convolutional layers are very similarly stretched out into certain rows as well. For instance, if you have 95 filters with a size of 11x11x3, you will get a matrix of w rows of size 96x363.

The result you get from your convolution will be equal to performing one huge matrix multiplication that evaluates the dot products between every receptive field and between every filter, resulting in the output of your dot product of every filter at every location. Once you get your result, you must reshape it back to the correct output dimension, which in this case is 55x55x96.

This is a great approach, but it has a downside. The main downside is that it uses a lot of memory, as the values contained in your input volume will be replicated several times. However, the main benefit of matrix multiplication is that many implementations can improve your model. In addition, this im2col approach can be re-used many times when you are performing a pooling operation.

Conclusion

Thanks for reading to the end!

Machine Learning with Python may be the answer that you are looking for in your latest project, Data Analysis task, or related endeavor. It is a simple approach that can teach your machine how to learn on its own, similar to what the human mind can do, but much faster and more efficiently. It has been a game-changer in many industries, and this guidebook's aim has been to show you the exact steps that you can take to put it into action.

There is just so much that a programmer can do when it comes to using Machine Learning in their code, and when you add this together with the Python coding language, you can take things even further, even as a beginner.

The next step is to start putting some of the knowledge that we discussed in this guidebook to good use. There are a lot of great things that you can do when it comes to Machine Learning, and in Python, there is nothing that we can't train our machine or our computer to do.

This guidebook has explored a lot of the different concepts related to Python Machine Learning. We looked at what Machine Learning is all about, how to work with it, and even did a crash course on using the Python language for the first time. Once that was done, we moved right into combining the two of these to work with a variety of Python libraries to get our projects moving.

If you have ever wanted to learn how to work with the Python coding language, or you want to see what Machine Learning can do for you, then this guidebook is the ultimate tool! Come back and read through it for reference to see just how powerful Python Machine Learning can be for you.

Python
Data Science

Introduction

When it comes to the locations and sources where a business can collect data, there are quite a few options that are open to the business. Many businesses will hire data scientists to help them collect information from sources like social media, sensors, digital videos, and pictures, purchased transactions that they get from their customers and even from surveys that the customers may have taken.

Because there are so many sources that the company can focus on when it comes to getting the information they want, it won't take much research before the company becomes flooded with all of the presented data. There is just so much data available, which is great, but we have to make sure that we know the right steps to handle the info and to learn what is there, rather than just collecting the information and calling it good.

The analysis that you will do on all of that data that comes in is a big part of Data Science. All this helps us to bring together a lot of professional skills to handle that info and put it to good use. Yes, it is going to include searching for the info, so it is a good idea to not forget it or skip over this part, but it can come in and help with understanding the info as well. To get all of this done, we need to have a few skills come together, either in one person or within the team, to make Data Science useful. Some of the things that Data Science, and the info we collect, will be able to help us out with will include.

- Reducing the number of costs that the business has to deal with.
- Helping to launch a brand-new service or product and knowing it will do well.
- To help gauge the effectiveness that we see in a new marketing campaign.
- To help tap into some different demographics along the way.
- To ensure that we can get into a new market and see success.

Of course, this is not an extensive list that we can look at, and knowing the right steps and all of the benefits that come with working in Data Science can help us to see some improvements and can make the business grow. No matter what items or services you sell, what your geographic location is, or what industry you are in, you can use Data Science to help your business become more successful.

Sometimes, it is hard for companies to see how they can use Data Science to help improve themselves. We may assume that this is just a bunch of hype, or that only a few companies have been able to see success with it. However, there are a ton of companies that can use this kind of information to get themselves ahead, including some of the big names like Amazon, Visa, and Google. While your business may or may not be on the same level as those three, it is still possible for you to put Data Science to work for your needs, improving what you can offer on the market, how you can help customers out, and so much more.

It is important to note that Data Science is a field that is already taking over the world, and it is helping companies in many different areas. For example, it is showing companies the best way to grow, how to reach their customers correctly and most efficiently, how to find new sources of value, and so much more. It often depends on the overall goal of the company for using this process of Data Science to determine what they will get out of it.

With all of the benefits that come with using this process of Data Science, and all of the big-name companies who are jumping on board and trying to gain some of the knowledge and benefits as well, we need to take a look at the life cycle that comes with Data Science, and the steps that it takes to make this project a big success. Let's dive into some of the things that we need to know about the data life cycle, so we know the basics of what needs to happen to see success with Data Science.

Data discovery

The first step that we are going to see with this life cycle is the idea that companies need to get out there and discover the info they want to use. This is the phase where we will search in a lot of different sources in order to discover the data that we need. Sometimes the data is going to be structured, such as in text format but other times it may come in a more unstructured format like videos and images. There are even some times when the data we find comes to us as a relational database system instead.

These are going to be considered some of the more traditional ways that you can collect the info that you need, but it is also possible for an organization to explore some different options as well. For example, many companies are relying on social media to help them reach their customers and to gain a better understanding of the mindset and buying decisions of these customers through this option.

Often this phase is going to include us starting with a big question that we would like answered, and then searching either for the data in the first place or if we already have the data, searching through the info that we have already collected. This makes it easier for us to get through all of that data and gain the insights that we are looking for.

Getting the data prepared

After we spend some time going through all of the different sources to find the information that we need, it is time to look at how we can use data, and data preparation will help out with this. There are a few steps that happen in this phase; basically we are going to do things like converting the information from all of those different sources into one common format so that they work together, and an algorithm that we pick out later will be able to handle the data without errors or mistakes.

This process is going to be more involved, but it is where the data scientist will start collecting clean subsets of data and then will insert the defaults and the parameters that are needed for you. In some cases, the methods that you use will be more complex, like identifying some of the values that are missing out of that data, and more.

Another step that needs to happen while you are here is to clean off the data. This is so important when you collect the data from more than one source because it ensures that it's the same and that the algorithm you pick will be able to read it all later. You also want to make sure that there isn't any information missing, that the duplicate values are gone, and there is nothing else found within the set of data you want to work with that will decrease the accuracy of the model that you are trying to make.

After you go through and clean off the data you would like to use, the next step is to do the integration and then create our conclusion based on the set of data for the analysis. This analysis is going to involve taking the data and then merging two or more tables that have the same objects, but different information. It can also include the process of aggregation, which is when we summarize the different fields found in the table as we go through the process.

During this whole process, the goal is for us to explore and then come up with an understanding of the patterns, as well as the values, that are going to show up in the data set that we are working with. This can take some time and some patience, but it is going to ensure that any mathematical models we work with later make sense and work the way that we want.

Mathematical models

When working with Data Science, all of the projects that you will want to work with will need to use mathematical models to help them get it all done. These are models that we can plan out ahead of time and then the data scientist is going to build them up to help suit the needs of the business or the question that they would like answered. In some cases, it is possible to work with a few different areas that fall in the world of mathematics, including linear regression, statistics, and logistics, to get these models done.

To get all of this done, we also have to make sure we are using the right tools and methods to make it easier. Some of the computing tools for statistics that come with R can help as well as working with some other advanced analytical tools, SQL, and Python, and any visualization tool that you need to make sure the data makes sense.

Also, we have to make sure that we are getting results that are satisfactory out of all the work and sometimes that means we need to bring in more than one algorithm or model to see the results. In this case, the data scientist has to go through and create a group of models that can work together to go through that info and answer any of the questions that the business has.

After measuring out the models that they would like to use, the data scientist can then revise some of the parameters that are in place, and do the fine-tuning that is needed as they go through the next round of modeling. This process is going to take up a few rounds to complete because you have to test it out more than once to make sure that it's going to work the way that you would like it to.

Putting it all into action

At this point, we have had a chance to prepare the data the way that it needs to be done, and we have been able to build up some of the models that we want to us. With this in mind, it is time to work with the models to get them to provide us with the kinds of results that need to show up. It is possible, depending on the data you have and the model you choose to go with, that there will be a few discrepancies, and you may have to go through a few levels of troubleshooting to deal with the process, but this is normal. Most data scientists have to make some changes to their models as they go through the process before coming up with the solution that is right for them.

Of course, to see how the model is going to play out in the real world, we need to first test out the model. This is the best way to see what will happen when the model is in use, rather than just a theory. You can try out a new algorithm with it as well to see if one type is a better option than any of the others. Sometimes, this is the part where we will decide to put in more than one algorithm to handle our data needs.

The importance of communication

While we are going through this life cycle of data, we need to spend a few moments talking about how important communication can be to the whole process. A good data scientist, or a good team of data scientists, is not going to be just working with the algorithms and the numbers; they are also going to handle the communication that has to go on. There is someone on the business end, such as the marketers and key decision-makers who will need to be able to read through this information, and the data scientist needs to be able to communicate in a manner that is easy to understand.

Communicating what has been found inside of the data, and through the various algorithms used, is going to be one of the important steps that we need to use in the data life cycle. During this stage, the professional is going to be able to talk between the different teams that are present, and they have to be skilled enough to communicate and to share their findings clearly and concisely.

Many different people need to have this kind of information, and not all of them are going to be data scientists or people who can understand some of the technical parts that come into play. The data scientist still has to share this information to make sure that these key decision-makers can understand the information and what insights have been found in the data. The decision-makers can then take that information and use it to decide which direction to take their company.

One thing to keep in mind here though is that a data scientist has to make sure that they are doing this communication in many different ways. Often this can include the written and the spoken word, so get ready to work on some of those public speaking skills and interpersonal skills to get things done.

But the written and the spoken words are not going to be the only places where the data scientist is going to need to know how to communicate. For example, the last part that comes with Data Science and its lifecycle is some kind of visualization of the information and the insights that are found in all that data. These visualizations can take all of the numbers and all of the data, and put it into some kind of image, like a bar chart, a graph, a pie chart or some other method or image.

This is useful because it can take a lot of information and put it into a form that we can just glance at and understand. Instead of having to go through all of the different pieces of information, and reading through all of that data, we can use these images to make it easier to see and understand what is going on, what relationships showed up for each part, and so much more.

The data life cycle is so important to help you understand what is in all of that data that you have collected over time. Companies can collect more data than ever, but they need to know how to take it and turn it into a form that can be used. This is often easier said than done, but by working with the life cycle of data that we talked about previously, you will be able to not only collect all of the data but also put it to good use to make some good business decisions.

1. History of Data Science

The history of Deep Learning can be traced back to 1943, when Warren McCulloch and Walter Pitts published a paper with a concept of Artificial Neuron (AN) to mimic the thought process. This Artificial Neuron was based on the characteristic of a biological neuron of either being fully active to stimulation or none at all. This behavior of biological neuron was observed in microelectrode readings from the brain.

In 1957, Frank and Rosenblatt presented Mark I Perceptron Machine as the first implementation of the perceptron algorithm. The idea was to resemble the working of a biological neuron to create an agent that can learn. This perceptron was a supervised binary linear classifier with adjustable weights. This functionality was implemented through the following function:

$$f(x) = \begin{cases} 1, & wX + B > 0 \\ 0, & otherwise \end{cases}$$

Where w is the weights vector, X is the input and b is the bias.

For each input and output pair, this formula provided classification results given by $f(x)$, the predicted value/output of the function.

In 1960, Widrow and Hoff stacked these perceptrons and built a 3-layered (input layer, hidden layer, output layer), fully connected, feed-forward architecture for classification as a hardware implementation, called ADALINE.

In 1960, Henry J. Kelley introduced a continuous back propagation model, which is currently used in the learning weights of the model. In 1962, a simpler version of backpropagation based on chain rule was introduced by Stuart Dreyfus, but these methods were inefficient. The backpropagation currently used in models was presented in the 1980s.

In 1979, Fukushima designed a multi-layered Convolutional Neural Network architecture, called Neocognitron, that could learn to recognize patterns in images. The network was similar to current day architectures but wasn't exactly the same. It also allowed to manually adjust the weight of certain connections. Many concepts from Neocognitron continue to be used. The layered connections in perceptrons sere useful to develop a variety of Neural Networks. For several patterns present in the data, the Selective Attention Model could distinguish and separate them.

In 1970, Seppo Linnainmaa presented automatic differentiation to efficiently compute the derivative of a differentiable composite function using the chain rule. Its application, later in 1986, led to the backpropagation of errors in multilayer perceptrons. This was when Geoff Hinton, Williams and Rumelhart presented a paper to demonstrate that backpropagation in Neural Networks provides interesting distribution representations. In 1989, Yann LeCun, currently, Director of AI Research Facebook, provided the first practical demonstration of backpropagation in Convolutional Neural Networks to read handwritten digits at Bell Labs.

Even though with backpropagation, deep Neural Networks were not being able to train well.

In 1995, Vapnik and Cortes introduced support vector machines for regression and classification of data. In 1997, Schmidhuber and Hochreiter introduced Long Short Term Memory (LSTM) for recurrent Neural Networks.

In all these years, a major hindering constraint was computed, but in 1999, computers started to become faster at processing data and Graphical Processing Units (GPUs) were introduced. This immensely increased the compute power.

In 2006, Hinton and Salakhutdinov presented a paper that reinvigorated research in Deep Learning. This was the first time when a proper 10-layer Convolutional Neural Network was trained properly. Instead of training 10 layers using backpropagation, they came up with an unsupervised pre-training scheme, called Restricted Boltzmann Machine. This was a 2-step approach for training. In the first step, each layer of the network was trained using an unsupervised objective. In the second step, all the layers were stacked together for backpropagation.

Later in 2009, Fei-Fei Li, a professor at Stanford University launched ImageNet, a large visual database designed for visual object recognition research containing more than 14 million hand-annotated images of 20,000 different object categories. This gave Neural Networks a huge edge as data of this order made it possible to train Neural Networks and achieve good results.

In 2010, Neural Networks got a lot of attention from the research community when Microsoft presented a paper on speech recognition and Neural Networks performed really well compared to other Machine

Learning tools like SVMs and kernels. Specifically, they introduced Neural Networks as a part of the GMM and HMM framework and achieved huge improvements.

In 2012, a paper by Krizhevsky, Sutskever and Hinton showed that huge improvements are achieved through Deep Learning in the visual recognition domain. Their model, AlexNet outperformed all the other traditional computer vision methods in visual recognition tasks and won several international competitions. Since then, the field has exploded and several network architectures and ideas have been introduced like GANs.

2. Working with Python for Data Science

Programming languages help us to expand our theoretical knowledge to something that can happen. Data Science, which usually needs a lot of data to make things happen, will by nature take advantage of programming languages to make the data organize well for further steps of the model development. So, let's start learning about Python for a better understanding of the topic.

Why is Python Important?

To illustrate this problem more vividly, we might assume that we have a small partner named Estella. She just got a job related to Data Science after graduating from the math department. On her first day at work, she was enthusiastic and eager to get in touch with this new industry. But she soon found herself facing a huge difficulty:

The data needed to process the work is not stored in her personal computer, but in remote servers, some in traditional relational databases, and some in Hadoop clusters. Unlike Windows, which is mostly used by personal computers, Linux-like systems are used on remote servers. Estella is not used to this operating system because the familiar graphical interface is missing. All operations, such as the simplest reading of files, need to be programmed by oneself. Therefore, Estella is eager to find a programming language that is simple to write, easy to learn and easy to use.

What is more fatal is that the familiar data modeling software, such as SPSS and MATLAB, cannot be used in the new working environment. However, Estella often uses some basic algorithms provided by this software in her daily work, such as linear regression and logical regression. Therefore, she hopes that the programming language she finds will also have a library of algorithms that can be used easily, and of course, it is better to be free of charge.

The whole process is very similar to Estella's favorite game, table tennis. The assumption is sent to the data as a "ball", and then the adjustment is made according to the "return ball" of the data, and the above actions are repeated. Therefore, Estella added one more item to her request: the programming language can be modified and used at any time without compilation. It is better to have an immediate response command window so that she can quickly verify her ideas. After a search, Estella excitedly told everyone that she had found an IT tool that met all her requirements that is Python.

I hope you have got a good layman's introduction on why programming language is important for Data Science. In the next sections, we will describe the language and its basic functions in detail.

What is Python?

Python is an object-oriented and interpretive computer program language. Its syntax is simple and contains a set of standard libraries with complete functions, which can easily accomplish many common tasks. Speaking of Python, its birth is also quite interesting. During the Christmas holidays in 1989, Dutch programmer Guido van Rossum stayed at home and found himself doing nothing. So, to pass the "boring" time, he wrote the first version of Python.

Python is widely used. According to statistics from GitHub, an open-source community, it has been one of the most popular programming languages in the past 10 years and is more popular than traditional C, C++ languages and C# which is very commonly used in Windows systems. After using Python for some time, Estella thinks it is a programming language specially designed for non-professional programmers.

Its grammatical structure is very concise, encouraging everyone to write as much code as possible that is easy to understand and write as little code as possible.

Functionally speaking, Python has a large number of standard libraries and third-party libraries. Estella develops her application based on these existing programs, which can get twice the result with half the effort and speed up the development progress.

More conveniently, Python can be shipped across platforms. For example, Estella often writes Python code under their familiar Windows system and then deploys the developed program to the server of the Linux system. To sum up, in one sentence Python is studious and easy to use.

The Role of Python in Data Science

After mastering Python as a programming language, Estella can do many interesting things, such as write a web crawler, collect data needed from the Internet, develop a task scheduling system, update the model regularly, etc.

Below we will describe how the Python is used by Estella for Data Science applications:

Data Cleaning

After obtaining the original data, Estella will first do preliminary processing on the data, such as unifying the case of the string, correcting the wrong data, etc. This is also the so-called "clean up" of "dirty" data to make the data more suitable for analysis. With Python and its third-party library pandas, Estella can easily complete this step of work.

Data Visualization

Estella uses Matplotlib to display data graphically. Before extracting the features, Estella can get the first intuitive feeling of the data from the graph and enlighten the thinking. When communicating with colleagues in other departments, information can be clearly and effectively conveyed and communicated with the help of graphics, so those insights can be put on paper.

Feature Extraction

In this step, Richard usually associates relevant data stored in different places, for example, integrating basic customer information and customer shopping information through customer ID. Then transform the data and extract the variables useful for modeling. These variables are called features. In this process, Estella will use Python's NumPy, SciPy, pandas, and PySpark.

Model Building

The open-source libraries sci-kit-learn, StatsModels, Spark ML, and TensorFlow cover almost all the commonly used basic algorithms. Based on these algorithm bases and according to the data characteristics and algorithm assumptions, Estella can easily build the basic algorithms together and create the model she wants.

The above four things are also the four core steps in Data Science. No wonder Estella, like most other data scientists, chose Python as a tool to complete his work.

Python Engineering Structure

This section discusses the engineering structure of Python projects. This part of the content for beginners may be more abstract. If readers find the following text difficult to understand, they can skip this section first, which does not affect the reading of other chapters in this book.

Suppose Estella has developed some scripts and put them in a file directory. Now, as a reader, when developing a new project, you hope to reuse the previous code like using a third-party library like NumPy. How should this be achieved? The answer is to create an __init__.py file full of "magic." Specifically, look at the following example.

First, create a mini_project directory with two subdirectories: components and tests. However, there are two Python scripts under components, namely counter.py and selecter.py.

- wordCount function is defined in counter.py script.
- getFrequentItem function is defined in selecter.py

This function depends on the wordCount function mentioned above, so import it at the beginning of the script with the following command:

[command for input] counter [to get]   function

- tests/test _ selector.py is the entrance to the program, that is, the script to be run directly, which will call the getFrequentItem function. Similarly, import getFrequentItem at the beginning of this script.

[command for input] frequency [to get]   function

If you use the "Python test _ selector.py" command to run the program at this time, you will get the following error prompt:

`error: not present as a module`

This is because Python does not regard the directory mini_project as a usable library, so the import failed. To fix this bug, just create an empty __init__.py file in each directory.

In essence, Python's library is a directory containing __init__.py files. __init__.py defines the properties and methods of this library. When we use the import command to import a library, we are importing the init__.py file. Under normal circumstances, there is no need to define anything in it, just an empty file is needed, Python will automatically process according to the default settings.

But without this file, Python would not regard the corresponding directory as a third-party library, and we would not be able to import and use it.

It is also worth reminding ourselves that when importing a library, you need to ensure that its corresponding directory is visible under the system path. To put it more bluntly, the corresponding library directory can be found under "sys.path." If not, then the corresponding path needs to be added to "sys. path"

By this, we have given a complete introduction to Python and why it can be considered as a good option for Data Science. In the next chapter, we will look at Python operations in more detail. This learning can help us with great Data Science projects. So why are you waiting? Let's dive into it.

3. How Machine Learning Fits with Data Science

The next topic that we need to take a look at is Machine Learning and how it comes into play when we work with Data Science and all of the neat things that we can do with this topic. Machine learning can definitely be an important part of the Data Science process, as long as we use it properly.

Remember, as we go through this process that part of Data Science is working on Data Analysis. This helps us to take a lot of the data we have collected along the way, and then actually see the insights and the predictions that are inside of it. To make this happen, we need to be able to create our models (that can sort through all of the data), find the hidden patterns, and provide us with our insights.

To define these models, and to make sure that they work the way that we want, we need to have a variety of good algorithms in place, and this is where Machine Learning is going to come into play quite a bit. You will find that with the help of Machine Learning, and the variety of algorithms that are present in Machine Learning, we can create models that can go through any kind of data we have, whether it is big or small, and provide us with the answers that we need here.

Machine learning is a process that we can use to make the system or the machine we are working with think in a manner that humans do. This allows the algorithm to go through and find hidden patterns in the same manner that a human would be able to do, but it can do it much faster and more efficiently than any human could do manually.

Think about how hard this would be to do manually for any human, or even for a group of people who are trying to get through all of that data. It could take them years to get through all of that data and find the insights that they need. And with how fast data is being generated and collected, those predictions and insights would be worthless by the time we got to that point anyway.

Machine learning can make this process so much easier. It allows us to have a way to think through the data and find the hidden patterns and insights that are inside for our needs. With the right Machine Learning algorithm, we can learn how the process works, and all of the steps that are necessary to make this happen for us. With this in mind, it is time to take a closer look at Machine Learning, and all of the parts that we need to know to make this work for our needs.

What is Machine Learning?

The first thing that we need to take a look at here is the basics of Machine Learning. Machine learning is going to be one of the applications of Artificial Intelligence that can provide a system with the ability to learn, all on its own, without the help of a programmer telling the system what to do. The system can even take this a bit further and can work to improve based on its own experience, and none of this is done with the system being explicitly programmed in the process. The idea of Machine Learning is going to be done with a focus on the development of programs on the computer that can access any data you have, and can then use that presented data to learn something new, and how you would like it to behave.

There are going to be a few different applications that we can look at when it comes to using Machine Learning. As we start to explore more about what Machine Learning can do, you may notice that over the years, it has been able to change and develop into something that programmers are going to enjoy working with more than ever. When you want to make your machine or system do a lot of the work on its own, without you having to step in and program every step, then Machine Learning is the right option for you.

When it comes to the world of technology, we will find that Machine Learning is pretty unique and can add a level of fun to the coding that we do. There are already a lot of companies, in a variety of industries (which we will talk about in a bit), that will use Machine Learning and are already receiving a ton of benefits from it.

There are a lot of different applications when it comes to using Machine Learning, and it is amazing what all we can do with this kind of Artificial Intelligence. Some of the best methods that we can follow and focus our time on when it comes to Machine Learning include:

Research on statistics: Machine learning is already making some headway when it comes to the world of IT. You will find that Machine Learning can help you go through a ton of complex data, looking for the large and important patterns that are in the data. Some of the different applications of Machine Learning under this category will include things like spam filtering, credit cards, and search engines.

An analysis of big data: There are a lot of companies who have spent time collecting what is known as Big Data, and now they have to find a way to sort through and learn from that data, in a short amount of time. These companies can use data to learn more about how money is spent by their customers, and even to help them make important decisions about the future. If we had someone go through and manually do the work, it would take much too long. But with Machine Learning, we can get it all done. Areas like the medical field, election campaigns, and even retail stores have started to turn to Machine Learning to gain some of these benefits.

The financial world: Many financial companies have been able to rely on Machine Learning. Stock trading online, for example, will rely on this kind of work, and we will find that Machine Learning can help with fraud detection, loan approvals, and more.

To help us get going with this one, and to understand how we can receive the value that we want out of Machine Learning, we have to make sure that we pair the best algorithms with the right processes and tools. If you are using the wrong kind of algorithm to sort through data, you are going to get a lot of inaccurate information, and the results will not give you the help that you need. Working with the right algorithm the whole time will make a big difference.

The cool thing that we will see with this one is that there are a lot of Machine Learning algorithms that we can choose from at this point to work on your model. Each of these works in a different manner than the others, but this ensures that you can handle any kind of problem that comes along with your project. With this in mind, though, you will notice that some of the different available algorithms include random forests, Neural Networks, clustering, support vector machines, and more.

As we are working on some of the models that we want to produce, we will also notice that there are a ton of tools and other processes that are available for us to work with. We need to make sure that we pick the right one to ensure that the algorithm and the model that you are working with will perform the way that you would like. The different tools that are available with Machine Learning will include:

1. Comprehensive management and data quality
2. Automated ensemble evaluation of the model to help see where the best performers will show up

3. GUIs for helping to build up the models that you want along with the process flows being built up as well
4. Easy deployment of this so that you can get results that are reliable and repeatable in a quick manner
5. Interactive exploration of the data and even some visualizations that help us to view the information easier
6. A platform that is integrated and end to end to help with the automation of some of the data to decision process that you would like to follow
7. A tool to compare the different models of Machine Learning to help us identify the best one to use quickly and efficiently

4. Data Science Algorithms and Models

This guidebook has taken some time to look through a lot of the different parts that come with Data Analysis. We took a look at what Data Analysis is all about, how to work with the Python language and why it is such a good thing for the Data Analysis, and even some of the basics of Machine Learning and why this should be a part of our process.

With all of this in mind, it is now time for us to move on to some of the other things that we can do when working on this process. We are going to explore some of the best algorithms and models that we can use to complete our Data Analysis with the help of the Python language. There are so many different algorithms that we can choose from, and all of them are going to be great options to get the work done. With this in mind, let's dive right in and see what some of the best algorithms and models are for completing your business Data Analysis with Python.

Neural Networks

It is hard to have a discussion about Machine Learning and Data Analysis without taking some time to talk about Neural Networks and how these forms of coding are meant to work. Neural Networks are a great addition to any Machine Learning model because they can work similarly to the human brain. When they get the answer right, they can learn from that, and some of the synapses that bring it all together will get stronger. The more times that this algorithm can get an answer right, the faster and more efficient it can become with its job as well.

With Neural Networks, each of the layers that you go through will spend a bit of time at that location, seeing if there is any pattern. This is often done with images or videos so it will go through each layer of that image and see whether or not it can find a new pattern. If the network does find one of these patterns, then it is going to instigate the process that it needs to move over to the following layer. This is a process that continues, with the neural network going through many layers until the algorithm has created a good idea of what the image is and can give an accurate prediction.

There are then going to be a few different parts that can show up when we reach this point, and it depends on how the program is set up to work. If the algorithm was able to go through the process above and could sort through all of the different layers, then it is going to make a prediction. If the prediction it provides is right, the neurons in the system will turn out stronger than ever. This is because the program is going to work with Artificial Intelligence to make the stronger connections and associations that we need to keep this process going. The more times that our neural network can come back with the correct answer, the more efficient this neural network will become in the future when we use it.

If the program has been set up properly, it is going to make the right prediction that there is a car in the picture. The program can come up with this prediction based on some of the features that it already knows belongs to the car, including the color, the number on the license plate, the placement of the doors, the headlights, and more.

When you are working with some of the available conventional coding methods, this process can be really difficult to do. You will find that the neural network system can make this a really easy system to work with.

For the algorithm to work, you would need to provide the system with an image of the car. The neural network would then be able to look over the picture. It would start with the first layer, which would be the outside edges of the car. Then it would go through some other layers that help the neural network understand if any unique characteristics are present in the picture that outlines that it is a car. If the program is good at doing the job, it is going to get better at finding some of the smallest details of the car, including things like its windows and even wheel patterns.

There could potentially be a lot of different layers that come with this one, but the more layers and details that the neural network can find, the more accurately it will be able to predict what kind of car is in front of it. If your neural network is accurate in identifying the car model, it is going to learn from this lesson. It will remember some of these patterns and characteristics that showed up in the car model and will store them for use later. The next time that they encounter the same kind of car model, they will be able to make a prediction pretty quickly.

When working with this algorithm, you are often going to choose one and use it, when you want to go through a large number of pictures and find some of the defining features that are inside of them. For example, there is often a big use for this kind of thing when you are working with face recognition software. All of the information wouldn't be available ahead of time with this method. And you can teach the computer how to recognize the right faces using this method instead. It is also one that is highly effective when you want it to recognize different animals, define the car models, and more.

As you can imagine, there are several advantages that we can see when we work with this kind of algorithm. One of these is that we can work with this method, and we won't have to worry as much about the statistics that come with it. Even if you need to work with the algorithm and you don't know the statistics or don't have them available, the neural network can be a great option to work with to ensure that any complex relationship will show up.

Naïve Bayes

We can also work with an algorithm that is known as the Naïve Bayes algorithm. This is a great algorithm to use any time that you have people who want to see some more of the information that you are working on, and who would like to get more involved in the process, but they are uncertain about how to do this, and may not understand the full extent of what you are doing. It is also helpful if they want to see these results before the algorithm is all the way done.

As you work through some of the other algorithms on this page and see what options are available for handling the data, you will notice that they often take on hundreds of thousands of points of data. This is why it takes some time to train and test the data, and it can be frustrating for those on the outside to find out they need to wait before they can learn anything about the process. Showing information to the people who make the decisions and the key shareholders can be a challenge when you are just getting started with the whole process.

This is where the Naïve Bayes algorithm comes in. It is able to simplify some of the work that you are doing. It will usually not be the final algorithm that you use, but it can often give a good idea to others outside of the process about what you are doing. It can answer questions, puts the work that you are doing in a much easier to understand the form, and can make sure that everyone will be on the same page.

Clustering algorithms

One of the best types of algorithms that you can work with is going to be the clustering algorithm. There are a variety of clustering algorithms out there to focus on, but they are going to help us ensure that the program can learn something on its own, and will be able to handle separating the different data points that we have. These clustering algorithms work best when you can keep things simple. It takes some of the data that you are working with and then makes some clusters that come together. Before we start with the program, though, we can choose the number of clusters that we want to fit the information too.

The number of clusters that you go with is going to depend on what kind of information you are working with as well. If you just want to separate your customers by gender, then you can work with just two clusters. If you would like to separate the customers by their age or some other feature, then you may need some more clusters to get this done. You can choose the number of clusters that you would like to work with.

The nice thing that comes with clustering algorithms is that they will handle most of the work of separating and understanding the data for you. This is because the algorithm is in charge of how many points of data go into each of the clusters you choose, whether there are two clusters or twenty that you want to work with. When you take a look at one of these clusters, you will notice that with all of the points inside, it is safe to assume that these data points are similar or share something important. This is why they fell into the same cluster with one another.

Once we can form some of these original clusters, it is possible to take each of the individual ones and divide them up to get some more sets of clusters because this can sometimes provide us with more insights. We can do this a few times, which helps to create more division as we go through the steps. In fact, it is possible to go through these iterations enough times that the centroids will no longer change. This is a sign that it is time to be done with the process.

Support Vector Machines

Another option that we need to work with is known as the Support Vector Machine or SVM. When we work with this one, it is important to take all of the items in our data set, and then work on plotting them into one n-dimensional space, rather than having them all over the place. N is going to be the number of features that should show up in this algorithm along with the rest of our information. We then have the option to take the value of all these features and translate them over to the value that is in your coordinates. From here, we determine where the hyperplane is because this will show us the differences that are there between our various classes.

You may notice while working on this kind of algorithm that more than one support vector is going to show up. Many of these are easy to ignore because they are just the coordinates of individual observations that are seen. You can then use the SVM as a frontier that can separate them into classes. The two support vectors that we need to focus on will be the hyperplane and the line.

To do this, we need to make sure that we know where the hyperplane is. As we go through this process, there can sometimes be more than one hyperplane to pick from depending on the kind of data we are working with. There can also be an additional challenge because we want to ensure that with these options, we go with the one that helps us to understand the data, not one that leads us astray. The good thing to consider here is that even if you do see more than one option to work with, there are a few steps that you can follow to make it easier to pick the right one. The steps that you can follow to make this happen will include:

- We are going to start with three hyperplanes that we will call 1, 2, and 3. Then we are going to spend time figuring out which hyperplane is right so that we can classify the star and the circle.
- The good news is there is a pretty simple rule that you can follow so that it becomes easier to identify which hyperplane is the right one. The hyperplane that you want to go with will be the one that segregates your classes the best.
- That one was easy to work with, but in the next one, our hyperplanes of 1, 2, and 3 are all going through the classes and they similarly segregate them. For example, all of the lines or these hyperplanes are going to run parallel with each other. From here, you may find that it is hard to pick which hyperplane is the right one.
- For the above issue, we will need to use what is known as the margin. This is the distance that occurs between the hyperplane and the nearest data point from either of the two classes. Then you will be able to get some numbers that can help you out. These numbers may be closer together, but they will point out

which hyperplane is going to be the best.

With the example that we have above, we see one of the times that this is a great tool to work within Machine Learning. When we look through some of the points of data that are available, and if you notice that there is a pretty good margin that separates some of the points, then this is a good place to work with the SVM model. It is effective and it can help us find some of the results that we want in the process as well.

Decision Trees

Decisions trees are also a good option that we can work with when we want to take a few available options, and then compare them to see what the possible outcome of each option is all about. We can even combine a few of these decision trees to make a random forest and get more results and predictions from this.

The decision tree is going to be one of the best ways to compare a lot of options, and then choose the path that is going to be the best for your needs. Sometimes there are a whole host of options that we can choose from, and many times they will all seem like great ideas. For businesses who need to choose from the best option out of the group, and need to know which one is likely to give them the results that they are looking for, the decision tree is the best option.

With the decision tree, we can place the data we have into it, and then see the likely outcome that is going to result from making a certain decision. This prediction can help us to make smart business decisions based on what we see. If we had a few different options with this and compare the likely outcomes from each one, it is much easier to determine which course of action is the best one for us to take.

K-Nearest Neighbors

The next algorithm that we can look at is known as the K-Nearest Neighbors algorithm or KNN. When we work with this algorithm, the goal is to search through all of the data that we have for the k most similar example of any instance that we want to work with. Once we can complete this process, then the algorithm can move on to the next step, which is where it will look through all of the information that you have and provide you with a summary. Then the algorithm will take those results and give you some of the predictions you need to make good business decisions.

With this learning algorithm, you will notice that the learning you are working with becomes more competitive. This works to your advantage because there will be a big competition going on between the different elements or the different parts in the models so that you can get the best solution or prediction based on the data you have at hand.

There are several benefits that we can receive when it comes to working with this algorithm. For example, it is a great one for cutting through all of that noise that sometimes shows up in our data. This noise, depending on the set of data that you use, can be really loud, and cutting this down a bit, can help make a big difference in the insights that you can see.

And if you are trying to handle and then go through some of the larger amounts of data that some companies have all at once, then this is a great algorithm to go with as well. Unlike some of the others that need to limit the set of data by a bit, the KNN algorithm is going to be able to handle all of your data, no matter how big the set is. Keep in mind that sometimes the computational costs are going to be higher with this kind of method, but in some cases, this is not such a big deal to work with.

To make the K-Nearest Neighbors algorithm work the way that you want, there are going to be a few steps that will make this process a little bit easier.

Working with this algorithm can help us to get a lot done when it is time to work with putting parts together, and seeing where all of our data is meant to lie. If you follow the steps that we have above, you will be able to complete this model for yourself, and see some of the great results in the process when it is time to make predictions and good business decisions.

The Markov Algorithm

Another type of unsupervised Machine Learning algorithm that you can work with is the Markov algorithm. This particular algorithm is going to take the data that you decide to input into it, and then it will translate it to help work in another coding language if you choose. The nice thing here is that you can pick out which rules you want to use with this algorithm ahead of time so that the algorithm will work the way that you want. Many programmers in Machine Learning find that this algorithm, and the fact they can set up their own rules ahead of time, is nice because it allows you to take a string of data and ensure that it is as useful as possible as you learn on the job and figure out the parameters of how the data will behave.

Another thing that you may like about this Markov algorithm is that you can work with it in several ways, rather than being stuck with just one method. One option to consider here is that this algorithm works well with things like DNA. For example, you could take the DNA sequence of someone, and then use this algorithm to translate the information that is inside that sequence into some numerical values. This can often make it easier for programmers, doctors, and scientists and more to know what information is present, and to make better predictions into the future. When you are working with programmers and computers, you will find that the numerical data is going to be much easier to sort through than other options of looking through DNA.

A good reason why you would need to use the Markov algorithm is that it is great at learning problems when you already know the input you want to use, but you are not sure about the parameters. This algorithm is going to be able to find insights that are inside the information. In some cases, these insights are hidden and this makes it hard for the other algorithms we have discussed to find them.

There are still some pitfalls to working with the Markov algorithm. This one can sometimes be difficult to work with because you do need to manually go through and create a new rule any time that you want to bring in a new programming language. If you only want to work with one type of programming language on your project, then this is not going to be a big deal. But many times, your program will need to work with several different languages, and going in and making the new rules a bunch of times can get tedious.

5. Regression Analysis (Linear and Logistic Regression)

Several industries across the globe are struggling with the best way to come up with the correct data or information that will eventually enable them to solve their incurring prediction problems. Several banks have made some losses, especially within their credit section as they could not correctly predict the trustfulness of the defaulters. In the health sector, you realize many have lost their lives because of poor planning and risk management, which come as a result of the lack of modeling to tool for more straightforward prediction. We also have other sectors such as weather forecasting where farmers were not advised on the occurrence of rain, as a result leading to more losses. Another area involved the payment of mortgage by homeowners. Due to all these, everyone across the universe went on a rampage looking for the best possible way to handle the prediction roles of the organizations. Later on, all these gave birth to what is termed regression analysis.

Therefore, regression analysis refers to statistical processes for prediction analysis using variables. In that, it helps in identifying the variables relationships. This analysis consists of both independent and dependent variables. In other words, regression analysis aids in understanding the effect of one independent variable on the dependent variable when other independent variables are kept constant. In most cases, regression analysis will try hard to predict the conditional expectation, especially of the dependent variable.

Regression analysis is applied in several areas such as weather forecasting and prediction. Here, it helps predict the outcome of the rain within a specific period. It is also applicable in other fields such as medical sectors for predicting the chances of diseases. Regression analysis comprises of the following: linear regression, logistic regression, polynomial, stepwise, ridge, lasso, and elastic net regression. All in all, this chapter will only tackle the most widely used regression analysis, such as linear regression and logistic regression. It is good to note that ElasticNet regression is a combination of the Lasso and Ridge regression.

Linear Regression

Linear regression refers to a statistical approach used for modeling a relationship between various variables in a particular set of different independent variables. In this chapter, you'll learn more about dependent variables such as response as well as independent variables, including features of simplicity. To be able to offer extensive search results and have a clear understanding of linear regression in Python, you need to be keen on a primary basis. We begin with the primary version of the subject. For instance, what is a simple linear regression?

By definition, simple linear regression refers to a significant approach that's used in predicting a significant response by utilizing a single feature. Therefore, it's assumed that the main two variables, in this case, are directly related. That's why it's vital to determine the linear function since it often predicts the main response value of the equation accurately. There are different regression models utilized in showing as well as predicting the main relationship between two different variables as well as factors. As such, it's important to note that the main factor that's being predicted is known as the dependent variable. But the factors utilized in predicting the main value of the dependent variable is identified as the independent variable. With that said, it's also vital to note that good data doesn't always narrate the entire story as it may be. Therefore, regression analysis is often used in the research as well as the establishment of the correlation of variables. However, correlation isn't the same as the subject of causation. Therefore, a line found in a simple linear regression that may be fitting into the data points appropriately may not indicate a definitive element regarding a major cause and effect relationship. When it comes to linear regression, every observation has two values. Therefore, one of the values is specifically for the dependent variable. The other is certainly for the independent variable.

Linear Regression in Python

When discussing the simple linear regression analysis, we are looking at some of the simplest forms of regression analysis that are used on various independent variables as well as one independent variable.

Consequently, in such a model, a straight line is often used in approximating the main relationship between an independent as well as a dependent variable. Multiple regression analysis occurs when there are 2 major independent variables applied in regression analysis. As a result, the model is not going to be a slightly simple linear one. Usually, this model ($y = \beta 0 + \beta 1 + E.$) represents a simple linear regression.

By applying the relevant mathematical convention, two main factors are herein involved. They include x and y, which are the main designations. Also, the equation often describes how y correlates with x. This is what is defined as the regression model. Apart from that, the linear regression model has an error term which is often represented by E. It can also be termed as the Greek letter epsilon. Usually, this error term is applied to mainly account for the variability found in y. However, this element cannot be explained in terms of the linear relationship found between x as well as y. It's also important to note that parameters are representing the major population being studied. Some of these parameters represent the main population that is being studied. Usually, a regression line can easily show how a unique positive linear relationship, no relationship, as well as a negative relationship.

With that said, if the line that has been graphed appears to be in a simple linear regression that's flat in any way, no relationship will be found in the two variables. On the other hand, if the regression line slopes upwards with the line's lower end located at y, on the graph, then there will be a positive linear relationship within the graph. But if the regression line tends to slope downward where the upper end of y that intercepts at the graph's axis. In the case where the parameters are well identified and known, the equation of the simple linear regression can utilize the computed meaning of the value of y. But in real practice, various parameter values aren't known. Therefore, they have to be estimated using some forms of data sampling from the actual population. Therefore, the parameters of these populations are often estimated using sample statistics. These statistics can be represented using $b_0 + b_1$.

It is clear that we live in a world that requires us to use tons of data coupled with powerful computers as well as Artificial Intelligence. While this may only be the beginning, there is a rise in the use of Data Science in various sectors across the world. Machine learning is also driving image recognition as well as autonomous vehicles development and decisions based in the sector of finance as well as the energy industry.

As such, linear regression in Python is still a fundamental statistical as well as Machine Learning technique. Therefore, for those who aspire to do statistics or scientific computing, there are high chances that this will be a requirement in the course work. Not only it is advisable to indulge in the learning process but also proceed to various complex methods appended to the studies.

It's important to understand the different types of linear regression. One of them includes multiple linear regressions that involve a unique case of the linear regression that has two to more independent variables. As such, in a case where there are two independent variables, it happens that the probable regression function is going to represent a major regression plane situated in a three-dimensional space. As such, the objective of the regression appears to be the value that will determine different weights. This also happens to be as close to the actual response as possible. In a different scenario, the case that exceeds two independent variables is often similar.

However, it's more general as well. In a similar case, you may regard polynomial regression as a major generalized issue of linear regression in Python. With that said, you can easily assume the polynomial dependence found between the output as well as inputs. In that case, your regression function may also be f which can include other non-linear terms.

Usually, linear regression is the initial Machine Learning algorithm that data scientists encounter in their practice. It's a vital model that everyone in the sector should master. This is because it helps in laying a strong foundation for different Machine Learning algorithms. For starters, it may be utilized in forecasting sales by analyzing sales data for initial months. Also, it may be used in gaining important insight regarding consumer behavior.

Logistic Regression

Logistic regression comprises of logistic model, logistic function, statistics model, and much more. Therefore, many organizations apply logistic regression in their day to day activities which is mainly composed of data predictions and analysis. You can always conduct this regression analysis, especially when the dependent variable is binary. That's dichotomous.

Just like other types of regression analyses, logistic regression is entirely applied in any analysis dealing with prediction. Its primary function, in this case, is to describe data. Also, logistic regression can be used to explain or illustrate the kind of relationship between the binary variable, which is the dependent one, and the other variables, which are the independent ones. This regression might look challenging to interpret, but with the help of specific tools such as Intellectus Statistics, you can easily undertake your Data Analysis.

Logistic regression knowledge can be easily applied in statistics with the help of the logistic model. In this case, the primary function of the logistic model is actually to come up with the correct results of certain predictions or classes with the help of probability. For example, probability works best in areas where you are only required to predict the outcome of the existing events. These events include: healthy or sick, win or lose, alive or dead, or even in places where you are making your analysis about the test where someone either fails or passes. Still, in this model, you will be able to fine-tune your result primarily through probability. In the case of an image, you will be able to extend your model to cover up various classes. You will be able to detect whether the image in your analysis is a lion or a cat, and so on. In this case, the individual variables within the image will have their probability numbers between 0 and 1. However, the sum here should be adding up to one.

Therefore, logistic regression refers to a basic statistical model that makes greater use of the available logistic function regardless of the complexity of more extensions that might exist. Logistic regression is part and parcel of the regression analysis, and on many occasions, it is applied in various analyses where logistic model parameters are estimated. Remember, the logistic model is like a form or a type of binary regression. Therefore, a binary regression consists of a binary logistic model. This model is composed of a dependent variable which includes two possible values of events. These values can be represented as pass/fail, alive/dead, good/bad, and much more. You need to note that the indicator variable actually denotes these possible values and always they have labeled 0 and 1. Within this logistic model, the odds logarithm that's log-odds, for the values of 1 represents a linear combination. In that, this combination has got one or more variables that are entirely independent. In this case, they are called predictors here.

Moreover, in logistic regression analysis, independent variables sometimes may each form a binary variable or sometimes a continuous variable. In the case of a binary variable, there must be the presence of two classes or events, and they have to be coded by the indicator variables. However, on the other hand, continuous variable represents real value. In the logistic regression analysis, the corresponding probability of these values always varies between 0 and 1 as has been denoted previously above. In this analysis, these log-odds, that's, algorithms of odds will be converted by logistic function into probability. Log odds are measured in logit which also a derivative of its name (logistic unit). Again, you can also use a probit model with a different sigmoid function to convert the log odds into a probability for easy analysis. You need to note that the probit model is an example of an analogous model which comprises of the sigmoid function.

All in all, you will realize that the logistic model is the most preferred in this conversion due to its defining attributes or characteristics. One such feature of the logistic model is its ability to increase the multiplicatively scales of each of the independent variables. As a result of this, it produces an outcome with parameters assigned to each independent variable at a constant rate. However, this will generalize the odd ratio if at all, it is part of a variable which is a binary dependent.

It is also good to note that there are extensions when it comes to dependent variables, especially in some regression such as binary logistic. However, this extension is only applicable where two or more levels are used. These two extensions include multinomial logistic regression which works best with categorical outputs, especially the one having several values that's, two values and above. The next type of logistic regression extension is the ordinal logistic regression which deals with a huge collection of multiple categories. A good example here is the ordinal logistic model dealing with the proportional odds. However, this system only does modeling and does not perform any classifications dealing with the statistics since it is not a classifier. Therefore, it will only convert the probability input into an output. Following this, let's discuss the applications of logistic regression in a real-life situation.

Applications of Logistic Regression

Logistic regression is applied in metrological and other forecasting stations which consist of meteorologists. The algorithm here is used to predict the probability of rain. This information is vital as it helps in many sectors such as agricultural, transport and so on. Time of planting can efficiently be planned for, and the right arrangement can be put into place.

This analysis is also applied in some risk management systems such as the credit control system. Here, the analysis will predict whether the account holder is a defaulter when it comes to payment or not. Still, on this, the regression analysis will predict the exact amount that someone can be given by using the previous records. This also enables many organizations to run, as they can control everything when it comes to risk management. All accounts will undergo a critical analysis before any credit is appended. Logistic regression is also applied in political sectors, especially during an election. Here, it gives out the probability of winning and losing each candidate owing to their strengths and resources they used. Again, this regression analysis will be able to predict the number of people who might fail to vote and who will vote at the end and to which particular candidate. Some factors help determine the prediction outcome here such as the age of the candidate, sex, the incomes of both the candidate and the voters, state of the residence of both and the total number of votes in the last elections.

Logistic regression is also applied in various medical fields. It is applied in epidemiology. Here, the analysis is used to identify all those risk factors that may eventually result in diseases. As a result, precautions and other preventive measures may be put into place. Its knowledge is usable in the Trauma and Injury Severity Score (TRISS) where predictions of mortality, especially in injured patients, are done. We have several medical scales that have been designed to check on the severity of patients across the globe.

All these medical scales have been developed or managed using logistic regression. In most cases, especially within the health sector, you can use this knowledge to predict the risk of acquiring some dangerous diseases. For example, diseases such as coronary heart disease, diabetes, and other forms of health-related complications can be easily controlled. These predictions are based on the day to day observable characteristics of the individual patient. The traits or characteristics here include the body mass index, sex, age, and even different results of their blood tests. This will eventually help in proper planning and risk management in the medical sector.

Again, this knowledge can be applied in the engineering sector. Here, it is used to predict the failure probability of a particular system, a new product, or even any kind of process. In the field of marketing, logistic regression analysis helps to determine the buyers' purchasing power, their propensity to purchase, and also this knowledge can be used to stop the various subscriptions of the companies. The technique is also applied in economics. Here, knowledge is used to predict the outcome of being involved in the public labor sector. We also have this technique in the issues to do with the probability of homeowners not paying a mortgage. Natural Language Processing uses conditional random fields which is also an extension of logistic regression, especially to sequential data.

Logistic Regression vs. Linear Regression

You may be wondering about the main difference between these two examples of regressions. In terms of the outcome, linear regression is responsible for the continuous prediction while there is a discrete outcome in logistic regression. A model predicting the price of a car will depend on various parameters like color, year of manufacture, and so on. Therefore, this value will always be different, indicating the continuous outcome. However, a discrete outcome is always one thing. That is, in case of sickness, you can either be sick or not.

Advantages of logistic regression

- It is very effective and efficient
- You can get an outcome without large computational resources
- You can easily interpret it
- No input features required for the scaling process
- No tuning required
- You can easily regularize logistic regression

How Does Machine Learning Compare to AI

One thing that we need to spend some time working on and understanding before we move on is the difference between Artificial Intelligence and Machine learning. Machine learning is going to do a lot of different tasks when we look at the field of Data Science, and it also fits into the category of Artificial Intelligence at the same time. But we have to understand that Data Science is a pretty broad term, and there are going to be many concepts that will fit into it. One of these concepts that fit under the umbrella of Data Science is Machine Learning, but we will also see other terms that include big data, Data Mining, and Artificial Intelligence. Data Science is a newer field that is growing more as people find more uses for computers and use these more often.

Another thing that you can focus on when you bring out Data Science is the field of statistics, and it is going to be put together often in Machine Learning. You can work with the focus on classical statistics, even when you are at the higher levels so that the data set will always stay consistent throughout the whole thing. Of course, the different methods that you use to make this happen will depend on the type of data that is put into this and how complex the information that you are using gets as well.

This brings up the question here about the differences that show up between Machine Learning and Artificial Intelligence and why they are not the same thing. There are a lot of similarities that come with these two options, but the major differences are what sets them apart, and any programmer who wants to work with Machine Learning has to understand some of the differences that show up. Let's take some time here to explore the different parts of Artificial Intelligence and Machine Learning so we can see how these are the same and how they are different.

What is Artificial Intelligence?

The first thing we are going to take a look at is Artificial Intelligence or AI. This is a term that was first brought about by a computer scientist named John McCarthy in the 1950s. AI was first described as a method that you would use for manufactured devices to learn how to copy the capabilities of humans concerning mental tasks.

However, the term has changed a bit in modern times, but you will find that the basic idea is the same. When you implement AI, you are enabling machines, such as computers, to operate and think just like the human brain can. This is a benefit that means that these AI devices are going to be more efficient at completing some tasks than the human brain.

At first glance, this may seem like AI is the same as Machine Learning, but they are not exactly the same. Some people who don't understand how these two terms work can think that they are the same, but the way that you use them in programming is going to make a big difference.

How is Machine Learning different?

Now that we have an idea of what Artificial Intelligence is all about, it is time to take a look at Machine Learning and how it is the same as Artificial Intelligence, and how it is different. When we look at Machine Learning, we are going to see that this is a bit newer than a few of the other options that come with Data Science as it is only about 20 years old. Even though it has been around for a few decades so far, it has been in the past few years that our technology and the machines that we have are finally able to catch up to this and Machine Learning is being used more.

Machine learning is unique because it is a part of Data Science that can focus just on having the program learn from the input, as well as the

302

data that the user gives to it. This is useful because the algorithm will be able to take that information and make some good predictions. Let's look at an example of using a search engine. For this to work, you would just need to put in a term to a search query, and then the search engine would be able to look through the information that is there to see what matches up with that and returns some results.

The first few times that you do these search queries, it is likely that the results will have something of interest, but you may have to go down the page a bit to find the information that you want. But as you keep doing this, the computer will take that information and learn from it to provide you with choices that are better in the future. The first time, you may click on like the sixth result, but over time, you may click on the first or second result because the computer has learned what you find valuable.

With traditional programming, this is not something that your computer can do on its own. Each person is going to do searches differently, and there are millions of pages to sort through. Plus, each person who is doing their searches online will have their preferences for what they want to show up. Conventional programming is going to run into issues when you try to do this kind of task because there are just too many variables. Machine learning has the capabilities to make it happen, though.

Of course, this is just one example of how you can use Machine Learning. In fact, Machine Learning can help you do some of these complex problems that you want the computer to solve. Sometimes, you can solve these issues with the human brain, but you will often find that Machine Learning is more efficient and faster than what the human brain can do.

Of course, it is possible to have someone manually go through and do this for you as well, but you can imagine that this would take too much time and be an enormous undertaking. There is too much information, they may have no idea where to even get started when it comes to sorting through it, the information can confuse them, and by the time they get through it all, too much time has passed and the information, as well as the predictions that come out of it, are no longer relevant to the company at all.

Machine Learning changes the game because it can keep up. The algorithms that you can use with it can handle all of the work while getting the results back that you need, in almost real-time. This is one of the big reasons that businesses find that it is one of the best options to go with to help them make good and sound decisions, to help them predict the future, and it is a welcome addition to their business model.

6. Interaction with Databases

Data management is not a scientific discipline per se. However, increasingly, it permeates the activities of basic scientific work. The increasing volume of data and increasing complexity has long exceeded manageability through simple spreadsheets.

Currently, the need to store quantitative, qualitative data and media of different formats (images, videos, sounds) is very common in an integrated platform from which they can be easily accessed for analysis, visualization or simply consultation.

The Python language has simple solutions to solve this need at its most different levels of sophistication. Following the Python included batteries, its standard library introduces us to the Pickle and cPickle module and, starting with Version 2.5, the SQLite3 relational database.

The Pickle Module

The pickle module and its fastest cPickle cousin implement algorithms that allow you to store Python-implemented objects in a file.

Example of using the pickle module

```
import pickle

class hi:
  def say_hi (self):
    print "hi"

a= hi()
f= open ('pic test','w')
pickle.dump(a, f)
f.close()

f= open ('pic test','r')
b=pickle.load (f)
b.say_hi()

hi
```

As we see in the example of using the pickle module, with the pickle module, we can store objects in a file, and retrieve it without problems for later use. However, an important feature of this module is not evident in example 8.1. When an object is stored using the pickle module, neither the class code nor its data is included, only the instance data.

```
class hi:
  def say_hi (self, name=' alex'):
    print'hi %s !'%name

f= open ('pictest','r')
b=pickle.load (f)
b.say_hi()
hi alex !
```

This way we can modify the class, and the stored instance will recognize the new code as it is restored from the file, as we can see above. This feature means that pickles do not become obsolete when the code they are based on is updated (of course this is only for modifications that do not remove attributes already included in the pickles).

The pickle module is not built simply for data storage but for complex computational objects that may contain data themselves. Despite this versatility, it is because it consists of a readable storage structure only by the pickle module itself in a Python program.

The SQLite3 Module

This module becomes part of the standard Python library from Version 2.5. Therefore, it becomes an excellent alternative for users who require the functionality of an SQL1-compliant relational database.

SQLite was born from a C library that had an extremely lightweight database and no concept client-server. In SQLite, the database is a file handled through the SQLite library.

To use SQLite in a Python program, we need to import the SQLite3 module.

```
import sqlite3
```

The next step is the creation of a connection object, through which we can execute SQL commands.

```
c= sqlite 3.connect (' /tmp/ example')
```

We now have an empty database consisting of the example file located in the / tmp directory. SQLite also allows the creation of RAM databases. To do this, simply replace the file name with the string: memory. To insert data into this database, we must first create a table.

```
c.execute (''' create table  specimens (name text, real
height, real weight)''')
< sqlite 3.Cursor object at 0 x83fed10 >
```

Note that SQL commands are sent as strings through the Connection object, execute method. The *create table* command creates a table; it must necessarily be followed by the table name and a list of typed variables (in parentheses), corresponding to the variables contained in this table. This command creates only the table structure. Each specified variable will correspond to one column of the table. Each subsequent entry will form a table row.

```
c.execute (''' insert  into  specimens values (' tom', 1
2.5, 2.3)'''
```

The insert command is another useful SQL command for inserting records into a table.

Although SQL commands are sent as strings over the connection, it is not recommended, for security reasons, to use the string formatting methods ('... values (% s,% s)'% (1,2)) of Python Instead, do the following:

```
t= (' tom',)
c.execute ('select from  specimens where name=?', t)
c.fetch all()
[(' tom', 1 2.5, 2.2 9 9 9 9 9 9 9 9 9 9 9 9 9 9 9 9 9 8)]
```

In the example above we use the fetchall method to retrieve the result of the operation. If we wanted to get a single record, we would use fetchone.

Below is how to insert more than one record from existing data structures. In this case, it is a matter of repeating the operation described in the previous example, with a sequence of tubes representing the sequence of records to be inserted.

```
T = ((' j e r r y', 5.1, 0.2), (' butch', 4 2.4, 1 0.3))
for i in t:
   c.execute (' insert into  specimens value s (?, ?, ?)',
i)
```

The cursor object can also be used as an iterator to get the result of a query.

```
c.execute (' selectfrom specimens by weight')
```

```
for reg in c:
  print reg
(' jerry', 5.1, 0.2)
(' tom', 1 2.5, 2.2 9 9 9 9 9 9 9 9 9 9 9 9 9 9 9 8)
(' butch', 4 2.4, 1 0.3)
```

The SQLite module is really versatile and useful, but it requires the user to know at least the rudiments of the SQL language. The following solution seeks to solve this problem in a more Pythonic way.

The SQLObject Package

The SQLObject2 package extends the solutions presented so far in two ways: it offers an object-oriented interface to relational databases, and also allows us to interact with multiple databases without having to change our code.

To exemplify sqlobject, we will continue to use SQLite because of its practicality.

Building a Digital Spider

In this example, we will have the opportunity to build a digital spider that will gather information from the web (Wikipedia3) and store it in an SQLite bank via sqlobject.

For this example, we will need some tools that go beyond the database. Let's explore the ability of the standard Python library to interact with the internet, and let's use an external package to decode the pages obtained.

The BeautifulSoup4package is a webpage breaker. One of the most common problems when dealing with Html pages is that many of them have minor design flaws that our browsers ignore, but can hinder further scrutiny.

Hence the value of BeautifulSoup: it is capable of handling faulty pages, returning a data structure with methods that allow quick and simple extraction of the desired information. Also, if the page was created using another encoding, BeautifulSoup, returns all Unicode content automatically without user intervention.

From the standard library, we will use the sys, os, urllib, urllib2 and re modules. The usefulness of each character becomes clear as we move forward in the example.

The first step is to specify the database. SQLObject allows us to choose from MySQL, PostgreSQL, SQLite, Firebird, MAXDB, Sybase,

MSSQL, or ADODBAPI. However, as we have already explained, we will restrict ourselves to using the SQLite bank.

Specifying the Database

```
johnsmith= os.path.expanduser ('~/. johnsmith' )
if not os.path.exists (at the dir):
os.mkdir (at the dir)
sqlhub.process Connection = connectionForURI
(' sqlite://'+johnsmithr +'/knowdb')
```

In specifying the database, we create the directory (os.mkdir) where the database will reside (if necessary) and we will natively connect to the database. We use os.path.exists to check if the directory exists. Since we want the directory in the user's folder, and we have no way of knowing beforehand what this directory is, we use os.path.expanduser to replace / home/user as it would normally on the Unix console.

On line 11 of Specifying the database, we see the command that creates the connection to be used by all objects created in this module.

Next, we specify our database table as a class, in which its attributes are the table columns.

Specifying the database ideatable.

```
class Idea (SQLObject): name= UnicodeCol() nlinks=
IntCol()
links= Pickle Col() address = StringCol
```

The class that represents our table is inherited from the SQLObject class. In this class, each attribute (table column) must be assigned an object that gives the type of data to be stored. In this example, we see four distinct types, but there are several others. UnicodeCol represents texts encoded as Unicode, i.e., it can contain characters from any language. IntCol is integer numbers. PickleCol is an exciting type as it allows you to store any type of Python object.

The most interesting thing about this type of column is that it does not require the user to invoke the pickle module to store or read this type of variable. Variables are automatically converted/converted according to the operation. Finally, we have StringCol, which is a simpler version of UnicodeCol, accepting only ASCII character strings. In SQL, it is common to have terms that specify different types according to the length of the text you want to store in a variable. In sqlobject, there is no limit to the size of the text that can be stored in either StringCol or UnicodeCol.

The functionality of our spider has been divided into two classes: Crawler, which is the creeper itself, and the UrlFac class that builds URLs from the word you want in Wikipedia.

Each page is pulled by the urllib2 module. The urlencode function of the urllib module makes it easy to add data to our request so as not to show that it comes from a digital spider. Without this disguise, Wikipedia refuses the connection.

The pages are then parsed by the VerResp method, where BeautifulSoup has a chance to do its work. Using the SoupStrainer function, we can find the rest of the document, which doesn't interest us, by analyzing only the links (tags 'a') whose destination is URLs beginning with the string/wiki/. All Wikipedia articles start this way. Thus, we avoid chasing external links. From the soup produced, we extract only the URLs, i.e. what comes after "href =".

7. Data Mining Techniques in Data Science

The basics of Math and Statistics help a data scientist to build, analyze, and create some complex analytics. To draw accurate insights about the data, data scientists are required to interact with the business side. Business Acumen is a necessity when it comes to analyzing data to help out the business. The results must also be in line with the expectations of the businesses. Therefore, the ability to verbally and visually communicate advanced results and observations to the business and help them easily understand. Data Mining is such a strategy used in Data Science that describes the process where raw data is structured in such a way where one can recognize patterns in the data via mathematical and computational algorithms. Let's do an overview of five major Data Mining Techniques that every data scientist must be aware of.

Mapreduce Technique

Data Mining applications manage vast amounts of data constantly. You must opt for a new software stack to tackle such applications. Stack software has its file system stored that is called a distributed file system. This file system is used for retrieving parallelism from a computing cluster or clusters. This distributed file system replicates data to enforce security against media failures. Other than this stack file system, there is a higher-level programming system developed to ease the process viz. Mapreduce. Mapreduce is a form of computed implemented in various systems, including Hadoop and Google. Mapreduce implementation is a Data Mining technique used to tackle large-scale computations. It is easy to implement, i.e.; you have to type only three functions viz. Map and Reduce. The system will automatically control parallel execution and task collaboration.

Distance Measures

The main limitation of Data Mining is that it is unable to track similar data/items. Consider an example where you have to track duplicate websites or web content while browsing various websites. Another example can be discovered similar images from a large database. To handle such problems, the Distance Measure technique is made available to you. Distance Measure helps to search for the nearest neighbors in a higher-dimensional space. It is very crucial to define what similarity is. Jaccard Similarity can be one of the examples. The methods used to identify similarity and define the Distance Measure Technique are:

- Shingling
- Min-Hashing
- Locality Sensitive Hashing
- A K-Shingle
- Locality-Sensitive Hashing

Link Analysis

Link Analysis is performed when you can scan the spam vulnerabilities. Earlier, most of the traditional search engines failed to scan the spam vulnerabilities. However, as technology got its wings, Google was able to Introduce some techniques to overcome this problem.

Pagerank

Pagerank techniques use the method of simulation. It monitors every page you are surfing to scan spam vulnerability. This whole process works iteratively, meaning pages that have a higher number of users are ranked better than pages without users visiting.

The Content

The content on every page is determined by some specific phrases used in a page to link with external pages. It is a piece of cake for spammers to modify the internal page where they are administrators, but it becomes difficult for them to modify the external pages. Every page is allocated a real number via a function. The page with a higher rank becomes more important than the page that does not have a considerable page rank. There are no algorithms set for assigning ranks to pages. But for highly confidential or connected Web Graphics, they have a transition matrix-based ranking. This principle is used for calculating the rank of a page.

Data Streaming

At times, it is difficult to know datasets in advance; also, the data appears in the form of a stream and gets processed before it disappears. The speed of arrival of the data is so fast that it is difficult to store it in the active storage. Here, data streaming comes into the picture. In the dataStream management system, an unlimited number of streams can be stored in a system. Each data stream produces elements at its own time. Elements have the same rate and time in a particular stream cycle. Such streams are archived into the store. By doing this, it is somewhat difficult to reply to queries already stored in the archival. But such situations are handled by specific retrieval methods. There is a working store as well as an active store that stores the summaries to reply to specific queries. There are certain data Streaming problems viz.

Sampling data in a Stream

You will select attributes to create some samples of the streams. To determine whether all the sample elements belong to the same key sample, you will have to rotate the hashing key of the incoming stream element.

Filtering Streams

To select specific tuples to fit a particular criterion, there is a separate process where the accepted tuples are carried forward, whereas others are terminated and eliminated. There is a modern technique known as Bloon Filtering that will allow you to filter out the foreign elements. The later process is that the selected elements are hashed and collected into buckets to form bits. Bits have a binary working, i.e., 0 and 1. Such bits are set to 1. After this, the elements are set to be tested.

Count Specific Elements in a Stream

If you require to count the unique elements that exist in a universal set, you might have to count each element from the initial step. Flajolet-Martin is a method that often hashes elements to integers, described as binary numbers. By using hash functions and integrating them may result in a reliable estimate.

Frequent Item – Set Analysis

In Frequent Item Set Analysis, we will check the market-basket model and the relationship between them. Every basket contains a set of items, whereas the market will have the data information. The total number of items is always higher than the number of items in the basket. This implies the number of items in the basket can fit in the memory. Baskets are the original and genuine files in the overall distributed system. Each basket is a set of item's type. To conclude on the market-basket technique, the characterization of the data depends on this technique to discover frequent itemset. Such sets of items are responsible for revealing most of the baskets. There are many use cases available over the Internet for this technique. This technique was applied previously in some big malls, supermarkets, and chain stores. To illustrate this case, such stores keep track of each of the basket that customer brings to the checkout counter. Here, the items represent the products sold by the store, whereas baskets are a set of items found in a single basket.

8. Decision Trees

Decision trees are built similarly to support vector machines, meaning they are a category of supervised machine learning algorithms that are capable of solving both regression and classification problems. They are powerful and used when working with a great deal of data.

You need to learn beyond the barebones basics so that you can process large and complex datasets. Furthermore, decision trees are used in creating random forests, which is arguably the most powerful learning algorithm. In this chapter, we are going to exclusively focus on decision trees explicitly because of their popular use and efficiency.

An Overview on Decision Trees

Decision trees are essentially a tool that supports a decision that will influence all the other decisions that will be made. This means that everything from the predicted outcomes to consequences and resource usage will be influenced in some way. Take note that decision trees are usually represented in a graph, which can be described as some kind of chart where the training tests appear as a node. For instance, the node can be the toss of a coin which can have two different results. Furthermore, branches sprout to individually represent the results and they also have leaves which are the class labels. Now you see why this algorithm is called a decision tree. The structure resembles an actual tree. As you probably guessed, random forests are exactly what they sound like. They are collections of decision trees, but enough about them.

Decision trees are one of the most powerful supervised learning methods you can use, especially as a beginner. Unlike other more complex algorithms, they are fairly easy to implement and they have a lot to offer. A decision tree can perform any common Data Science task and the results you obtain at the end of the training process are highly accurate. With that in mind, let's analyze a few other advantages, as well as disadvantages, to gain a better understanding of their use and implementation.

Let's begin with the positives:

Decision trees are simple in design and therefore easy to implement even if you are a beginner without a formal education in Data Science or machine learning. The concept behind this algorithm can be summarized with a sort of a formula that follows a common type of programming statement: If this, then that, else that. Furthermore, the results you will obtain are very easy to interpret, especially due to the graphic representation.

The second advantage is that a decision tree is one of the most efficient methods in exploring and determining the most important variables, as well as discovering the connection between them. Also, you can build new features easily to gain better measurements and predictions. Don't forget that data exploration is one of the most important stages in working with data, especially when there is a large number of variables involved. You need to be able to detect the most valuable ones in order to avoid a time-consuming process, and decision trees excel at this.

Another benefit of implementing decision trees is the fact that they are excellent at clearing up some of the outliers in your data. Don't forget that outliers are noise that reduces the accuracy of your predictions. In addition, decision trees aren't that strongly affected by noise. In many cases, outliers have such a small impact on this algorithm that you can even choose to ignore them if you don't need to maximize the accuracy scores.

Finally, there's the fact that decision trees can work with both numerical as well as categorical variables. Remember that some of the algorithms we already discussed can only be used with one data type or the other. Decision trees, on the other hand, are proven to be versatile and handle a much more varied set of tasks.

As you can see, decision trees are powerful, versatile, and easy to implement, so why should we ever bother using anything else? As usual, nothing is perfect, so let's discuss the negative side of working with this type of algorithm:

One of the biggest issues encountered during a decision tree implementation is overfitting. Take note that this algorithm tends to sometimes create very complicated decision trees that will have issues generalizing data due to their complexity. This is known as overfitting and it is encountered when implementing other learning algorithms as well, however, not to the same degree. Fortunately, this doesn't mean you should stay away from using decision trees. All you need to do is invest some time to implement certain parameter limitations to reduce the impact of overfitting.

Decision trees can have issues with continuous variables. When continuous numerical variables are involved, the decision trees lose a certain amount of information. This problem occurs when the variables are categorized. If you aren't familiar with these variables, a continuous variable can be a value that is set to be within a range of numbers. For example, if people between ages 18 and 26 are considered to be of student age, then this numerical range becomes a continuous variable because it can hold any value between the declared minimum and maximum.

While some disadvantages can add to additional work in the implementation of decision trees, the advantages still outweigh them by far.

Classification and Regression Trees

We discussed earlier that decision trees are used for both regression tasks as well as classification tasks. However, this doesn't mean you implement the exact same decision trees in both cases. Decision trees need to be divided into classification and regression trees. They handle different problems; however, they are similar in some ways since they are both types of decision trees.

Take note that classification decision trees are implemented when there's a categorical dependent variable. On the other side, a regression tree is only implemented in the case of a continuous dependent variable. Furthermore, in the case of a classification tree, the result from the training data is the mode of the total relevant observations. This means that any observations that we cannot define will be predicted based on this value, which represents the observation that we identify most frequently.

Regression trees, on the other hand, work slightly differently. The value that results from the training stage is not the mode value, but the mean of the total observations. This way, the unidentified observations are declared with the mean value which results from the known observations.

Both types of decision trees undergo a binary split; going from the top to bottom. This means that the observations in one area will spawn two branches that are then divided inside the predictor space. This is also known as a greedy approach because the learning algorithm is seeking the most relevant variable in the split while ignoring the future splits that could lead to the development of an even more powerful and accurate decision tree.

317

As you can see, there are some differences as well as similarities between the two. However, what you should note from all of this is that the splitting is what has the most effect on the accuracy scores of the decision tree implementation. Decision tree nodes are divided into subnodes, no matter the type of tree. This tree split is performed to lead to a more uniform set of nodes.

Now that you understand the fundamentals behind decision trees, let's dig a bit deeper into the problem of overfitting.

The Overfitting Problem

You learned earlier that overfitting is one of the main problems when working with decision trees and sometimes it can have a severe impact on the results. Decision trees can lead to a 100% accuracy score for the training set if we do not impose any limits. However, the major downside here is that overfitting creeps in when the algorithm seeks to eliminate the training errors, but by doing so it actually increases the testing errors. This imbalance, despite the score, leads to terrible prediction accuracy in the result. Why does this happen? In this case, the decision trees grow many branches and that's the cause of overfitting. To solve this, you need to impose limitations on how much the decision tree can develop and how many branches it can spawn. Furthermore, you can also prune the tree to keep it under control, much like how you would do with a real tree in order to make sure it produces plenty of fruit.

To limit the size of the decision tree, you need to determine new parameters during the definition of the tree. Let's analyze these parameters:

min_samples_split

The first thing you can do is change this parameter to specify how many observations a node will require to be able to perform the splitting. You can declare anything with a range of one sample to maximum samples. Just keep in mind that to limit the training model from determining the connections that are very common to a particular decision tree, you need to increase the value. In other words, you can limit the decision tree with higher values.

min_samples_leaf

This is the parameter you need to tweak to determine how many observations are required by a node, or in other words, a leaf. The overfitting control mechanism works the same way as for the sample split parameter.

max_features

Adjust this parameter in order to control the features that are selected randomly. These features are the ones that are used to perform the best split. To determine the most efficient value, you should calculate the square root of the total features. Just keep in mind that in this case, the higher value tends to lead to the overfitting problem we are trying to fix. Therefore, you should experiment with the value you set. Furthermore, not all cases are the same. Sometimes a higher value will work without resulting in overfitting.

max_depth

Finally, we have the depth parameter, which consists of the depth value of the decision tree. To limit the overfitting problem, however, we are only interested in the maximum depth value. Take note that a high value translates to a high number of splits, therefore a high amount of information. By tweaking this value you will have control over how the training model learns the connections in a sample.

Modifying these parameters is only one aspect of gaining control of our decision trees in order to reduce overfitting and boost performance and accuracy. The next step after applying these limits is to prune the trees.

Pruning

This technique might sound too silly to be real; however, it is a legitimate machine learning concept that is used to improve your decision tree by nearly eliminating the overfitting issue. As with real trees, what pruning does is reduce the size of the trees in order to focus the resources on providing highly accurate results. However, you should keep in mind that the segments that are pruned are not entirely randomly selected, which is a good thing. The sections that are eliminated are those that don't help with the classification process and don't lead to any performance boosts. Less complex decision trees lead to a better-optimized model.

In order to better understand the difference between an unmodified decision tree and one that was pruned and optimized, you should visualize the following scenario. Let's say that there's a highway that has a lane for vehicles that travel at 80 mph and a second lane for the slower vehicles that travel at 50 mph. Now let's assume you are on this highway in a red car and you are facing a decision. You have the option to move on the fast lane to pass a slow-moving car; however, this means that you will have a truck in front of you that can't achieve the high speed he should have in the left lane and therefore you will be stuck on that lane. In this case, the cars that are in the other lane are slowly starting to overtake you because the truck can't keep up. The other option is staying in your lane without attempting to overtake. The most optimal choice here is the one that allows you to travel a longer distance for a certain amount of time. Therefore, if you choose to stay in the slow lane until you gradually pass the truck that is blocking the fast lane, you will eventually be able to switch to that lane and pass all the other vehicles. As you can see, the second option might look slow at the time of consideration; however, in the long run, it ends up being the most efficient one. Decision trees are the same. If you apply limits to your trees, they won't get greedy by switching you to the left lane where you will be stuck behind a truck. However, if you prune the decision tree, it will allow you to examine your surroundings in more detail and allow you predict a higher number of options you have to be able to make a better choice.

As you can see, performing the pruning process does yield some benefits that cannot be ignored. However, the implementation of this technique requires a number of steps and conditions. For instance, for a decision tree to be suitable for pruning, it needs to have a high depth value. Furthermore, the process needs to start at the bottom to avoid any negative returns. This issue needs to be avoided because if we have a negative node split at the bottom and another one occurs at the top, we will end up with a decision tree that will stop when the first division occurs. If the tree is pruned, it will not stop there and you will have higher gains.

Visualizing decision trees can sometimes be difficult when all you have is the theory, so let's start with a step by step implementation to see them in action.

Decision Tree Implementation

Creating a decision tree starts from the root node. The first step is to select one of the data attributes and set up a logical test based on it. Once you have a set of results you can branch out and create another set of tests, which you will use to create the subnode. Once we have at least a subnode, we can apply a recursive splitting process to it in order to determine that we have clean decision tree leaves. Keep in mind that the level of purity is determined based on the number of cases that sprout from a single class. At this stage, you can start pruning the tree to eliminate anything that doesn't improve the accuracy of the classification stage. Furthermore, you will also have to evaluate every single split that is performed based on each attribute. This step needs to be performed in order to determine which is the most optimal attribute, as well as split.

But enough theory for now. All you should focus on at this point is the fundamental idea behind decision trees and how to make them efficient. Once you think you grasped the basics, you need to start the implementation.

In the following example, we will once again rely on the Iris dataset for the data and the Scikit-learn library which contains it.

K-means Clustering

As mentioned, unsupervised learning methods are ideal for working with unlabeled data. However, to be more specific, one of the best techniques, if not the best, is to use a type of clustering algorithm. The main idea behind this approach is the cluster analysis which involves reducing data observations to clusters, or subdivisions of data, where each cluster contains information that is similar to that of a predefined attribute. Clustering involves several techniques that all achieve the same goal because they are all about forming a variety of theories regarding the data structure.

One of the most popular unsupervised learning algorithms and clustering techniques is known as k-means clustering. This concept revolves around building data clusters based on the similarity of the values. The first step is to determine the value of k, which is represented by the total number of clusters we define. These clusters are built as k-many points, which hold the average value that represents the entire cluster. Furthermore, the values are assigned based on the value, which is the closest average. Keep in mind that clusters have a core that is defined as an average value that pushes the other averages aside, changing them. After enough iterations, the core value will shift itself to a point where the performance metric is lower. When this stage is reached, we have the solutions because there aren't any observations available to be designated.

If you're confused by now by all this theory, that's ok. You will see that this technique is a lot easier than it sounds. Let's take a look at the practical implementation. In this example we will use the UCI handwritten digits dataset. It is freely available and you don't need to download if you are using Scikit-learn along with the book. With that being said, here's the code:

```
from time import time
import numpy as np
import matplotlib.pyplot as plt
from sklearn import datasets
np.random.seed()
digits = datasets.load_digits()
data = scale(digits.data)
n_samples, n_features = data.shape
n_digits = len(np.unique(digits.target))
labels = digits.target
sample_size = 300
print("n_digits: %d, \t n_samples %d, \t n_features %d"
% (n_digits, n_samples, n_features))
print(79 * '_')
print('% 9s' %
'init'       time     inertia     homo     compl    v-meas
ARI AMI   silhouette')
def bench_k_means(estimator, name, data):
t0 = time()
estimator.fit(data)
print('% 9s %.2fs %i %.3f %.3f %.3f %.3f %.3f %.3f'
% (name, (time() - t0), estimator.inertia_,
metrics.homogeneity_score(labels, estimator.labels_),
metrics.completeness_score(labels, estimator.labels_),
metrics.v_measure_score(labels, estimator.labels_),
metrics.adjusted_rand_score(labels, estimator.labels_),
metrics.silhouette_score(data, estimator.labels_,
metric='euclidean',
sample_size=sample_size)))
(Source: K Means clustering - Implementing k Means.
Adapted from https://techwithtim.net/tutorials/machine-
learning-Python/k-means-2/ accessed in October 2019)
```

If you analyze the code line by line you will notice that the implementation is fairly simple, logical, and easy to understand. In fact, it is somewhat similar in parts to other techniques we used so far. However, there is one major difference that is important to mention, namely the performance measurements we are using in order to accurately interpret the data.

First, we have a homogeneity score. This metric can have a value between zero and one. It mainly seeks the clusters that make room only for one class system. The idea is that if we have a score that is close to the value of one, then the cluster is mostly built from the samples that belong to a single class. On the other hand, if the score is close to zero, then we have achieved a low homogeneity.

Next, we have the completeness score. This metric compliments the homogeneity measure. Its purpose is to give us information on how the measurements became part of a specific class. The two scores allow us to form the conclusion that we either managed to perform perfect clustering, or we simply failed.

The third metric is known as the V-metric, or sometimes the V-measure. This score is calculated as the harmonic mean of the previous two scores. The V-metric essentially checks on the homogeneity and the completeness score by assigning a zero to one value that verifies the validity.

Next, we have the adjusted Rand index metric. This is a score that is used to verify the similarity of the labeling. Using a value between zero and one, the Rand index simply determines the relation between the distribution sets.

Finally, we have the silhouette metric, which is used to verify whether the performance of the clustering is sufficient without having labeled data. The measurement goes from a negative value to a positive one and it determines whether the clusters are well-structured or not. If the value is negative, then we are dealing with bad clusters. To make sure we have dense clusters, we need to achieve a score close to a positive one. Keep in mind that in this case, we can also have a score that is close to zero. In this case, the silhouette measurement tells us that we have clusters that are overlapping each other.

Now that you understand the measurement system, we have to apply one more step to this implementation and make sure that the results are accurate. To verify the clustering scores, we can use the bench_k_means function like so:

```
bench_k_means(KMeans(init='k-means++',
n_clusters=n_digits, n_ init=10),
name="k-means++", data=data)
print(79 * '_')
```

Now let's see what conclusion we can draw from the scores. Here's how your results should look:

```
n_digits 10        n_samples 1797      n_features 64
init               time inertia        homo compl
k-means++          0.25s 69517         0.596 0.643
init               v-meas ARI          AMI silhouette
k-means++          0.619 0.465         0.592 0.123
```

As you can see, with a basic k-means implementation, we have fairly decent scores; however, there is a lot we could improve. Clustering is sufficient, but we could perfect the scores by implementing other supervised or unsupervised learning techniques. For instance, in this case, you might consider using the principal component analysis algorithm as well. Another option would be applying various dimensionality reduction methods. However, to learn how to implement the K-means clustering algorithm, these results will suffice. However, you should keep in mind that in the real world of Data Science, you will often implement several algorithms and techniques together. You will rarely be able to get useful results with just one algorithm, especially when working with raw datasets instead of the practice ones.

In this chapter, we have focused on learning about unsupervised learning algorithms, namely K-means clustering. The purpose of this section was to show you a technique that can be used on more complex datasets. Clustering algorithms are the staple of Data Science and frequently used, especially in combination with other algorithms and learning techniques. Furthermore, as you will learn later, clustering techniques, especially K-means clustering, are highly efficient in dealing with Big Data.

9. Real World Applications

The application of Big Data and Big Data Analytics are benefitting both small and big companies across various industrial domains. In this chapter, we are going to explore more in detail such applications.

eCommerce

Over 2.6 billion and counting active social media users include customers and potential customers for every company out there. The race is on to create more effective marketing and social media strategies, powered by machine learning, aimed at providing enhanced customer experience to turn prospective customers into raving fans. The process of sifting through and analyzing a massive amount of data has not only become feasible, but it's easy now. The ability to bridge the gap between execution and big Data Analysis has been supplemented by Artificial Intelligence marketing solutions. Artificial Intelligence (AI) marketing can be defined as a method of using Artificial Intelligence consonants like machine learning on available customer data to anticipate customer's needs and expectations while significantly improving the customer's journey. Marketers can boost their campaign performance and return on investment read a little to no extra effort in the light of big data insights provided by Artificial Intelligence marketing solutions. The key elements that make AI marketing as powerful are:

- Big data - A marketing company's ability to aggregate and segment a huge dump of data with minimal manual work is referred to as Big Data. The marketer can then leverage the desired medium to ensure the appropriate message is being delivered to the target audience at the right time.
- Machine learning - Machine learning platforms enable marketers to identify trends or common occurrences and gather effective insights and responses, thereby deciphering the root cause and probability of recurring events.
- Intuitive platform – Super fast and easy to operate applications are integral to AI marketing. Artificial Intelligence technology is capable of interpreting emotions and communicating like a

human, allowing AI-based platforms to understand open form content like email responses and social media.

Predictive Analysis

All Artificial Intelligence technology-based solutions are capable of extracting information from data assets to predict future trends. AI technology has made it possible to model trends that could previously be determined only retroactively. These predictive analysis models can be reliably used in decision-making and to analyze customers' purchase behavior. The model can successfully determine when the consumer is more likely to purchase something new or reorder an old purchase. The marketing companies are now able to reverse engineer customers' experiences and actions to create more lucrative marketing strategies. For example, FedEx and Sprint are using predictive analytics to identify customers who are at potential risk of defecting to a competitor.

Smart searches

Only a decade ago, if you typed in "women's flip flops" on Nike.com, the probability of you finding what you were looking for would be next to zero. However, today's search engines are not only accurate but also much faster. This upgrade has largely been brought on by innovations like "semantic search" and "Natural Language Processing" that enable search engines to identify links between products and provide relevant search results, recommend similar items, and auto-correct typing errors. Artificial Intelligence technology and big data solutions can rapidly analyze user search patterns and identify key areas that the marketing companies should focus on.

In 2015, Google introduced the first Artificial Intelligence-based search algorithm called "RankBrain." Following Google's lead, other major e-commerce websites, including Amazon have incorporated Big Data Analysis and Artificial Intelligence into their search engines to offer smart search experience for their customers, who can find desired products even when they don't know exactly what they're looking for. Even small e-commerce stores have access to Smart search technologies like "Elasticsearch." The data-as-a-service companies like "Indix" allow companies to learn from other larger data sources to train their product search models.

Recommendation Engines

Recommendation engines have quickly evolved into fan favorites and are loved by customers just as much as the marketing companies. "Apple Music" already knows your taste in music better than your partner, and Amazon always presents you with a list of products that you might be interested in buying. This kind of discovery aide that can sift through millions of available options and hone in on an individual's needs are proving indispensable for large companies with huge physical and digital inventories.

In 1998, Swedish computational linguist, Jussi Karlgren, explored the practice of clustering customer behaviors to predict future behaviors in his report titled "Digital bookshelves". The same year, Amazon implemented collaborative filtering to generate recommendations for their customers. The gathering and analysis of consumer data paired with individual profile information and demographics, by the predictive analysis-based systems allow the system to continually learn and adapt based on consumer activities such as likes and dislikes on the products in real-time. For example, the company "Sky" has implemented a predictive analysis-based model that is capable of recommending content according to the viewer's mode. The smart customer is looking for such an enhanced experience not only from their music and on-demand entertainment suppliers but also from all other e-commerce websites.

Product Categorization and Pricing

E-commerce businesses and marketing companies have increasingly adopted Artificial Intelligence in their process of categorization and tagging of the inventory. The Marketing companies are required to deal with awful data just as much, if not more than amazingly organized, clean data. This bag of positive and negative examples serves as training resources for predictive analysis-based classification tools. For example, different retailers can have different descriptions for the same product, such as sneakers, basketball shoes, trainers, or Jordan's, but the AI algorithm can identify that these are all the same products and tag them accordingly. Alternatively, if the data set is missing the primary keyword like skirts or shirts, the Artificial Intelligence algorithm can identify and classify the item or product as skirts or shirts based solely on the surrounding context.

327

We are familiar with the seasonal rate changes of hotel rooms, but with the advent of Artificial Intelligence, product prices can be optimized to meet the demand with a whole new level of precision. The machine learning algorithms are being used for dynamic pricing by analyzing customer's data patterns and making near accurate predictions of what they are willing to pay for that particular product as well as their receptiveness to special offers. This empowers businesses to target their consumers with high precision and calculated whether or not a discount is needed to confirm the sale. Dynamic pricing also allows businesses to compare their product pricing with the market leaders and competitors and adjust their prices accordingly to pull in the sale. For example, "Airbnb" has developed its dynamic pricing system, which provides 'Price Tips' to the property owners to help them determine the best possible listing price for their property. The system takes into account a variety of influencing factors such as geographical location, local events, property pictures, property reviews, listing features, and most importantly, the booking timings and the market demand. The final decision of the property owner to follow or ignore the provided 'price tips' and the success of the listing are also monitored by the system, which will then process the results and adjust its algorithm accordingly.

Customer Targeting and Segmentation

For the marketing companies to be able to reach their customers with a high level of personalization, they are required to target increasingly granular segments. The Artificial Intelligence technology can draw on the existing customer data and train Machine learning algorithms against "gold standard" training sets to identify common properties and significant variables. The data segments could be as simple as location, gender, and age, or as complex as the buyer's persona and past behavior. With AI Dynamics, segmentation is feasible which accounts for the fact that customers' behaviors are ever-changing, and people can take on different people in different situations.

Sales and Marketing Forecast

One of the most straightforward Artificial Intelligence applications in marketing is in the development of sales and marketing forecasting models. The high volume of quantifiable data such as clicks, purchases, email responses, and time spent on webpages serve as training resources for the machine learning algorithms. Some of the leading business intelligence and production companies in the market are Sisense,

328

Rapidminer, and Birst. Marketing companies are continuously upgrading their marketing efforts, and with the help of AI and machine learning, they can predict the success of their marketing initiatives or email campaigns. Artificial Intelligence technology can analyze past sales data, economic trends, as well as industrywide comparisons to predict short and long-term sales performance and forecast sales outcomes. The sales forecasts model aids in the estimation of product demand and to help companies manage their production to optimize sales.

Programmatic Advertisement Targeting

With the introduction of Artificial Intelligence technology, bidding on and targeting program-based advertisement has become significantly more efficient. Programmatic advertising can be defined as "the automated process of buying and selling ad inventory to an exchange which connects advertisers to publishers." To allow real-time bidding for inventory across social media channels and mobile devices as well as television, Artificial Intelligence technology is used. This also goes back to predictive analysis and the ability to model data that could previously only be determined retroactively. Artificial Intelligence is able to assist the best time of the day to serve a particular ad, the probability of an ad turning into sales, the receptiveness of the user, and the likelihood of engagement with the ad.

Programmatic companies can gather and analyze visiting customers' data and behaviors to optimize real-time campaigns and to target the audience more precisely. Programmatic media buying includes the use of "demand-side platforms" (to facilitate the process of buying ad inventory on the open market) and "data management platforms" (to provide the marketing company an ability to reach their target audience). In order to empower the marketing rep to make informed decisions regarding their prospective customers, the data management platforms are designed to collect and analyze the big volume of website "cookie data." For example, search engine marketing (SEM) advertising is practiced by channels like Facebook, Twitter, and Google. To efficiently manage a huge inventory of the website and application viewers, programmatic ads provide a significant edge over competitors. Google and Facebook serve as the gold standard for efficient and effective advertising and are geared to words providing a user-friendly platform that will allow non-technical marketing companies to start, run and measure their initiatives and campaigns online.

Visual Search and Image Recognition

Leaps and bounds in the advancements in Artificial Intelligence-based image recognition and analysis technology have resulted in uncanny visual search functionalities. With the introduction of technology like Google Lens and platforms like Pinterest, people can now find results that are visually similar to one another using visual search functionality. The visual search works in the same way as traditional text-based searches that display results on a similar topic. Major retailers and marketing companies are increasingly using the visual search to offer an enhanced and more engaging customer experience. Visual search can be used to improve merchandising and provide product recommendations based on the style of the product instead of the consumer's past behavior or purchases.

Major investments have been made by Target and Asos in visual search technology development for their e-commerce websites. In 2017, Target announced a partnership with Pinterest that allows integration of Pinterest's visual search application called "Pinterest lens" into Target's mobile application. As a result, shoppers can take a picture of products that they would like to purchase while they are out and about and find similar items on Target's e-commerce site. Similarly, the visual search application launched by Asos called "Asos' Style Match" allows shoppers to snap a photo or upload an image on the Asos website or application and search their product catalog for similar items. These tools attract shoppers to retailers for items that they might come across in a magazine or while out and about by helping them to shop for the ideal product even if they do not know what the product is.

Image recognition has greatly helped marketers get a head start on social media by allowing them to find a variety of uses for their brands' logos and products to keep up with visual trends. This phenomenon is also called "visual social listening" and allows companies to identify and understand where and how customers are interacting with their brand, logo, and product even when the company is not referred directly by its name.

Healthcare Industry

With the increasing availability of healthcare data, Big Data Analysis has brought on a paradigm shift to healthcare. The primary focus of big Data Analytics in the healthcare industry is the analysis of relationships between patient outcomes and the treatment or prevention technique used. Big Data Analysis driven Artificial Intelligence programs have successfully been developed for patient diagnostics, treatment protocol generation, drug development, as well as patient monitoring and care. The powerful AI techniques can sift through a massive amount of clinical data and help unlock clinically relevant information to assist in decision making.

Some medical specialties with increasing Big Data Analysis based AI research and applications are:

- Radiology – The ability of AI to interpret imaging results supplements the clinician's ability to detect changes in an image that can easily be missed by the human eye. An AI algorithm recently created at Stanford University can detect specific sites in the lungs of the pneumonia patients.

- Electronic Health Records – The need for digital health records to optimize the information spread and access requires fast and accurate logging of all health-related data in the systems. A human is prone to errors and may be affected by cognitive overload and burnout. This process has been successfully automated by AI. The use of Predictive models on the electronic health records data allowed the prediction of individualized treatment response with 70-72% accuracy at baseline.

- Imaging – Ongoing AI research is helping doctors in evaluating the outcome of corrective jaw surgery as well as in assessing the cleft palate therapy to predict facial attractiveness.

Entertainment Industry

Big Data Analysis, in coordination with Artificial Intelligence, is increasingly running in the background of entertainment sources from video games to movies and serving us a richer, engaging, and more realistic experience. Entertainment providers such as Netflix and Hulu are using Big Data Analysis to provide users with personalized recommendations derived from individual user's historical activity and behavior. Computer graphics and digital media content producers have been leveraging big Data Analysis based tools to enhance the pace and efficiency of their production processes. Movie companies are increasingly using machine learning algorithms in the development of film trailers and advertisements as well as pre-and post-production processes. For example, big Data Analysis and an Artificial Intelligence-powered tool called "RivetAI" allow producers to automate and excellently read the processes of movie script breakdown, storyboard as well as budgeting, scheduling, and generation of shot-list. Certain time-consuming tasks carried out during the post-production of the movies such as synchronization and assembly of the movie clips can be easily automated using Artificial Intelligence.

Marketing and Advertising

A machine learning algorithm developed as a result of big Data Analysis can be easily trained with texts, stills, and video segments as data sources. It can then extract objects and concepts from these sources and recommend efficient marketing and advertising solutions. For example, a tool called "Luban" was developed by Alibaba that can create banners at lightning speed in comparison to a human designer. In 2016, for the Chinese online shopping extravaganza called "Singles Day," Luban generated 117 million banner designs at a speed of 8000 banner designs per second.

20th Century Fox collaborated with IBM to use their AI system "Watson" for the creation of the trailer of their horror movie "Morgan." To learn the appropriate "moments" or clips that should appear in a standard horror movie trailer, Watson was trained to classify and analyze input "moments" from audio-visual and other composition elements from over a hundred horror movies. This training resulted in the creation of a six-minute movie trailer by Watson in a mere 24 hours, which would have taken human professional weeks to produce.

With the use of Machine Learning, computer vision technology, Natural Language Processing, and predictive analytics, the marketing process can be accelerated exponentially through an AI marketing platform. For example, the Artificial Intelligence-based marketing platform developed by Albert Intelligence Marketing can generate autonomous campaign management strategies, create custom solutions, and perform audience targeting. The company reported a 183% improvement in customer transaction rate and over 600% higher conversation efficiency credited to the use of their AI-based platform.

In March 2016, the Artificial Intelligence-based creative director called "AI-CD ß" was launched by McCann Erickson Japan as the first robotic creative director ever developed. "AI-CD ß" was given training on select elements of various TV shows and the winners from the past 10 years of All Japan Radio and Television CM festival. With the use of

Data Mining capabilities, "AI-CD ß" can extract ideas and themes fulfilling every client's individual campaign needs.

Personalization of User Experience

The expectations of the on-demand entertainment users for a rich and engaging personal user experience are ever-growing. One of the leading on-demand entertainment platforms, Netflix, rolled out Artificial Intelligence-based workflow management and scheduling application called "Meson," comprised of various "machine learning pipelines" that are capable of creating, training, and validating personalization algorithms to provide personalized recommendations to users. Netflix collaborated with the University of Southern California to develop new Machine Learning algorithms that can compress video for high-quality streaming without degrading image quality called "Dynamic Optimizer." This Artificial Intelligence technology will address streaming problems in developing nations and mobile device users by optimizing video fluency and definition.

IBM Watson recently collaborated with IRIS.TV to offer a business-to-business service to media companies such as CBS, The Hollywood Reporter, and Hearst Digital Media by tracking and improving the introduction of their customers with their web content. IBM Watson is boosting IRIS.TV company's Machine learning algorithms that can 'learn' from users' search history and recommend similar content. Reportedly, a 50% increase in view or retention or a small PDF three months was achieved by the Hollywood reporter with the use of IRIS.TV application.

Search Optimization and Classification

The ability to transform text, audio, and video content into digital copies has led to an explosion of media availability on the Internet, making it difficult for people to find exactly what they're looking for. To optimize the accuracy of search results, advancements are being made in machine learning technology. For example, Google is using Artificial Intelligence to augment its platform for accurate image searching. People can now simply upload a sample picture to Google Image instead of typing in keywords for their search. The image recognition technology used by Google image will automatically identify and manage features of the uploaded user image and provide search results with similar pictures. Google is also using Artificial Intelligence technology in advertisement positioning across the platform. For example, a pet food ad will only appear on the pet-related website, but a chicken wings advertisement will not appear on a site targeted to vegetarians.

The company Vintage Cloud has partnered with an Artificial Intelligence-based startup called "ClarifAI" to develop a film digitalization platform. With the use of computer vision API provided by ClarifAI, Vintage Cloud succeeded in burgeoning the speed of movie content classification and categorization.

A visual assets management platform integrated with machine learning algorithms has been developed by a company called "Zorroa." This platform enables users to search for specific content within large databases called an "Analysis Pipeline." The database contains processors that can tag each visual asset uniquely and Machine learning algorithms that have been 'trained' to identify specific components of the visual data. This visual content is then organized and cataloged to deliver high-quality search results.

10. Data in the Cloud

Data Science is a mixture of many concepts. To become a data scientist, it is important to have some programming skills. Even though you might not know all the programming concepts related to infrastructure, having basic skills in computer science concepts is a must. You must install the two most common and used programming languages i.e., R and Python, on your computer. With the ever-expanding advanced analytics, Data Science continues to spread its wings in different directions. This requires collaborative solutions like predictive analysis and recommendation systems. Collaboration solutions include research and notebook tools integrated with code source control. Data ScienceScience is also related to the cloud. The information is also stored in the cloud. So, this lesson will enlighten you with some facts about the "data in the Cloud." So let's understand what cloud means and how the data is stored and how it works.

What is the Cloud?

Cloud can be described as a global server network, each having different unique functions. Understanding networks is required to study the cloud. Networks can be simple or complex clusters of information or data.

Network

As specified earlier, networks can have a simple or small group of computers connected or large groups of computers connected. The largest network can be the Internet. The small groups can be home local networks like Wi-Fi, and Local Area Network that is limited to certain computers or locality. There are shared networks such as media, web pages, app servers, data storage, and printers, and scanners. Networks have nodes, where a computer is referred to as a node. The communication between these computers is established by using protocols. Protocols are the intermediary rules set for a computer. Protocols like HTTP, TCP, and IP are used on a large scale. All the information is stored on the computer, but it becomes difficult to search for information on the computer every time. Such information is usually stored in a Data Centre. A Data Centre is designed in such a way that it is equipped with support security and protection for the data. Since the cost of computers and storage has decreased substantially, multiple organizations opt to make use of multiple computers that work together when one wants to scale. This differs from other scaling solutions like buying other computing devices. The intent behind this is to keep the work going continuously even if a computer fails; the other will continue the operation. There is a need to scale some cloud applications, as well. Having a broad look at some computing applications like YouTube, Netflix, and Facebook that require some scaling. We rarely experience such applications failing, as they have set up their systems on the cloud. There is a network cluster in the cloud, where many computers are connected to the same networks and accomplish similar tasks. You can call it as a single source of information or a single computer that manages everything to improve performance, scalability, and availability.

Data Science in the Cloud

The whole process of Data Science takes place in the local machine, i.e., a computer or laptop provided to the data scientist. The computer or laptop has inbuilt programming languages and a few more prerequisites installed. This can include common programming languages and some algorithms. The data scientist later has to install relevant software and development packages as per his/her project. Development packages can be installed using managers such as Anaconda or similar managers. You can opt for installing them manually too. Once you install and enter into the development environment, then your first step, i.e., the workflow starts where your companion is only data. It is not mandatory to carry out the task related to Data Science or Big Data on different development machines. Check out the reasons behind this:

1. The processing time required to carry out tasks on the development environment fails due to processing power failure.
2. Presence of large data sets that cannot be contained in the development environment's system memory.
3. Deliverables must be arrayed into a production environment and incorporated as a component in a large application.
4. It is advised to use a machine that is fast and powerful.

Data scientist explores many options when they face such issues; they make use of on-premise machines or virtual machines that run on the

336

cloud. Using virtual machines and auto-scaling clusters has various benefits, such as they can span up and discard it anytime in case it is required. Virtual machines are customized in a way that will fulfill one's computing power and storage needs. Deployment of the information in a production environment to push it in a large data pipeline may have certain challenges. These challenges are to be understood and analyzed by the data scientist. This can be understood by having a gist of software architectures and quality attributes.

Software Architecture and Quality Attributes

A cloud-based software system is developed by Software Architects. Such systems may be product or service that depends on the computing system. If you are building software, the main task includes the selection of the right programming language that is to be programmed. The purpose of the system can be questioned; hence, it needs to be considered. Developing and working with software architecture must be done by a highly skilled person. Most of the organizations have started implementing effective and reliable cloud environment using cloud computing. These cloud environments are deployed over to various servers, storage, and networking resources. This is used in abundance due to its less cost and high ROI.

The main benefit to data scientists or their teams is that they are using the big space in the cloud to explore more data and create important use cases. You can release a feature and have it tested the next second and check whether it adds value, or it is not useful to carry forward. All this immediate action is possible due to cloud computing.

Sharing Big Data in the Cloud

The role of Big Data is also vital while dealing with the cloud as it makes it easier to track and analyze insights. Once this is established, big data creates great value for users.

The traditional way was to process wired data. It became difficult for the team to share their information with this technique. The usual problems included transferring large amounts of data and collaboration of the same. This is where cloud computing started sowing its seed in the competitive world. All these problems were eliminated due to cloud computing, and gradually, teams were able to work together from different locations and overseas as well. Therefore, cloud computing is very vital in both Data Science as well as Big Data. Most of the organizations make use of the cloud. To illustrate, a few companies that use the cloud are Swiggy, Uber, Airbnb, etc. They use cloud computing for sharing information and data.

Cloud and Big data Governance

Working with the cloud is a great experience as it reduces resource cost, time, and manual efforts. But the question arises that how organizations deal with security, compliance, governance? Regulation of the same is a challenge for most companies. Not limited to Big Data problems, but working with the cloud also has its issues related to privacy and security. Hence, it is required to develop a strong governance policy in your cloud solutions. To ensure that your cloud solutions are reliable, robust, and governable, you must keep it as an open architecture.

Need for Data Cloud Tools to Deliver High Value of Data

Demand for a data scientist in this era is increasing rapidly. They are responsible for helping big and small organizations to develop useful information from the data or data set that is provided. Large organizations carry massive data that needs to analyze continuously. As per recent reports, almost 80% of the unstructured data received by the organizations are in the form of social media, emails, i.e., Outlook, Gmail, etc., videos, images, etc. With the rapid growth of cloud computing, data scientists deal with various new workloads that come from IoT, AI, Blockchain, Analytics, etc. Pipeline. Working with all these new workloads requires a stable, efficient, and centralized platform across all teams. With all this, there is a need for managing and recording new data as well as legacy documents. Once a data scientist is given a task, and he/she has the dataset to work on, he/she must possess the right skills to analyze the ever-increasing volumes through cloud technologies. They need to convert the data into useful insights that would be responsible for uplifting the business. The data scientist has to build an algorithm and code the program. They mostly utilize 80% of their time to gathering information, creating and modifying data, cleaning if required, and organizing data. The rest, 20%, is utilized for analyzing the data with effective programming. This calls for the requirement of having specific cloud tools to help the data scientist to reduce their time searching for appropriate information. Organizations should make available new cloud services and cloud tools to their respective data scientists so that they can organize massive data quickly.

Therefore, cloud tools are very important for a data scientist to analyze large amounts of data at a shorter period. It will save the company's time and help build strong and robust Data Models.

Conclusion

Thank you for making it through to the end! The next step is to get started by seeing how Data Science is going to be able to work for your business. You will find that there are a lot of different ways that you can use the large amount of info that you have access to, and all of the data that you have been able to collect over time. Collecting data is just the first step to the process. We also need to make sure that we can gain all of the insights and predictions that come out of that information, and this is where the process of Data Science is going to come into play.

This guidebook has taken some time to explore what Data Science is all about, and how it can help benefit your company in so many ways. We looked at some of the tasks that Data Science can help out with, what Data Science is and how to work with the life cycle of data, the future of data, and so much more. This helps us to see some of the parts that come to Data Analysis, and even how beneficial gathering and using all of that information can be to grow your business.

But this is not the only step that we can work with. We also need to take this a bit further and not just collect data, but also be able to analyze that data and see what information it holds. This is a part of the Data Science life cycle, but it deserves some special attention because, without it, the data would just sit there without being used.

In this guidebook, we worked with the Python coding language and how this was able to help us to work through all of that data, collecting models and more, so we could learn something useful and make predictions about the data as well. This guidebook spent some time introducing Python and how it works and then moved on to some of the best libraries that you can use to not only write codes in Python but to use Python to work on the different models for analyzing the data you have.

Data Science is a great thing to add to your business, and it can help you to make sure customer satisfaction is high, that waste is low, that you can make more money and can even help with predictions in the future, such as what products you should develop and put out on the market. But learning all of this is not something that just happens on its own. Working with Data Science, and adding in some Python language and the different libraries that are included with it can make the difference. When you are ready to work with Python Data Science to improve many different aspects of your own business and to beat out the competition, make sure to check out this guidebook again to help you get started with it right away.

Made in the USA
Columbia, SC
28 June 2022

62432354R00187